THE MARKETING OF FOODSTUFFS IN THE GAMBIA, 1400–1980

To mum and dad
and
the people of The Gambia

The Marketing of Foodstuffs in The Gambia, 1400–1980

A Geographical Analysis

HAZEL R. BARRETT
Derbyshire College of Higher Education

Avebury

Aldershot · Brookfield USA · Hong Kong · Singapore · Sydney

© H.R. Barrett, 1988

Published by
Avebury
Gower Publishing Company Limited,
Gower House, Croft Road, Aldershot,
Hants. GU11 3HR, England

Gower Publishing Company,
Old Post Road, Brookfield, Vermont 05036,
United States of America

British Library Cataloguing in Publication Data

Barrett, Hazel R.
   The marketing of foodstuffs in the Gambia,
   1400-1980: a geographical analysis.
   1. Food ———— Gambia ———— Marketing
   I. Title
   380.1'456413'0096651   HD9017.G/

ISBN 0 566 05487 6

Printed and bound in Great Britain by
Athanaeum Press Limited, Newcastle-upon-Tyne

Contents

Tables

Figures

Acknowledgements

Over the period that I have been working on this piece of research, I have received advice and encouragement from many people all over the world. It is impossible for me to mention them all by name here. Only those to whom I owe a special debt will be acknowledged, to the friends and colleagues not named - thank you.

This study was made possible through a two-year award from the Social Science Research Council towards a PhD degree in West African Studies, at the University of Birmingham. The finance given funded the author's fieldwork in The Gambia (September 1979 until October 1980). During the author's fieldwork in West Africa, numerous people cooperated in the study including market masters and market users, both sellers and customers, without their cooperation the fieldwork would have been a failure. I must acknowledge the help given to me by Mr. M. Gibril (then Director of Central Statistics) who was my local supervisor. I also wish to thank my interpreters, Mr. K. Krubally, Mr. J. Mendeh, and especially Mr. B. Jatta, for their patience and dedication. Their cheerfulness under, sometimes very trying circumstances, made my task much easier and more enjoyable. My biggest debt of obligation is, however, owed to Mr. J.J. Cates and Mr. A.S. Jatta. Mr. J.J. Cates, affectionately known as Uncle Joe, treated me like a daughter, and without his advice and assistance the fieldwork for this study would never have been started. Words cannot express my gratitude to my dear friend Mr. A.S. Jatta, whose guidance, support and devotion, helped to make my stay in West Africa an exciting, happy and memorable experience.

Back home I would like to thank all my friends and colleagues in the Centre of West African Studies, University of Birmingham, particularly Dr. P.K. Mitchell, Dr. J. Crisp, Dr. H. Main and Mr. R. Gervais. At Derbyshire College of Higher Education, Derby, I would like to thank Mr. A. Skinner for his skillful cartographic work, Mr. P. Holdcroft and Miss M. Wood for their technical help, Mrs. A. Rathbone for her excellent typing job and Mr. R. Pearson for his comments on the script. Last, but not least, I wish to thank my parents, Leslie and Hilda Barrett, whose faith and confidence in me has been an inspiration at all stages of this study.

To you all - a sincere thank you.

1 Introduction

Introduction

West Africa is distinguished from the rest of Africa by the number, extent and variety of its marketplaces, as well as by the importance of marketing as an economic activity. It is known that markets existed in West Africa from at least the ninth century onwards, when they were mentioned in the writings of Arab travellers. [1] Much later, European explorers such as Cadamosto (1937), Jobson (1932) and Barth (1859), frequently commented on the extent of commercial activity in West Africa, often advocating trade with its peoples. Today markets still thrive and are familiar and vital elements of the socio-economic life of the region, forming an integral part of the spatial economic system of the area.

This book sets out to examine the historical development of the traditional marketplace network from the fifteenth century to the 1980s, emphasising the effect that groundnut production has had on both the production and marketing of foodstuffs in The Gambia. In an empirical piece of research the author has attempted to look at the Gambian situation on its own terms, not through the confines of prevailing standardised models and theories. When these become relevant and appropriate to the situation under investigation, this has been pointed out and discussed.

The Gambia : background

The Gambia, once a terminus of the trans–Sudanic salt trade, was
one of the first parts of West Africa to be visited by Europeans
and subsequently colonised.   Here, trade and commerce were
important constituents of the economy. When the first Europeans
arrived in the river, in the early part of the fifteenth century
markets existed and were operating on a periodic basis, not only
to serve the needs of the long distance traders, but also to
provide the subsistence needs of the local villagers.
Marketplaces (apart from a brief period in the eighteenth and
nineteenth centuries when they temporarily disappear), have
continued to be an important part of the Gambian way of life. The
term 'traditional' is used in the title of this book in
recognition of that history and to distinguish the marketing
network based on marketplaces, operating in the traditional style,
from the other marketing networks, notably those of the
supermarkets and other retail outlets and the Groundnut Produce
Marketing Board (GPMB) buying agencies. Today, more than at any
other time in the past, as a consequence of the groundnut
revolution of the nineteenth century, marketplaces play a vital
role in the local economy of The Gambia, providing the food
requirements for most of the population.

The Gambia is one of the smallest countries in Africa (11,000
sq. km) with an average breadth of 32 kilometres and an east–west
length of 480 kilometres.   The River Gambia, after which the
country is named, is the dominant relief feature.   This small
country is surrounded on its three landward borders by Senegal.
The curious geographical shape of the country is explained by the
carving up of the area in the late nineteenth century by French
and British colonial interests, the French claiming Senegal and
The Gambia becoming part of the British Colonial Empire. This
small British enclave was given its independence in February 1965
and in February 1982, after an abortive coup d'etat in July 1981,
was formally confederated with its neighbour to form the
Senegambian Confederation.

Like the majority of West African colonial demographic
enterprises, the censuses of The Gambia prior to 1963 are not very
reliable.   The whole country was covered by only four Travelling
Commissioners, each with a staff of one clerk. The Commissioner
personally, over the space of months, counted the people of each
village, as he toured his area. The first attempts at estimating
the population were made in 1881 and 1891. But estimates derived
from these attempts are not comparable with figures from later
censuses, due to boundary changes. The population of the country
at successive censuses is given in Table 1:1. The period between
1921 to 1931 shows a negative rate of growth. This apparent
decline in population over the decade is a mystery, as there were
no major disasters, out-migrations or evidence of declining
birthrates.   The probable explanation is an under-count of

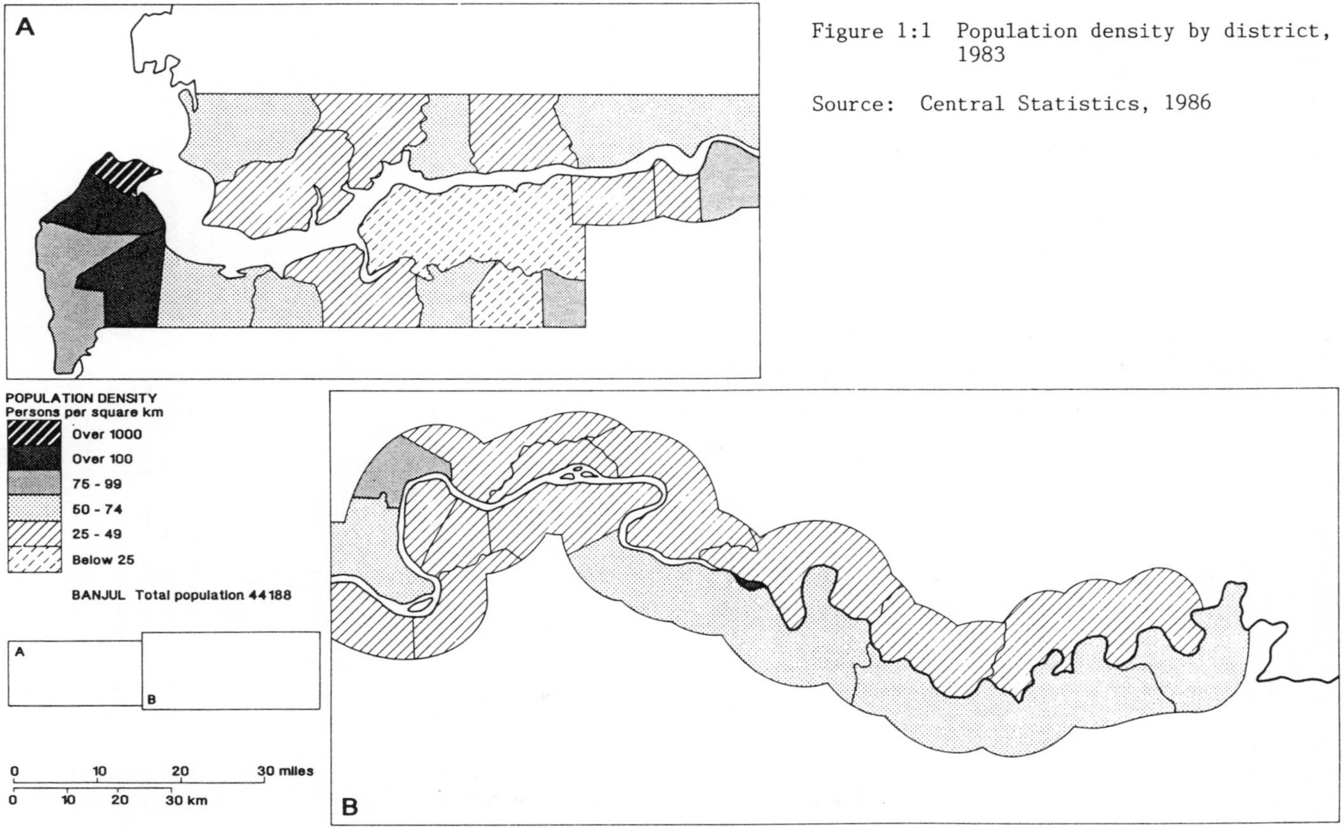

Figure 1:1 Population density by district, 1983

Source: Central Statistics, 1986

POPULATION DENSITY
Persons per square km

Over 1000
Over 100
75 - 99
50 - 74
25 - 49
Below 25

BANJUL Total population 44188

A

B

0   10   20   30 miles
0   10   20   30 km

A

B

3

population. Between 1931 and 1963 no censuses were conducted in The Gambia. In 1944 only Bathurst was enumerated and in 1951 only Kombo St. Mary. The 1963 census was the first simultaneous census to be carried out in the country, with the most recent one carried out in 1983. [2] The provisional 1983 census report indicates a total population in the country of 687,817. The spatial distribution of the Gambian population, by district in 1983 is shown in Figure 1:1. The most densely populated districts are Banjul, Kombo St. Mary and Brikama with the later two experiencing high rates of in-migration. The districts of Kiang West and Foni Bondali are the least densely populated in the country, followed by the north bank districts of MacCarthy Island and Upper River Divisions.

Table 1:1
The population of The Gambia at successive censuses

Year	Population	Average Annual Growth Rate	Total Increase
		%	
1901	90,404	–	–
1911	196,101	4.9	105,697
1921	210,611	3.7	14,510
1931	199,520	−0.6	−11,091
1963	315,486	1.4	115,966
1973	493,499	4.6	178,013
1983	687,817	3.4	194,318

Politically The Gambia is a parliamentary democratic republic, with free elections taking place every five years. [4] Since independence the ruling party has been the Peoples Progressive Party (PPP) headed by Sir Dawda Jawara, the elected president of the republic. The country is administered from the capital, Banjul (formerly Bathurst) through seven local government divisions, which are shown on Figure 1:2. There are two urban local government areas, Banjul and Kombo St. Mary (Kanifing being the administrative centre) and five rural areas, North Bank Division (NBD), Lower River Division (LRD), Western Division (WD), MacCarthy Island Division (MID) and Upper River Division (URD). MacCarthy Island Division is further divided into a north bank area, administered from Kuntaur and a south bank area, administered from Georgetown. It is a system that appears to operate reasonably satisfactorily, taking into account the poor communications of the country.

Figure 1:2 Administrative areas of The Gambia

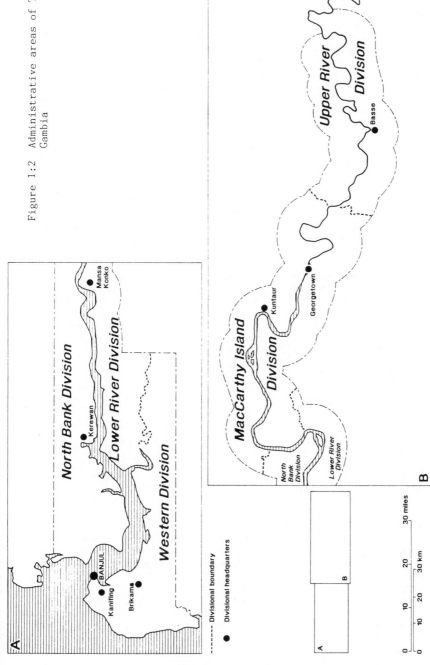

5

Unlike other areas of Africa, transportation has never been a problem in The Gambia. Traditionally, the major internal communication in the country has been by means of the river and no part of the territory is more than 14 kilometres from its bank. This is still the main method by which the groundnut crop is evacuated to the GPMB depots at Kaur and Banjul. Unlike other regions [5] where the lack of efficient communications hindered the spread of the capitalist economy, the River Gambia facilitated export expansion and speeded the process of specialisation in the region. Indeed it could be argued that The Gambia is the direct political expression of mercantile use of the river as a transport mode.

The colonial government realised the importance of the river and in 1952 (Bunning 1952) published a report which came down heavily on the side of river transport expansion.

The River Gambia . . . provides cheap and easy evacuation for groundnuts and other crops and for the distribution of imports to and from River ports, I cannot see how the setting up of heavy trunk roads is likely to produce one more pound of rice or one more bag of groundnuts. (Bunning 1952, p.4)

In fact the building of roads was actively discouraged.

The Gambia is blessed with one of the finest rivers in Africa, as far as navigation is concerned . . . Therefore, to permit an industry to grow up in competition with this natural highway is to upset the economic balance of The Gambia, which while very finely adjusted, should be perfectly satisfactory as long as reasonable principles are maintained. (Bunning 1952, p.4)

More explicitly the report concluded,

I do not see how anything beyond the absolute minimum by way of road communications for feeder services and for light vehicles for administrative, etc., purposes can help in the general development of The Gambia. (Bunning 1952, p.5)

So until independence in 1965, the river was the main means of transportation in the country. Apart from the groundnut cutters, two boats plied up and down the river from Banjul to Basse. The boats were slow but more comfortable than attempting the journey by road, especially in the rainy season.

With independence, the emphasis changed, and the new government's strategy for transport included, as well as the usual improvements for the river network, the completion of the national trunk road network, and the improvement of feeder road links from the relatively important and potentially important agricultural areas to the main road and river network. The objective was to eliminate serious transport bottlenecks and to stimulate agricultural activity and trade. By 1975, a national highway existed along 90% of the south bank of the river and 60% along the north bank, with two north-south routes traversing these, one near the coast running through Banjul and the other in the middle of the country running through Farafenni and Soma (the Trans-Gambian

6

Highway). But four areas were still isolated from any reliable all-weather road; the north-east from Lamin Koto to Bassimus; the south-east tip from Basse to Fatoto; Western Kiang; and an area on the north bank south-east of Barra. By 1982 a bituminous surfaced road was open all the way to Basse, with a poor all-weather gravel road continuing onto the eastern border with Senegal via Fatoto. On the north bank a bituminous surfaced road ran from the ferry terminal at Barra, north to the border with Senegal. At Essau an all-weather gravel road branched off to the east and ran as far as the ferry terminal opposite MacCarthy Island. From here a poor, track-like road continued to Sutukoba. This area is the most remote, and explains why the Wuli and Sandu districts rely so heavily on the river boat for essential supplies. (See Figure 4:7).

The roads described so far are the major ones; there are, however, gravel feeder-roads which connect villages with one another and with the main roads and, in some instances, the river. However, many of these roads are impassable by motor vehicles, particularly in the rainy season. The main roads are passable all year round – with bridges crossing the creeks. The only unbridged creek is at the Mini Minium Bolon near Kerewan, where there is a ferry. Travelling north or south of the river by road is relatively easy, crossing the river is not. There is no bridge across the river within the boundaries of The Gambia. The lowest bridging point is in Senegal at Goulombo, 60 kilometres east-north-east of Basse, where the paved road from Tambacounda to Kolda crosses the river. However, the river can be crossed by ferry. There are seven ferry crossing points within The Gambia: Banjul-Barra, the Trans-Gambian Highway, Kuntaur, Georgetown, Bansang, Basse and Fatoto, all shown on Figure 4:7.

The most well used piece of road in The Gambia is the Trans-Gambian Highway, which crosses the river at Yellitenda. The Highway was opened in 1957 and at once became the busiest road in the country. From 1962 to 1968 the number of vehicles using the ferry crossing on the Highway more than doubled, rising from 22,901 to 46,999 (1968 being the latest figures available). (Kolp 1970) In 1980 the ferry was in continual use in daylight hours and even then the average waiting time to use it was three days.

Other roads are not so busy, with most of the traffic taking the form of the odd taxi or lorry. The main centres of population are connected by a regular and popular taxi service, the fares for which are fixed by the government. In 1978, to supplement the taxi service, a less frequent and efficient bus service was established. This service is most developed and most frequent in the Banjul-Kombo St. Mary region. Although there are services along the south bank on the tarmaced road, these are not reliable. As there is only one short stretch of tarmaced road on the north bank, there is no bus service as yet.

The land area of The Gambia is part of an extensive sedimentary basin which developed during the Tertiary period, and consists of the highly weathered Continental Terminal formation made up of layers of clayey sandstone, quartz gravel, sand and clay. Since its deposition, this sandstone has been dissected by the River Gambia and a series of iron pan (cuirasse) layers have developed. The highest remaining surface forms part of the Senegambian Plateau at 40-50 metres above mean sea level and is frequently marked by the outcrop of the uppermost iron pan level. Below this level, dissection has produced a series of gentle colluvial slopes and alluvium has been deposited in the floodplain of the River Gambia and its tributaries.

The distribution of soils is closely related to the landforms described above. They can be divided into two major categories, the soils of the recent alluvium and those soils developed on the Continental Terminal. The soils of the recent alluvium (fluvisols) show a high degree of variability in both morphology and chemical characteristics. Basically most of the alluvial soils are hydromorphic and fine-textured, usually comprising more than 80 per cent silt-plus-clay throughout. The soils developed on the Continental Terminal also have certain common characteristics. They are of low chemical fertility and are poorly structured and become hard when dry. Most of them are sandy loams or sandy clays, with only the depth of the upper horizon differentiating them. Soils with less then 25 cm of upper horizon are characteristically associated with plateau situations, whereas on the colluvial slopes this horizon is thicker.

The depth of soil available for exploitation by the growing crop is an essential factor in determining the amount of water and nutrients available to it. In the alluvial soils, effective rooting depth is often limited by the water table. Except for a few specially adapted plants such as rice, plant roots cannot penetrate the water table very far because of lack of oxygen. Most of the alluvial areas west of approximately 15°W (Kundang, 218 km up river) are seasonally waterlogged and much of the area is flooded throughout the year, at least during high tides. East of this area, the alluvial soils can be divided into those which are subject to seasonal inundation and support grassland vegetation, and those which are rarely flooded and support shrub or woodland. Another limitation on the exploitation of the alluvial soils is inundation by salt water, this has led to saline salt in much of the alluvial area lying west of approximately 15°W. At the height of the wet season the salt/freshwater mixing zone may be located near Kerewan (70 km upstream from Banjul). As the flood declines, this zone moves up river as a result of diffusion, tidal mixing and mass flow, at an observed rate of 15-20 kilometres per month, at its peak reaching between Kaur/Kuntaur (155-220 km upstream). [6] The extraction of freshwater upriver of the saline limit (1 part per 1,000) for irrigation during the dry season causes the salt-water to move further up the river,

8

with potentially disastrous consequences for present irrigation schemes in the eastern part of the country. Calculations indicate [7] that 1 m^3/s continuous extraction above Kuntaur throughout the dry season moves the saline mixing zone up river by approximately one kilometre per month depending on the volume of the river at the position of the mixing zone and the rate of inflow from upstream. This obviously has serious implications for the future use of the alluvial soils and perhaps helps explain their underutilisation. Agricultural exploitation of the upland soils is inhibited by inadequate soil depth. The problem with these soils is the depth to the iron pan, which limits effective rooting depth.

All these factors limit the production potentials of Gambian soils leaving only a small proportion suitable for agricultural exploitation. A survey undertaken by the Land Resource Survey team (Dunsmore 1976) tried to estimate the amount of land suitable for farming. Table 1:2 records the results of this survey. Soils are divided into five groups and the percentage of each in the seven geographical regions is shown. If it is assumed that land in groups three, four and five are generally suitable for crop production it will be seen that Lower River Division has the lowest proportion of cultivable land (36 per cent), whilst Western Division has the highest (67 per cent). Groundnuts and upland cereals are principally grown on the colluvial slopes (group four). Over the country as a whole 75 per cent of these soils had either been cultivated or lay under a recent fallow in 1972. It is obvious then that potential for further expansion of farming in these areas is limited. By comparison only 22 per cent of the suitable and irrigable soils (group five) were in current cultivation or recent fallow. Their fine texture, however, makes them difficult to work and their exploitation is limited by the availability of irrigation water in the dry season, and saline intrusion.

In West African savanna regions, water is a limiting resource and determines the extent to which other resources can be developed or efficiently utilised. Table 1:3 shows the mean monthly and annual rainfall totals for various stations in The Gambia, and clearly demonstrates the seasonality of the rainfall regime. This juxtaposition of five months of intense rainfall, with seven months dry season, imposes a severe constraint on the country's agriculture, most of which is rainfed. As the most common cause of plant death in the tropics is the lack of sufficient water to replace that lost by transpiration, even a temporary water deficit can sometimes be fatal. Not only is the amount of rainfall important, but also its distribution, as crops that have not matured by the time the rains have ended, have to rely partly or completely on residual soil moisture for yield formation and maturation. Photosensitive sorghums and millets form their yields and mature on residual soil moisture because they are susceptible to head mould and insect damage if they

Table 1:2

Soil suitability groups by geographical region.areas in hectare and percentage of regional total

Soil suitability group	Western	Lower River	North Bank	MacCarthy Island (N)	MacCarthy Island (S)	Upper River (N)	Upper River (S)	The Gambia
1. Unsuitable	31,981 18%	79,795 52%	81,811 37%	52,485 35%	39,389 28%	34,679 39%	36,197 34%	356,337 34%
2. Marginal	25,348 15%	18,225 12%	14,790 7%	30,638 21%	16,312 11%	13,409 15%	7,239 7%	125,961 12%
3. Suitable with qualifications	39,117 22%	21,693 14%	30,731 14%	8,681 6%	23,661 17%	11,253 12%	12,278 11%	147,414 14%
4. Suitable	78,340 45%	34,085 22%	93,676 42%	40,740 28%	33,860 24%	15,476 17%	30,780 29%	326,957 32%
5. Suitable and	0	0	0	15,065 10%	28,917 20%	14,809 17%	20,592 19%	79,383 8%
% total of 3, 4 and 5	67%	36%	56%	44%	61%	46%	59%	54%

Source: Dunsmore (1976), p.243

mature before the end of the rains. Other crops such as groundnuts, cowpeas and maize, when sown on time, do not generally rely on residual soil moisture for maturation.

The inability of the soil to retain and provide the growing crop with sufficient moisture over a long enough period is a severe limitation to potential agricultural production in The Gambia, and restricts the growing season to the rainy period only. However, the traditional cultivars and cropping systems used by the farmer have evolved over a long period of time, and the farmer knows the potential of the ecological environment in which he finds himself. It was just fortunate that the alien cultivar, the groundnut, suited the conditions so well.

Little work has been published on The Gambia. There are a few generalised histories, such as those of Gailey (1964) and Gray (1966) both published around the time of Independence. Gray's book gives emphasis to European explorers, traders and administrators between the fifteenth and nineteenth centuries, whilst Gailey concentrates on the constitutional and political development of the country since the late nineteenth century. There are few geographical texts, the most notable being those of Jarrett (1948, 1949, 1950) published also during the colonial era, which tend to be short and static. Gamble (1955, 1967), who is basically an anthropologist, has made a valuable contribution with his work on the Wolof ethnic group. Recent changes mean this is now more historical, than current, anthropology. In terms of agricultural economics, Haswell (1975) has made a unique contribution with her three studies of the village of Genieri, which span a twenty-five year period. However, no work has been undertaken at all on the traditional marketing system and few references are made to it. The author therefore found herself working in virgin territory.

It was for this reason that the study had to broaden its outlook, from its original purpose, which was to investigate foodcrop marketing in present-day Gambia. It became necessary to examine both pre-colonial and colonial marketplace development. This brief look at Gambian history demonstrated how profoundly the adoption of the groundnut as a cash crop by the Gambian farmer has influenced present-day commerce in the region and is primarily responsible for the present-day pattern of local markets. Hence it became necessary to trace the development of groundnut cultivation in The Gambia, emphasising the effects that this has had on both the production and marketing of foodcrops. In The Gambia, a situation occurred where colonial cash crop production, in the form of the groundnut, displaced foodcrops by reallocating labour time and land. The precise conditions of cash crop expansion in relation to food supply can only be pieced together from inadequate archival materials. However, it can be seen quite clearly that groundnuts made profound inroads into the Gambian food economy. In fact, we have a situation where most of the

Table 1:3

Mean monthly and annual rainfall totals (in mm) for various stations in The Gambia

Station	Period	No. of Years*	Dec–April	May	June	July	Aug	Sept	Oct	Nov	Annual
Gunjur	1951–60	8		3	63	404	449	370	146	15	1,447
Yundum (Airport)	1946–73	28		4	70	269	462	300	94	6	1,205
Banjul (Marina)	1886–1950	64		5	65	259	489	275	89	4	1,185
Bwiam	1945–63	18	rainfall ecologically insignificant	4	84	260	375	279	102	4	1,126
Kaur	1950–63	8		9	66	187	336	211	110	6	926
Sapu	1956–62	7		4	124	203	319	204	81	1	935
Georgetown	1908–25) 1949–73)	43		11	115	203	305	246	84	4	967
Basse	1942–72	26		19	127	209	338	242	90	10	1,035

* some data are missing and dubious data were omitted

Source: Compiled from Dunsmore, 1976, p.26

Gambian population participate in the world economy in order to sell their cash crop and purchase subsistence needs, yet the traditional marketing system has changed little since pre-colonial days.

Using Bohannan and Dalton's classification in their introduction to Markets in Africa (1962) The Gambia can be described as a "market society", that is, a society in which:

> There is, on the one hand, dependence on the sale of a cash crop which makes the market of extreme importance to the producers of that crop; with the cash income they receive, they buy on the market not only the imported and luxury goods that they have come to demand, but also all or the major portion of their daily subsistence requirements.
> (Bohannan and Dalton 1962, p.2)

It is a society in which the market principle (i.e. the determination of prices by the forces of supply and demand regardless of the site of the transactions) is important, and supersedes the physical marketplace. [8] In the Gambia, groundnuts, the income from which forms the basis of the economy, by-pass the traditional markets, which are left to perform the function of providing the population with its subsistence needs.

Sources and fieldwork methods

Pre-colonial historical geography

Sources of information about Gambian exchange institutions and trade patterns before colonial times are very scant. As oral histories of this period are now at least second- or third-hand, no great reliance can be placed upon them. Only when oral accounts are backed up by evidence from the journals of early European travellers, are they used in this book.

Travel accounts of early European visitors to the Gambian region provide most valuable primary source material on pre-colonial geography. Of particular value are the journals of Cadamosto (1937), Pereira (1937) and Jobson (1932) which describe in some detail the trade of the region, especially the salt trade which was thriving in the fifteenth and sixteenth centuries. Also consulted were the few modern historical and ethnographic publications on the Gambia region, such as Gailey (1964), Gray (1966), Gamble (1955, 1967), Jarrett (1948, 1949, 1950) and Quinn (1972). None of these works are concerned specifically with the trade or internal exchange mechanisms of The Gambia in the pre-colonial period, but they do provide some useful information and general background.

13

Trade and markets in the colonial period

The advent of British administration encouraged the institutionalisation of record keeping although it is not until the second half of the nineteenth century that the records become comprehensive and well organised. Thus from about 1890 onwards there is a continuous documentation of government actions (concerned both with the colony and the protectorate), which influenced economic change in the region. Access to these materials, which are to be found in the Public Records Office at Kew in London and the Banjul Archives in Banjul, The Gambia, are essential in order to assess the range of decisions, trends and forces which combined to shape the pattern of marketplace development in The Gambia. The records vary considerably in scope and depth of coverage, consistency and general quality, but nevertheless are the most important source materials for this period.

It is fair to claim that extensive and hitherto unused documentary and other material exists for the study of the development of trade and markets in The Gambia, during the colonial period. This book explores the material with the aim of contributing to an understanding of the evolution of the country's marketing network and to assess how groundnut cultivation has affected and influenced the present-day pattern of marketplaces.

The marketing of foodstuffs in the post-independence era

Before the research reported here, there had been no comprehensive investigation of the distribution of markets; no government report, statistical abstract or even complete map, providing the overview of where markets were operating. Material was therefore collected by the author during a twelve-month period of fieldwork (September 1979–October 1980). [9] Every major market centre was visited and sixteen were surveyed in detail, with a total of 1,188 traders and 830 customers being interviewed. Further intensive study was undertaken in the busier markets, namely, Banjul, Serrekunda, Farafenni and Basse.

Marketplaces everywhere are congested, noisy and extremely fluid gatherings. In The Gambia they vary from congregations of less than fifty to over one thousand people. Crowded conditions, along with a 'floating' consumer population and a trader population which is constantly changing, make a rigorous sampling procedure impractical. For this reason, procedures used to select subjects for interview had to be flexible. It is the results of these interviews, supplemented by general discussions within the marketplace, that form the basis of the discussion of the present-day network.

Organisation of the book

The book begins with a brief survey of pre-colonial trade and
markets. Two types of marketplaces are identified and described
in Chapter Two. Firstly, the country 'fair' type of market that
was associated with long-distance trade, particularly the trans-
Sudanic salt trade; and secondly, local subsistence markets which
served an area of about five miles radius. From the available
evidence it would appear that markets only operated in the region
east of Balanghar. With the decline in the salt trade and the
emergence of the slave trade in the eighteenth century, the
eastern markets declined and the economic nucleus of the region
shifted to the coastal areas, where the Europeans set up trading
factories. However, from 1700 until 1900 local markets seem to
disappear from the region (possible explanations are given in
Chapter Two), but in 1900 they reappear as daily institutions, not
as the periodic phenomenon they had previously been.

This 'reappearance' of the marketplaces coincides with colonial
domination of the region in the 1890s, and can be mainly
attributed to the increased production of the groundnut.
Groundnuts were first exported from the River Gambia in the 1830s,
where their adoption and cultivation by the local people can be
explained by 'vent-for-surplus' theory. But with the colonial
government's "encouragement" of the cash crop in the twentieth
century, which is dealt with in Chapter Three, this theory is no
longer applicable.

By 1900, groundnuts were very successfully competing with food
crops, particularly the upland cereals, for land and labour. The
result of this conflict is described in Chapter Four. Firstly,
the factors of production, although not being transformed into the
capitalist mode, took up added importance with more and more land,
labour and capital being devoted to cash crop production, at the
expense of food cultivation. With this added emphasis being given
to the groundnut, increasing quantities of rice were being
imported to make up the food deficit. Secondly, a marked
seasonality of the money supply developed, associated with the
sale of the groundnut crop in the dry season. This affected local
markets and commodity sales. Thirdly, the colonial government
devised a system for marketing the groundnut crop which by-passed
the traditional marketing network. It took the form of the Gambia
Oilseeds Marketing Board (GOMB). As a consequence, the
traditional network was virtually ignored by the colonial
government, and few improvements took place.

Under these conditions, the local marketing network was slow to
develop, with no markets existing west of Kaur, until after 1935.
The evolution of the present-day network is discussed in Chapter
Five, in which two phases are identified. The first phase is the
period up to 1935, when all markets were located in the eastern
half of the country. The second phase is the period after 1935,

when with increased purchasing power associated with groundnut cultivation in the east, and the diffusion of modernising influences from the west, marketplaces became nationwide phenomenon. After 1950, the network readjusted to the shift in emphasis from river to road communications that occurred with independence. Marketplaces relocated away from the wharftowns, to the main roads.

In Chapter Six, the present-day system of marketplaces is described. Using the results of the author's fieldwork, a distinction is made between official and unofficial markets; and markets are classified as either rural, peri-urban or urban. The inter-relationships of these various categories or markets are discussed, isolating two nodes where wholesale activity is beginning to develop, namely around Banjul and Kombo St. Mary and in the Farafenni/Kaur _luma_ area.

Having discussed market types and their interaction, Chapters Seven, Eight and Nine take particular food categories and describe how they move from producer, through the marketplace, to the consumer. The marketing of cereals is dealt with in Chapter Seven, in which the government controlled network and price structure controls for rice, (both imported and locally produced) is described and contrasted with the traditional system, which still operates for the upland cereals. The effect that one has upon the other is examined. Chapter Eight describes the disastrous attempt by the government to nationalise the meat and fish sectors, by establishing marketing boards. The pre-marketing board system are considered and the instigation of the marketing boards is discussed, along with their failure and ultimate dissolution. The least government-interfered-with part of the food marketing system, that of fruit and vegetables, is dealt with in Chapter Nine. In contrast to the previous two sectors, government involvement in fruit and vegetable marketing has been a recent occurrence and one that has turned out to be totally incompetent. As the example of the onion growing scheme shows, much more research needs to be undertaken on the marketing of foodstuffs in The Gambia, in order that mistakes can be avoided and improvements speeded up, for the benefit of both producers and consumers.

Notes

[1]   See al-Masudi; Ibn Haukal; al-Bakri; al-Idrisi; Ibn Battuta;
        and Ibn Khaldun, cited by E.W. Bovill (1958).
[2]   The 1983 census report is not yet published, but a
        provisional report of some of the results was published in
        March 1986 by the Central Statistics Department, Banjul.
[3]   Between 1973 and 1983, Kombo St. Mary experienced a 157.6
        per cent increase in population, with the Brikama local
        government area experiencing a 50.8 per cent increase.

[4]   The most recent election took place on 11th March 1987. For
      more details see the relevant editions of <u>West Africa</u>.
[5]   For example with the opening of the Dakar-St. Louis railway
      in 1885, exports of groundnuts from Senegal increased from
      65,000 tons in 1894 to 140,000 tons in 1900.   The Kano
      region of Northern Nigeria, also, only became an important
      groundnut exporting area after the opening of the Lagos-Kano
      railway in 1912. See Hogendorn (1966, 1975).
[6]   Dunsmore (1976).
[7]   1 m^3s continuous extraction of water is adequate for growing
      one crop of rice over an area of about 590 ha.
[8]   Many definitions of what constitutes a marketplace have been
      made, the one most widely quoted being that of the UK Royal
      Commission on Market Rights and Tolls, 1891, where a
      marketplace is defined as:
         An authorised concourse of buyers and sellers of
         commodities meeting at a place, more or less strictly
         limited or defined, at an appointed time.
         (cited by P. Hill 1966).
      Hodder takes a similar stance defining markets as:
         an authorised public gathering of buyers and sellers of
         commodities meeting at an appointed place at regular
         intervals. (B.W. Hodder 1965)
      Smith, however, takes a broader view:
         West African marketplaces are the sites at which people
         meet regularly in order to acquire and/or dispose of
         locally produced and imported goods and services, to
         exchange information with relatives, friends and strangers
         and to engage in recreational activities.
         (R.H.T. Smith 1971).
[9]   The fieldwork was financed by the Social Science Research
      Council.

2 Trade and the local marketing system in the pre-colonial riverine region of The Gambia

Introduction

This chapter investigates the relationship between long distance trade and the development of a marketing network in the Gambian region during the pre-colonial period.   The Gambian region has consistently been an export region, trade in salt was followed by hides, then by slaves.   After the abolition of the slave trade, gum, hides and beeswax were the main items of trade until superceded in the 1840s by the groundnut.   From the available evidence it would appear that two types of marketplace were operating during this period, in the area east of Balanghar. First, the country 'fair' type of market that was associated with long distance trade, particularly the trans-Sudanic salt trade; and secondly, local subsistence markets. With the decline of the salt trade and the emergence of the slave trade in the eighteenth century, the eastern markets declined and the economic nucleus of the region shifted to the coastal areas, where the Europeans set up trading factories.   However, from 1700-1900 local marketplaces seem to disappear from the region, to reappear in 1900 as daily institutions, not as the periodic phenomena they had previously been.   This chapter demonstrates the complex and intricate relationship that existed between long distance trade and local marketplace systems in the Gambian region of West Africa in the period before colonial domination.

Trade and marketing in the Gambian region, pre 1700: the period of
the salt trade and local periodic markets

A familiar theme in the literature on markets and exchange
mechanisms, concerns their origins, development and change. It is
a controversial debate, with Hodder (1965) suggesting that local
markets were the result of exchange stimulated by long distance
commerce, a hypothesis confirmed by Good (1970, 1973) and M.G.
Smith (1962) in their study areas, Ankole in Uganda and Hausaland
in Nigeria. Meillassoux (1971) on the other hand suggests that
local exchange was more important in marketplace development than
Hodder allowed for. Work done in Sierra Leone by Riddell (1972,
1974) and Howard (1981) shows there is no universal answer. For,
although there is evidence of external trade in the north of pre-
colonial Sierra Leone, it did not elicit a response in the form of
a local marketing system. The debate goes on, and as Hopkins
says, the historical evidence provides no clear answer: 'that
local exchange needs were important in the creation of local
markets, and that long distance trade had a stimulating effect on
marketing activity at all levels' is clear (1973, p.54).

The example of the evolution of the marketing system in The
Gambia, does not provide an answer to this problem. Both long
distance trade and local exchange were important in the region
long before the first Europeans arrived along the coast. All that
can be done from the available evidence is to give a picture of
how the two interacted.

Sources of information about the Gambian exchange institutions
and trade patterns before colonial times are very scant. Travel
accounts of early European visitors to the Gambian region provide
the most valuable primary source material on the geography of the
area. Of particular value are the journals of Cadamosto (1485),
Pereira (1505-8) and Jobson (1620) which describe in some detail
the trade of the region. From these accounts it is possible to
reconstruct something of the pattern of the Gambian marketing
system of the fifteenth and sixteenth centuries.

At this time the economy of the region is dominated by the salt
trade, with its important trans-Saharan and trans-Sudanic
networks. The western Sudan drew most of its supplies of salt
from five major deposits situated in or close to the Sahara
(Awlil, Bilma, Idjil, Teghaza and Taondeni). (See Figure 2:1)
These supplies were often interrupted by wars and invasions, as
happened at Teghaza in 1585 when it was captured by the Moroccans.
[1] For these reasons the Sudanese had to look for other sources
to supplement their Saharan supplies. It would appear that like
the supplies of salt from Awlil (near the estuary of the River
Senegal), salt from the River Gambia also fulfilled this role.

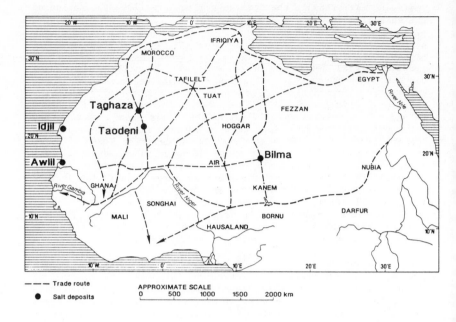

Figure 2:1   Saharan trade routes in the pre-colonial period

    It is impossible to estimate the quantity of salt produced in the Gambian region before the end of the nineteenth century. Curtin (1975) estimates that in the later half of the nineteenth century, 1,000–2,000 metric tons per year was produced, of which 500–1,000 metric tons would have been exported out of the region by the caravans.   This he estimates as corresponding to 25 per cent of all salt reaching the interior, quite a significant quantity if the figures are correct.   However, it is doubtful if all this reached the entrepot centres of Timbuctu and Gao, the southern termini of the major western trans-Saharan trade routes. It is suspected that a large proportion of this seasalt found its way to the gold fields to the east of Senegambia, known to the Arabs as 'wangara'.   Bovill (1958) argues that this gold field was probably what is known today as the Bambuk-Lobi gold field, an area lying between the upper Senegal, Faleme, Niger and Tinkisso rivers. [2]   It is known that in this region the lack of salt was chronic. [3]   Sundstrom (1965) notes that the Lobi area had practically no outside salt supply in pre-colonial days.   The fact that large quantities of gold were to be found on the River Gambia when the first Europeans arrived there in the fifteenth century suggests that at least some Gambian produced salt was being exchanged for gold in the Bambuk-Lobi region.

20

It was in the kingdom of Bursall that salt was produced in large quantities along the River Gambia, in the area known as Lower and Upper Niumi. Jobson, in 1620, describes the production of salt which was refined from brackish river water in calabashes which were exposed to the sun. The salt was then transported by canoe as far as the Barrakunda Falls where it was exchanged for slaves. He noted that a village near the Falls called Setico (present-day Sutokoba) sent slaves to the coast in exchange for this salt, which was then taken further east to be traded for gold.

> The inhabitant heere [Setico], who are all Marybuckes, [4] are the only people, who follow a continual trade from their owne houses downe to the king of Bursall whose dwellings is sayd to be by the seaside; at which place, the seashore doth naturally yeeld great store of salt ... to buy, which they carry downe, as their chiefest commoditie, the slaves or people of the country, whereof the King of Bursall doth make such profit ... This commodity [salt] the people doe carry likewise faire up into the Country, for amongst themselves we can perceive they make little use there of so as their travell is long and tedious; the returne they make is not discerned to be anything but gold, and a kind of nuts they call kola, which is in great esteeme amongst them. (Jobson 1932, p.101)

The salt trade as here described is obviously conducted outside the marketplace on a client-landlord basis, a situation described by Howard (1981) for the caravans involved in the kola trade in northern pre-colonial Sierra Leone. The mechanisms of this trade are discussed by Wright (1977) who describes the role of Mandinka clans in this extensive commerce:

> Nearly all of the overland long distance trade that passed from the upper Niger to and along the Gambia River - a major commercial axis of the Western Sudanic network - was carried by one of several traditional jula [5] clans. (Wright 1977, p.36)

Wright identifies several Mandinka clans active in this trade; the Singateh, Kinteh, Bayo, Danso, Fofanna and Nyaringa, but concentrates only on the role of the Darbo clan. He described how the trade was conducted:

> Like segments of other Mandinka jula clans' extended families of Darbo jula were settled in commercial villages along the river, where over the years they had developed social and economic ties with local residents and with members of the ruling families of the appropriate Gambian Mandinka states. From these locations, and with the aid of their strong local and regional influence, Darbo jula were able to participate actively and regularly in the long-distance trade of the Gambia-Niger commercial axis. (Wright 1977, p.33)

It was this trans-Sudanic trade in salt, iron and cloth that the first European travellers to the region describe in their journals with Setico as one of the termini. Setico was described by Jobson as 'the greatest towne or place that I have seen' (Jobson 1932, p.131) on his journey so far, and for him was the most important trading settlement of the region, as well as being the centre of the salt trade. This may well be an exaggerated report, but there is no doubt of the importance of Setico to the salt trade. As far back as 1456 Cadamosto had made a similar observation.

> I went up the river as far as Cantor, [6] which is a large town near the riverside ... when the report spread throughout the country round, that the Christians were in Cantor, the natives came together from all quarters, viz, from Tambucutu, in the north, from the Serre Geley in the south, and there came also people from Quioquun. [Gao] (Cadamosto 1937, p.93)

It is interesting to note the mention of at least two of the three southern termini of the trans-Saharan trade, but Serre Geley cannot be identified.

Cantor, the kingdom in which Setico was located, played an important part in the salt trade, due to its role as a break of bulk point. It was at this point that salt had to be unloaded from canoes onto caravans of asses before the journey east could proceed. This was due to the barrier to river navigation caused by the Barrakunda Falls. This area thus attracted much attention from the earliest European travellers, including the Portugese explorer Pereira, who travelled up the river in 1505-8. He has left us with a vivid account of the great fair at Sutucoo (Jobson's Setico), in which he stresses the role of the Mandinka traders in the network.

> 150 leagues from its mouth is a district called Cantor where there are four towns, the principal of which is called Sutucoo and has some 4,000 inhabitants, the names of the other three are Jalancoo, Dabancoo and Jamnamsura; they are all enclosed with wooden palisades and are distant from the river half a league, a league, and a league and a half. At Sutucoo is held a great fair, to which the Mandinguas, when the country is at peace and there are no wars, come to our ships ... and buy common red, blue and green cloth, kerchiefs, thin coloured silk, brass bracelets, caps, hats, the stones called "alequequas" [7] and much more merchandise, so that in time of peace as we have said, 5-6,000 doubloons of good gold are brought hence to Portugal. (Pereira 1937, p.87)

However, Pereira goes on in his account to tell of the silent trade between the Mandinka traders and the 'dogface' people of the interior, possibly in present-day Burkina Fasso, (Pereira 1937, p.89) in which slaves were supposedly exchanged for gold. As Pereira states, 'I have spoken with men who have seen this'. (Pereira 1937, p.89) We must then question how much of his account is oral tradition and how much his own personal experience. Nonetheless, there can be no doubt as to the important trading role played by this area.

Salt was not the only commodity to be traded along the River Gambia. In 1585 Donelha (1977) sailed up the river and noted the importance of present day Kaur and Kassang as trading ports, particularly in cloths, cotton, wax, ivory, gold and hides, and on his arrival at Kassang he found seven ships trading in the port, with two more following. He described the busy port thus:

> The town of Casan [Kassang] stands a pistol shot away from the
> port. The port is handy, we disembark on dry land, and there
> is a certain amount of sand. Near the port are some high
> trees, under which the ground is as bare as if it had been
> swept, and here the black women hold a market when ships are
> in port; they bring for sale rice, 'milho', 'cuscus', hens,
> eggs, milk, butter, country fruit and other things. (Donelha
> 1977, p.149)

He goes on to say:

> In Kassang: "There is great trade in cloths, cotton, wax,
> ivory, gold and hides of various animals, but all the gold,
> wax, ivory and hides they take to the Jalofo coast, to the
> French, English and other nations. [These foreigners] even
> came up the Gambia to undertake this trade with the blacks,
> and they draw immense profit from this river. (Donelha 1977,
> p.155)

These markets give the impression of being 'country fair' types
of markets, which dealt in luxury items such as gold, beeswax and
ivory, and which served the needs of long distance trade, i.e. the
salt trade and the European vessels trading in the river. These
markets are reported only in the area east of Balanghar. At the
same time local markets were in operation designed to serve the
local populace. These local markets were very different from
those described above. In 1455-56 Cadamosto visited a local
market inland from Kaur. It is obviously a local subsistence
orientated exchange market that met in a field on Mondays and
Fridays. (Cadamosto 1937, pp.48-9) Items that were sold there
included cotton, cloth, vegetables, oil, millet, wooden bowls, and
palm mats. Seventy years later, Jobson describes a similar
market, or even the same one at Balanghar, four miles west of
Kaur.

> While we were in the River, at a place called Mangegar
> [Balanghar], against which we had occasion to ride with our
> ship, both up and down, in the open fields, about a mile
> distance from any housing, is every Monday a market kept;
> which is in the middle of the week, unto which would come
> great resort of people, from round about, as here in our
> country, who would disperse and settle themselves, with their
> commodities under the shady trees, and take up a good space of
> ground and anything what the country did yield was there
> brought in and bought and sold amongst them. (Jobson 1937,
> p.156)

These markets are clearly local exchange markets serving nearby
villages and having no direct relation with the salt trade further
east. This is demonstrated by the fact that early accounts of
these markets do not mention luxury goods such as ivory or gold;
only pure subsistence locally produced goods, mainly food such as
millet, rice, milk, eggs and fruit are mentioned as being offered
for sale.

So, from the travel accounts of this period we can draw a rough picture of marketing in the Gambian region prior to 1700. Firstly local markets are known to have existed from Balanghar eastwards. They were probably part of a network of interconnected markets covering the whole Senegambian region. This is supported by the fact that Cadamosto describes similar markets in operation in the territory which is now present-day Senegal. From the fact that the goods exchanged within them were not luxury items, but subsistence goods, we can conclude that the salt trade was not an important factor in their existence and functioning, especially as it would appear that the salt trade was conducted from outside the marketplace. However, it seems probable that the salt trade did stimulate certain local markets, such as Sutokoba, temporarily exaggerating their regional importance. This would occur at break of bulk points such as the extreme eastern point of present-day Gambia, where continued river communications become impossible.

Trade and markets in the Gambia, 1700-1900: the period of the slave trade, legitimate trade and the beginnings of the groundnut trade

By the beginning of the eighteenth century the salt trade of the River Gambia had begun to decline. Quinn (1971) suggests that this was a direct result of the decline of the great trading towns of Timbuctu, Gao and Jenne, caused by the invasion of the Songhai Empire by the Morrocans in 1591. The resulting disorder along the western trans-Saharan routes eventually diverted traffic away from the western Sudan, to the Kano-Wadai route. Most important, however, was that new states emerged to the east of the Senegambian region with the decline of the Songhai Empire, namely the Bambara kingdoms of Segu and Kaarta. (Fage 1969, p.30) These states became the eastern limits of Gambian trade. Park (1878) points out that from the country to the east of Bambara came merchants who 'speak a different language from Bambara or any other kingdom which they [the Bambara] are acquainted.' The Gambian Mandinka trading links had thus been cut short. The Bambara kingdoms were now the furthest states to the east in which they could feel secure, where they could be understood and trade in peace.

The political map of the Senegambian region had also been redrawn with the disintegration of the Jolof and Mali Empires. This left a series of medium sized kingdoms along the river, falling under the broad hegemony of whichever was the strongest at any particular time (see Figure 2:2). In the east, the once powerful kingdoms of Wuli and Kantora were in decay, and were threatened by invasion by the Fulbe of Futa Jalon. These kingdoms, once being the terminus of the flourishing west-east salt trade, were insecure with the journey now made dangerous by a two day crossing of wilderness which had appeared between Wuli and the Fula kingdoms of Bundu, due to the sustained hostilities

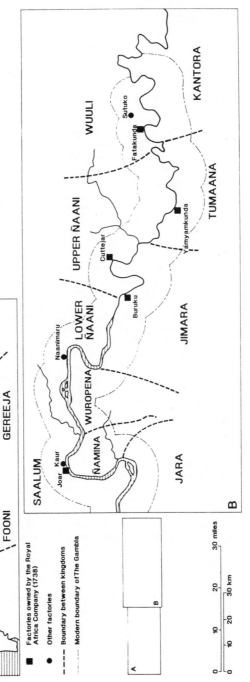

Figure 2:2 Factories owned by the Royal Africa Company on the River Gambia, about 1735.

(Adapted from Curtin, 1975, p.106)

Wally Factory and Samy Factory could not be located.

■ Factories owned by the Royal Africa Company (1738)
● Other factories
--- Boundary between kingdoms
...... Modern boundary of The Gambia

0 10 20 30 miles
0 10 20 30 km

25

between the two. (Curtin 1975, p.75; Quinn 1972, p.32) Enhanced by the appearance of European traders in the river estuary, the once weak states in the west had become stronger. The king of Niumi, for example, imposed customs on all vessels and traders who entered or left his kingdom with merchandise. (Moore 1738, pp.20-45) Park in 1799, regarded him as 'more formidable to Europeans than any other chieftain on the river'. (Park 1878, p.4)

The insecurity in the eastern part of the region obviously discouraged trade along the river, as did the high taxes demanded by the kingdoms at the river's mouth. This change in the internal political organisations of the Gambian region, combined with the disturbances in the western Sudan, caused the shift eastwards of trans-Saharan trade resulting in the decline of the Gambian salt trade, which by the nineteenth century had been reduced to a trickle. (Quinn 1972, p.8) The economic nucleus of the river had thus shifted from the east to the west, encouraging the English to set up a trading post at James Island in 1661, with the French establishing one opposite at Albreda.

The earliest European traders to the river were principally interested in gold. For this reason the gold trade is described in some detail by the early travellers. [8] But as this ambition become frustrated it was found that other goods were just as attractive as trading items. Slaves, hides, ivory and beeswax were exchanged for gin, guns, cloth, tobacco and ornaments. A thriving trade developed in these articles so that by 1730, Moore (1738) was able to write, 'The chief trade of this country is gold, slaves, elephants teeth and beeswax', and by the 1730s this trade was undertaken at fourteen factories along the river owned by the Royal African Company. Figure 2:2, shows the location of these factories, demonstrating their relatively even distribution along the river. By the eighteenth century, the principal objective of the European trading companies in the river had become the procurement of slaves for the West Indian plantations. Senegambia was one of the first sub-Saharan sources of slaves to be shipped across the Atlantic. The main pattern of Senegambian slave origins was simple: a small supply of slaves from the coast, with a larger supply coming from the Bambara core area, which seems to be associated with the foundation of the kingdom of Segu.

Compared with areas further to the east, the Gambian region had not been a major slave exporting area in the eighteenth century. Slaves had, however, been the principal article of export at that time. (See Table 2:1) With the British Government proclamation abolishing the slave trade in 1807, the Gambian region was to experience a period of economic uncertainty. Merchants trading in the region were desperately seeking a legitimate form of commerce as a substitute for the slave trade. One possibility was gum.

Table 2:1
Changing proportions of major Senegambian exports
at half century intervals, 1680s-1830s

Commodity	Percentage of major exports			
	1680s	1730s	1780s	1830s
Gold	5.0	7.8	0.2	3.0
Gum	8.1	9.4	12.0	71.8
Hides	8.5	-	-	8.1
Ivory	12.4	4.0	0.2	2.8
Slaves	55.3	64.3	86.5	1.9
Wax	10.8	14.5	1.1	9.9
Groundnuts	-	-	-	2.6
Total	100.0	100.0	100.0	100.0

Source: Curtin 1975, p.327

Gum arabic was one of the earliest exotic commodities to be imported regularly into Europe. Initially, supplies were obtained from Arabia and Nilotic Sudan, but from the sixteenth century onwards West Africa, most notably the Senegambian region, had begun to contribute to the trade. By the eighteenth century the Senegambia had become the only significant supplier to Europe, where gum was used for paper making, confectionary production and in the textile industry. Up to 1750 European consumption of gum is thought to have been less than 500 metric tons a year. But in the 1740s Senegambian gum suddenly became important, with the French Compagnie des Indes shipping more than 1,000 metric tons in 1743 and 1746. As demand rose so did the price, increasing five times on the old price in the 1770s, ten times the old price in the 1780s and fifteen times the old price in the period 1823-27. However by the 1840s the high prices had brought other sources onto the market, so demand for Senegambian gum levelled off.

After 1833 the export of gum from the Gambia River was overtaken in value by the export of hides and was never able to reassert itself. (See figure 2:3) In that year, hides and beeswax both contributed 23 per cent of the total export income of the Gambia with gum at 20 per cent, a downward trend that was to continue. Hides began to be an important export from Senegambia in the sixteenth century, when the number exported was about 6,000-7,000 hides per year. Curtin estimates that exports may have reached

27

150,000 per year in the 1660s due to an increase in European demand for leather. In the eighteenth century the price for hides fell to only £2 per hundred, from a price of £7.8s in 1680, and the market slumped. It was not until the early nineteenth century that prices recovered, reaching £12.10s per hundred in the 1820s and £20 per hundred in the 1830s and 1840s. Stimulated by this dramatic price rise in the early nineteenth century, hide exports rose to an annual average of 176,000. (Curtin 1975, pp.220-1) By 1830-31 hide exports from The Gambia made up 30 per cent of total exports by value. Hides kept its proportion in the export league until 1845, when its share of the export trade fell to less than 10 per cent and was never to recover.

As early as 1810, the dominant export item from the River Gambia was beeswax. In 1817 beeswax is reported to have accounted for 90 per cent of the total value of all Gambian exports. (Gray 1966, p.379) In 1829, total exports from the River were valued at £65,130 - wax accounting for 41 per cent, hides 14 per cent, teak 13 per cent, [9] gum 10 per cent, ivory six per cent, rice five per cent, gold four per cent and corn three per cent. [10] Beeswax retained its dominance as The Gambia's principal export until 1844, when it was overtaken by groundnuts. In that year, the percentage share of groundnuts had risen by 40 per cent in twelve months, to a record 64 per cent. This gave beeswax a poor second with 20 per cent, hides with 12 per cent and gum with three per cent. By 1861, the value of groundnuts exported from the River was £101,060 and represented 74 per cent of the total value of exports, with wax and hides contributing a combined 17 per cent. Figure 2:3 shows the percentage of total export earnings contributed by groundnuts, gum, hides and beeswax for the period 1825-1900, demonstrating how these commodities fluctuated in importance, with groundnuts quickly becoming firmly established as the river's chief export.

During this hundred year period the region saw much political upheaval. In the first half of the century the affairs of the Gambian riverine kingdoms were very stormy. There was no overlord with sovereign power over any extensive area on the river, political authority among the indigenous peoples being uneasily shared by numerous chiefs. With the spread of Islam a large proliferation of Muslim political institutions had sprung up, threatening the established Mandinka authority. This uneasy peace ended in 1861, with the beginning of the Soninke-Marabout wars which were not to end until 1901, with the death of Fodi Kabba, one of the principal Muslim leaders.

By the 1880s the economy of the river was showing signs of these strains. Groundnut production was minimal, in 1886 only 5,996 tons (6,092 metric tons) (valued at £38,400) were exported and in the following year the tonnage was down to 2,999 (3,047 metric tons) with a value of only £26,001, and representing only 30 per cent of the total value of exports. (Blue Books) Famine was widespread and noted in the Governor's report in 1876.

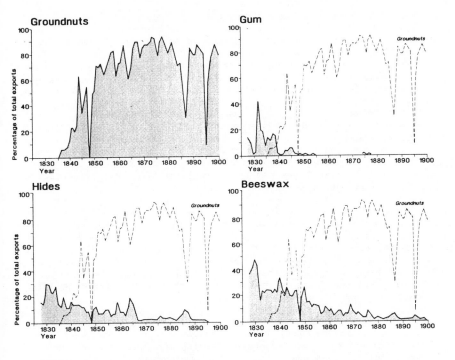

Figure 2:3   Groundnut, gum, hide and beeswax exports from The
Gambia, as percentages of total exports, 1825–1900

Source: Blue Books

> There was much privation felt among the natives on the upper
> river many of whom died from starvation.   The scarcity of food
> was owing to two causes, the native wars prevented in some
> cases the culture of provisions and predatory bands of so
> called warriors scoured the country, pillaging as they went.
> (Annual Report 1876, p.140)

Against this sombre background the British and French sought to
extend their commercial and political power.   The primary
objective of both colonial powers in the Senegambia was to re-
establish trade through the establishment of peace and order.   In
1889, the French and British agreed to partition the Senegambia to
protect their respective commercial interests and signed the
Anglo-French Convention in August of that year.   The Gambia became
a British protectorate.

29

The disappearance of marketplaces

During the period 1700 to 1900 much is written about the trade of the Gambia River, but we know nothing of the local marketing system. Travellers make no mention of local markets. In their journals, neither Moore (1738), Adanson (1759), Park (1878), nor Mollien (1820), mention local markets, nor do the colonial reports of the period. Moore, who travelled extensively for a number of years in the Gambian region in the employ of the Royal African Company, not once mentions a market. Similarly, Park, who spent a lot of time in The Gambia and who was at great pains to describe the country and its people, omits to mention markets. It seems unlikely that these eighteenth and nineteenth century travellers were blind to a phenomenon that had attracted their predecessors and other contemporaries elsewhere.

This lack of documentary evidence has led Ames (1962) to comment that 'Markets, it seems were absent' in the Senegambian region. His argument rests on the evidence that 'early observers of the Gambia, like Jobson and Moore, give many descriptions of the local scene, but never refer to a marketplace', (Ames 1962, p.31) and leads him to conclude that 'Native Gambian marketplaces seem to have developed long after the Europeans had established trading centres'.

This was clearly not the case. Ames had not read Jobson carefully enough and had neglected other travel accounts, particularly those of Cadamosto, Pereira and Donelha. He seems to have fallen into the trap of the anthropologists' 'changeless past'. He is correct, though, to a certain degree, since sources do seem to suggest that marketplaces had disappeared in the eighteenth and nineteenth centuries. There could be two explanations for this. Firstly, that the marketplace did temporarily disappear from the Gambian scene or, secondly, that the markets continued to function at customary places, but were not documented.

Marketplaces temporarily disappear

It is possible that with the widespread violence and warfare in the region, particularly in the nineteenth century, markets were not able to function effectively, and in fact did not open. This perhaps accounts for the food shortages and famines that were common at this time. However this is surprising in a region with such a long history of commercial exchange and economic specialisation.

After 1857, there is evidence to suggest that north bank farmers were neglecting the cultivation of food crops. It appears that they were growing more groundnuts to the detriment of their food crops, on the assumption that they could buy food from the proceeds of the export crop. In this way, the farmers created a cash demand for locally produced foodstuffs, as well as for imported rice. This dilemma was clearly expressed by Governor D'Arcy in a report of 1861, in which he wrote that the people of Baddibu

> ... need food, considerable quantities of which come from the south bank of the river - the Baddibu people themselves growing ever increasing quantities of groundnuts but rarely do they now grow sufficient food to feed themselves. The situation is the same in neighbouring Niumi. The men are no longer devoting effort to food cultivation. They leave this task entirely to the women, while they pursue groundnuts in earnest ... It is my opinion that this situation is a great ill that the extension of commerce has recently brought to the river ... I am acquainted with the Negro mind; as long as groundnuts pay to cultivate, the people will continue to devote their time to the cash crop, using the rewards of commerce to purchase imported rice, and local foodstuffs where available. (CO87/71, 1861)

Jeng (1978) points out that it was the traditionally more productive and relatively well populated north bank that concentrated on groundnut production to the detriment of food cultivation, while the more sparsely populated and less productive south bank emphasised food production. In 1860 Governor D'Arcy visited Gunjur in Kombo and reported that 'It is pleasing to see the people have not forgotten their food crops of cereals and vegetables'. (CO87/69, 1860) In the same year he visited Yundum, also in Kombo and reported a similar pattern, observing that 'natives come from various districts, even from the other side of the river, to buy food'. (CO87/69, 1860) How they procured their food is not described, but it was not via the marketplace, otherwise he would not have had to organise a fair at Sukuta in 1861. This fair he states

> afforded me an opportunity to observe the productions of the soil. Many people repaired to Sabiji [Sukuta] from villages in Niumi on the North Bank, returning home with foodstuffs. It was gratifying to observe that Sabiji people are resisting the growing habit of neglecting foodcrops that is so widespread in the river. (CO87/71, 1861)

At Lincoln, near the mouth of the Casamance River, the people were producing large quantities of foodstuffs, and the Governor disclosed to the Colonial Office that Lincoln was supplying Bathurst with rice. (Jeng 1978, p.152) The local marketing system, whatever its form, was obviously failing to supply the colony.

It is clear that the farmers in the south bank responded to the expansion in groundnut cultivation by specialising in food production. It might be expected that this specialisation would have led to an expansion of the internal market, made manifest in marketplaces, but this does not appear to have occurred. However, it is improbable that no indigenous exchange took place at all. Rather it is suspected that due to the slave trade and the

31

unsettled political situation in the region at the time, exchange was undertaken outside of the marketplace, by other mechanisms. These could be indigenous, such as the 'house trade' described by Hill (1969, 1971) in Northern Nigeria, or by itinerant peddlars and seasonal fairs. Alternatively, it is plausible to suggest that exchange was closely linked with the slave (and later 'legitimate') traders and their imported commodity factories, similar to the commodity stores used by the United Africa Company and others. These factories stocked food, cloth, tobacco and other items, which were sold or advanced so that the producers were obliged to sell at the traders' weights and prices. This meant that the traders functioned as wholesalers in the local foodstuff market.

Marketplaces functioned, but were not documented by travellers

It is possible that markets described by earlier travellers continued to function but were not documented. There are three reasons why this may have occurred. Firstly, the trader could perform his business without leaving the trading post. Slaves were brought from coastal African merchants and therefore the trader had no need to leave the factory. It seems that the inland states were well organised to bring trade to the coast; Europeans did not need to go inland, therefore they had no reason to come into contact with local markets and report them. Fage states this clearly:

> Europeans had no need to penetrate beyond the immediate coastlands and the interior communities were content to do their business by sending their traders to lodge with mechants at the coast who acted as agents for, and intermediaries in, the trade with the Europeans. (Fage 1969,. p.96)

Secondly, it may be that markets were no longer held in open fields, as had previously been the case. Perhaps because of the hostilities along the river and the fear of slave raiding, local markets were now held inside the stockades of the villages - areas where Europeans were not welcome. It is plain that certain villages were important trading points, particularly Kaur. Moore described it in 1730 as 'the chief town on the whole river; and as I hinted before, the best place for trade'. (Moore 1738, p.102) A hundred years later, Ingram described the town:

> The trade of this town is considerable; the principal articles of produce being corn, millet, hides, country cloths called pangs or paynes, groundnuts, ivory and wax. (Ingram 1847, pp.150-5)

It would seem unlikely that such an eminent trading village producing both subsistence and export goods did not have a local market, but neither Moore nor Ingram mentions one. The third reason why, perhaps, markets were not recorded by these journalists, is that they were such common occurrences that it was just assumed that each major settlement would have one, and the obvious would not be stated in the journals. The only market to be mentioned by the journals kept by Europeans at this time is the

32

Albert Market in the colony of Bathurst. Burton in 1863 describes
it beautifully.

> The scene as we approach the neat market "Albert" and dome
> with zinc or iron roof – built by Govenor O'Connor – becomes
> amusing. Men and women sit under the tall cotton trees and
> the stately banyans, selling oranges, limes and paw paws,
> vegetables of all kinds, especially the Bhendi of India, here,
> as in the Southern States of North America, called okra, or
> okros and making the best thickening for soups; tomatoes which
> would grow wild upon the coast as in the interior, and form an
> admirable corrective to the climate, yams, batatas or sweet
> potatoes, and baskets of groundnuts, which up river even
> pigeons are fed. There are kolanuts both for retail in
> baskets and packed in bundles with bamboo matting – here they
> are imported and become costly. The livestock consists of a
> few geese and turkeys, Manilla ducks . . . (Burton 1863,
> pp.152-3)

There appears to be quite a variety of foodstuffs available in
the Albert Market suggesting that not all these were produced on
the island. Many goods must have come in from the Kombos or
possibly across the river, from Niumi. Burton goes on to
emphasise the role played by Georgetown: 'It is however, the key
of the interior, and a depot of trade, without which Bathurst
would soon see an empty market.' (Burton 1863, pp.168-9) The
fact that many of the goods came from outside Banjul Island is
supported by Whitford, who visited the Colony between 1853 and
1875 and who writes, 'Representatives of many tribes come by long
distances by river, to barter produce for goods', in a very
crowded market. (Whitford 1967, pp.18-19) This strongly suggests
that there was no functioning marketplace system upriver
performing the tasks of mediating between rural producer and
ultimate urban consumer.

From the available evidence, it seems clear that marketplaces
did in fact 'disappear' from the Gambian region in the eighteenth
and nineteenth centuries. However, it does not follow that there
were no exchange transactions. The fact that the market at
Bathurst was well supplied and that Governor D'Arcy reported
people crossing the river to 'procure' food from the Kombos,
indicates that exchange did occur, although it was not undertaken
in the marketplace.

Conclusion

From the evidence presented, it can be said that two market
networks existed in the Gambian region on the pre-colonial period;
firstly, the local subsistence orientated marketing network which
supplied local people with their everyday needs; secondly, similar
markets that had been temporarily given added economic importance
by the stimulus of long distance trade, be it the salt, slave or
groundnut trade. In these markets more luxurious items could be

purchased. The location of the second type of market depended on
the good being traded and the location of the demand for it. In
the fifteenth and sixteenth centuries these markets were located
in the eastern Kantora region of the river, as break-of-bulk
points for the Sudanese salt trade. With the shift in emphasis
from the Sudan to the Atlantic, brought about by the trans-
Atlantic slave trade, there was a shift of these prominent long
distance trade orientated markets from the eastern region, to
convenient river locations in the west. These riverine markets
were later reinforced by the need to buy and ship out large
quantities of groundnuts, grown in the interior, during the
nineteenth and twentieth centuries.

One rather odd phenomenon of the Gambian region is the apparent
disappearance of markets in the region in the eighteenth and
nineteenth centuries. As no written record of a Gambian
marketplace appears to survive, the problem is whether there were
functioning marketplaces during these two hundred years which went
unrecorded, or did they temporarily disappear, trade and exchange
being effected through other mechanisms. Evidence is scant, but
it is hypothesised that, due to the political upheavals in the
region at this time and the growth of the slave trade,
marketplaces did in fact disappear, but exchange continued through
other mechanisms. With colonial domination of the region at the
turn of the twentieth century, markets re-emerge. (Barrett 1986)

The Gambian region has consistently been an export region.
Since the early seventeenth century one product has made up more
than half the total value of its exports. Firstly, it was salt,
followed by hides; in the late seventeenth century slaves
dominated. By the 1830s, gum was important, followed by a
confused period in which hides and beeswax vied for supremacy,
which by the 1840s had been superceded by the groundnut. In
short, the Gambian region adjusted again and again over three
centuries to a combination of changing external demand and
changing supply conditions at home. The groundnut revolution of
the nineteenth century was only the last of a series of commercial
revolutions in the region.

The groundnut trade has had the most profound influence on
present-day commerce in the region, and is primarily responsible
for the present-day pattern of local markets. The development of
the trade under colonial rule will be discussed in the next
chapter, with its influence on the local exchange network being
described in Chapter Five.

Notes

[1]   See J.D. Fage 1969, p.28.
[2]   McIntosh (1981) puts forward the argument that 'Wangara' was
       in fact the Inland Delta of the Niger.

[3]   Bovill 1958, p.193.
[4]   Religious teachers, (Muslim marabouts), probably of Mandinka origin.
[5]   Jula is Mandinka for 'trader', and is not to be confused with the jola, an ethnic group of the region.
[6]   A kingdom in the eastern part of present day Gambia, extending as far east as the Barrakunda Falls.
[7]   Bloodstones.
[8]   Jobson actually entitled the journal of his expedition up the River Gambia The Golden Trade.
[9]   In 1822, timber, particularly mahogany, began to be exported, but it was a short lived experiment, largely because the tectona forests were unstable and quickly destroyed.
[10] Blue Book 1829. 'Corn' would be millets and sorghums, and possibly maize; rice was listed separately.
[11] In this area, due to the seclusion of the women in Islamic tradition, the women continue to trade, but in the comfort and security of their own compound. The information network is so efficient that customers know which compound to visit for which commodity, with children acting as couriers.

3 The adoption of the groundnut into the Gambian economy

Introduction

This chapter investigates the adoption of the groundnut into the
economy of the Gambian region in the nineteenth and twentieth
centuries. The importance of the cash crop can be traced back to
the 1830s when demand for vegetable oils in Europe suddenly
expanded and continued to expand in association with the growth of
the margarine industry. It is suggested that in the first few
decades of commercial groundnut production, the farmer was
following a 'vent for surplus' policy, however by the turn of the
twentieth century and the imposition of colonial rule, this is no
longer the case. The effect of colonial policy is analysed
emphasising the effect of taxation and the implementation of a
colonial marketing board system on groundnut production. The
chapter continues by examining the policies of the independent
Gambian government demonstrating how the structure of the
cooperative movement and many agricultural development projects
favour the cultivation of the cash crop despite government calls
for increased food production. The chapter concludes by analysing
farm economies, which show that the Gambian farmer makes a totally
rational economic decision when he plants his fields with
groundnuts rather than food crops. The result is an increasing
dependency on the world market, both for the sale of the cash crop
and for the purchase of food.

The groundnut as a 'vent for surplus' crop, 1830-90

The groundnut (arachis hypogaea) is a legume indigenous to South
America and is almost certainly native to Brazil. It is thought
to have been introduced to Africa by the Portuguese in the
sixteenth century. (Brooks 1975) However, it attracted little
attention from European observers until the late eighteenth
century. Even the French botanist Adanson (1759) in the account
of his research in Senegambia from 1749-53 did not describe
groundnut cultivation although he was familiar with the plant. As
late as 1824 an observant European visitor to The Gambia (Brooks
1975, p.32) remarked on groundnut cultivation only because the
tops of the plant were fed to horses, which was alleged to be the
reason why Gambian horses were stronger and longer lived than
elsewhere in West Africa.

In the course of the two centuries preceding the 1830s the
groundnut has been introduced and absorbed into the domestic
economy of the Gambian household. However, before the 1830s the
crop was simply a minor item in the diverse list of crops grown
strictly for home consumption and exchange in the local market.
Most producers regarded the groundnut mainly as an insurance
against millet failure. This two century period is seen by Curtin
as a broad epoch of "comparative stability in agricultural
technology". (Curtin 1975, p.13) After 1830, groundnuts began
conspicuously to dominate the export sector. It is important to
note that there was not the introduction of novel, exotic and
improved technology, which is usually associated with such a
change. The stable agricultural technology described by Curtin
continued to function after 1830, despite the disruption to
agriculture and trade caused by the Soninke-Marabout wars of the
second half of the nineteenth century.

The first groundnuts were recorded as being exported from the
Gambian region in 1830 and were shipped to the West Indies, it is
assumed to be tested at the Institute of Tropical Agriculture
there. The next recorded exports are in 1834, when 213 baskets
(Blue Books 1834) were shipped to London, probably to Forster and
Smith, who were the leading company in initiating the
commercialisation of groundnuts. Once this trade had been
initiated, groundnut exports from The Gambia increased at a
phenomenal rate. By the 1840s thousands of tons of nuts were
being exported (see Figure 3:1), and exports have continued to
rise steadily since then.

Hogendorn (1976) argues that the adoption of the groundnut by
Gambian farmers in the nineteenth century can be explained by
'vent for surplus' theory. This theory was first publicised by
Myint in 1958, in an attempt to explain the rapid growth of
agricultural exports from Asia and Africa in the eighteenth and
nineteenth centuries. He claimed that the dramatic growth of
exports in these areas had been directly attributable to the

existence of surplus factors of production present in previously
isolated, under utilised areas which, when exposed to the
international market and thereby provided with a vent, were
capable of increasing exports while simultaneously maintaining
production for domestic consumption. In the Gambian region in the
nineteenth century, there was plenty of open land, a demand
existed for European goods and groundnuts could be interplanted
with food crops; all the necessary conditions for 'vent for
surplus' were fulfilled.

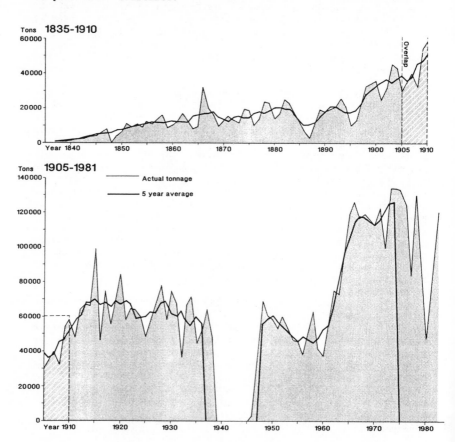

Figure 3:1   Tonnages of groundnuts exported from The Gambia, 1835–
1981

Source: Blue Books, GPMB Reports

Recently, the theory has been widely criticised for neglecting other important indigenous factors (see Freund 1977; Hart 1982). Hart argues that internal class struggles were important in the adoption of the new cash crop in the Senegambia, a factor 'vent for surplus' omits. He states that the transition of the Gambian region into an export orientated cash crop economy, was due to the collapse of the slave market and a rise in demand for vegetable oils, which meant that:

> The coastal and near-coastal elites badly needed to restore their income, maintain their prestige, and find a new place of power in the emergent European-dominated system. (Hart 1982, p.112)

They did this by turning to groundnut cultivation. Using Senegal as an example, Hart elaborates:

> The traditional hierarchies of slaves, soldiers, chiefs and hunters were undermined in the nineteenth century by an early French policy of colonization, by the abolition of slavery, and by loss of feudal taxes. Once they became sedentary, these peoples chose groundnuts as a source of money, to shore up their shattered prestige and then set freed slaves to work growing them. (Hart 1982, p.67)

It is difficult to find evidence to support this argument, but it is obviously a factor that must be examined in more depth, although it is out of the sphere of this study. It should be added, however, that it was not only the elite along with their slaves that produced groundnuts in the Senegambian region during this period, many peasant farmers also participated in the trade. They did so in an effort to raise their living standards and purchase some of the many imported European goods that were offered by the European firms in exchange for groundnuts.

After 1860, and particularly with colonial domination of the region in the 1890s, the situation changed and groundnut cultivation can no longer be seen in terms of 'vent for surplus'. Production of the profitable cash crop was directly and indirectly encouraged by the colonial government, hastening a process that had begun in the early nineteenth century and ensuring the dominance of the crop in the present-day Gambian economy.

The encouragement of groundnut production by the Colonial Government

In 1888 The Gambia became a British protectorate with Bathurst and environs (Kombo St. Mary) remaining a Crown Colony. During the period 1888 to 1939 The Gambia acquired many of the classic features of British rule. The colonial government was established at Bathurst and consisted of a Governor, a few expatriate assistants and an Executive and a Legislative council. The main concern of the administration was to keep the peace and collect taxes. Outside Bathurst, the position of the traditional chiefs was confirmed and in areas where the chieftaincy was vacant, new

ones were appointed by the British. However, their position had
been altered in that they were now responsible to the Travelling
Commissioner, an expatriate appointed by the colonial government.
[2] Under Section 14 of the 1894 Protectorate Ordinance, it was
stipulated that chiefs shall "obey all orders given by the
Commissioner for the order and general good management of the
district". (Crowder 1968) As there were only two Travelling
Commissioners (one responsible for the north bank and the other
the south bank of the river), when they were absent from an area,
the chiefs presided over their own courts. The chiefs were also
responsible for the upkeep of roads and the collection of the Yard
Tax (see below). This system proved so successful that in 1933
Governor Palmer introduced the Native Authority system in The
Gambia. These Native Authorities usually consisted of a single
chief, empowered to issue orders enforceable through Native
Authority Tribunals, and also to make rules, subject to the
Governor's approval for "the peace, good order and welfare of
those within their jurisdiction". (Hailey 1951, p.336) The
impact of British rule during this period was very limited and its
principal effect was to consolidate the status quo rather than to
begin a process of cumulative economic, political or social
change.

During these years groundnuts continued to be the mainstay of
the economy. In 1888, 10,207 tons (10,370 metric tons) of
groundnuts were exported from the area, in 1900 35,805 tons
(36,378 metric tons), in 1910 58,456 tons (59,391 metric tons) and
in 1920 exports of the cash crop had reached 85,190 tons (86,553
metric tons). (See Figure 3:1) This rapid rise in groundnut
exports can be directly attributed to the increased European
demand for margarine. (McPhee 1926) The original demand for
groundnuts had come from France, where groundnut oil was used in
soap making, and as a cheap substitute for olive oil in cooking.
For a time (1836-40) a large share was exported to USA, 75 per
cent by value in 1838/9, but this was much reduced by the US
Tariff Act of 1842 which curtailed imports of foreign nuts.
However, at the turn of the century, margarine was invented, with
two Dutch companies, Anton Jurgens and Van den Bergh having
captured most of the market in Germany, the Low Countries and
Britain. From 1906-13, the consumption of margarine doubled in
Britain, and from 1906-14 in Germany, demand increased by 250 per
cent. [3] With the hydrogenation process perfected in 1909,
liquid oil could be used in margarine production in place of the
animal fat product, oleo. This led to a huge increase in demand
for groundnut oil, which was much cheaper than oleo. In Jurgen's
factories in June 1907, margarine production consisted of 63 per
cent animal fat, but by January 1914 this figure had dropped to
only 14 per cent. (Hogendorn 1976, p.23) This technical
breakthrough helps to explain the huge export of groundnuts from
The Gambia during this period, which reached what was then an all
time high of 96,152 tons (97,690 metric tons) in 1915, a figure
that was not to be bettered until 1965.

Despite this huge external demand for nuts, it was felt by the trading community that the Gambian farmer was not producing as many nuts as he could. It was felt that he needed more incentive. This 'incentive' was given to him by the colonial government when they introduced taxes that had to be paid in specie. This necessitated the earning of money, which in turn 'stimulated' cash cropping, as it was the only method by which most Gambians could pay the new taxes.

The first tax to be imposed in The Gambia by the colonial administration was the Trader's Licences Ordinance, implemented in 1893, followed shortly afterwards by a tax on strange farmers. [4] These were justified by the colonial government on the grounds that in the past, the high rents demanded by landlords from strange farmers had discouraged them from farming in The Gambia; and that the traders' licences were necessary to minimise conflict between chiefs and traders.

The Traders' Licence Ordinance abolished the long established practice of trader payment of 'custom' to the various chiefs for permission to trade in the interior. From 1893 traders were required to pay for licences in Bathurst and then merely to show them to the chiefs in the interior who would receive a percentage of the fee from the government. This ordinance reflected the government's concern to minimise conflicts between chiefs and traders and in this way improve the conditions for groundnut trading. The licence fees did not contribute large sums of money to the colonial coffer, but did help to establish the supremacy of the colonial administration in the Protectorate by, in effect, turning the chiefs into salaried officials of the colonial bureaucracy; they were now expected to collaborate with the colonial government if they wanted to receive any cash handouts. In 1895, the traders protested vigorously against the imposition of the licences, calling them "unconstitutional", but their objections failed to sway the Governor and the Colonial Office. Traders' Licences had come to stay. Whereas traders' licences affected both the merchants and the chiefs, the tax on strange farmers affected only the chiefs, and helped emphasise their new position in the colonial bureaucracy. Previous to colonial administration, each strange farmer paid a sum of money to the chief, who gave the relevant alakali (village head) a share. The colonial government saw this traditional 'rent' as too high and, concerned that it was discouraging strange farmers from coming into the region to cultivate groundnuts, imposed a fixed rent. This was fixed at 4s for each strange farmer, out of which 1s went to the chief, 2s was shared out between the chiefs alakalis and 1s was retained by the government. It was not until after the establishment of both these taxes that the Protectorate Yard Tax Ordinance was introduced in 1895. The Gambian producers themselves were now being directly taxed by the government. Each yard containing huts was taxed according to the number of huts and whether they were occupied by members of the family or by strangers. [5]

It has been argued that taxation of agricultural producers by colonial governments forces producers to undertake cash crop production. Amin writes about the "taxation of peasants in money which forced them to produce what the monopolists offered to buy". (Amin 1972, p.520) Hogendorn explains more fully:

> The economic philosophy behind a system of direct cash taxation in the African colonial context is simple enough. It was the most effective tool through which subsistence farmers could be drawn into the money economy; it could not be avoided even by those who did not want to buy imported goods or preferred leisure to work. Every taxpayer had either to work for wages or to sell some product for which there was a market. (Hogendorn 1975, p.302)

There is evidence from The Gambia during this period, which strongly confirms Hogendorn's analysis. In 1899 Travelling Commissioner Ozanne wrote that:

> since the introduction of direct taxation, the area of cultivation under groundnuts increases considerably every year, whilst that under corn, cotton and indigo is decreasing proportionately, as the natives now even more than in the past prefer to grow groundnuts for which they can get cash to pay the taxes and then as has been the practise buy other things from the Jollops in the interior. (CO87/159, 1899)

In 1900 Travelling Commissioner Sitwell disclosed how the Jolas on the south bank of the river, who were traditional food crop cultivators (see Chapter Two), now had to enter groundnut production:

> Before I went on leave last year I directed the Jolahs at Foni to plant groundnuts for the payment of tax, and I am pleased to report that on my tour through I noted that each stockade had its small heap of nuts. (CO87/160, 1900)

It must be noted that direct taxation in The Gambia was not accepted without some protest. But resistance was in no way comparable in scale or complexity to the Sierra Leone hut tax riots of 1897-98. (Crowder 1968) Many Gambian chiefs did protest against direct taxation and many

> flatly refused to entertain any idea of the laws with regard to Traders' Licences' Farm Rents and slavery; they maintained that they had a right to the "customs" from the traders and the Farm Rents, and that they would go on slave-dealing, and further that if the Government attempted to enforce these laws they would leave and go over to French country. (CO87/143, 1893)

In 1897 eleven north and south bank chiefs met at Brikama to talk and protest against the hut tax. The chiefs reached the unanimous decision that their people would not pay the hut tax because "they were all too poor to bear taxation". (CO87/154, 1897) Between 1897 and 1899 the Travelling Commissioners had little success in persuading the chiefs to accept taxation, so in 1900 a "Protectorate Punitive Expedition" had to be organised. By such methods the chiefs were finally forced to accept the new colonial order. The evidence suggests that after the implementation of direct taxation in The Gambia, there was an increase in groundnut production accompanied by an increase in the area under groundnut cultivation. Direct taxation had produced the desired result.

One aspect of the groundnut trade in which the colonial government was directly active was the distribution of seed nuts. In December 1893 there had been a disastrous rain, which seriously affected seednuts and resulted in bad harvests for the next three years. In order to assist farmers restore production the colonial government in 1896 imported a quantity of seednuts from Senegal to issue to farmers on credit, and by 1909 this had become an annual undertaking by the government. However, a period of bad harvests and low prices meant that farmers became heavily indebted to the government. In 1925, debts of £33,000 had to be written off and in 1932 advances of rice and seednuts were discontinued. The passing of the Native Authority Ordinance in 1933 enabled the Native Authority in each district to make a rule to remedy the situation. The owner of each groundnut farm was required, after the winnowing of the season's crop, to deposit five bushels of seednuts in the village store which would then be distributed to farmers the following season. The scheme met with the full cooperation of the chiefs and people and has been very successful, operating up to the present.

Another important positive step taken by the government during this period was the setting up of an Agricultural Department. This department, set up in 1924, was to deal primarily with groundnut cultivation. A number of agricultural stations were opened in the Protectorate and field experiments were carried out. Rotary screens were introduced for the purpose of cleaning the nuts at the time of purchase and thus ensuring that they were shipped clean. However, all this government interest was disturbed by the Second World War which heralded a renewed interest in the groundnut trade by the colonial government and resulted in its eventual control by the government through a marketing board.

After World War Two, the British government began to modify its ideas and more money was spent in the colonies. In The Gambia, Bathurst harbour was improved and a start was made on modernising the colony's roads. The government also began to interfere directly in the economy, and the years 1948-51 saw a major attempt to diversify exports. The most notable failure of the period was the Yundum egg scheme, which lost almost £1 million, and left the colony just as dependent on groundnuts as before. However during this period the Gambia Oilseeds Marketing Board (GOMB), later to become the Groundnut Produce Marketing Board (GPMB), was set up. The origins of the GOMB lie primarily in the emergency commodity control measures instituted by the UK in her colonies during the

Second World War. [7] In 1942 the West African Produce Control Board (WAPCB) had been established with a statutory monopoly over the export of groundnuts, oil palm produce and cocoa. Its aims were to deny supplies to the enemy, to prevent a collapse in prices and to maintain or increase exports. In 1949 the WAPCB was disbanded and the GOMB came into being, its purpose was to determine producer prices and the quality of groundnuts and palm kernels to be marketed. It also had the power to determine the structure of the marketing system, its participants and their remuneration. The GOMB was as closely associated with the colonial government as the WAPCB had been. As Blandford states, "In many Less Developed Countries the Export Marketing Board has tended to become increasingly entwined in government strategy for economic growth and development". (Blandford 1976, p.2) This is most definitely the case in The Gambia.

There is a lot of controversy over the value of export marketing boards, [8] mostly concerning their potential use by the government to manipulate the rural population and monitor their income. It raises some very contentious public policy questions. The existence of a marketing board lends itself to use by the government as a fiscal device. Thus, governments impose export taxes upon the produce they handle (in the case of The Gambia, groundnuts), they then fix the buying price, and then 'utilise' the 'surpluses' retained by the marketing boards. In the Gambian context this reserve fund (known as the 'Farmers' Fund') was used, not to stabilise prices as originally intended, but instead to set up the Fish Marketing Corporation and the Livestock Marketing Board, both of which were put into liquidation only two years after their establishment, [9] thus in effect wasting the groundnut producers' forced savings. This type of problem has led Bauer to comment, "suggestions that they [Export Marketing Boards] are devised for price stabilisation or that they are individual commercial organisations only obscure their nature and function". (Bauer 1954, p.316) This was part of a strong attack by Bauer on the policies of the statutory marketing boards. However, what concerns us here is how the setting up of a marketing board helped stimulate groundnut production in The Gambia after the Second World War.

The GPMB (formerly the GOMB), was created in 1949 to facilitate the collection and export of groundnuts. Whilst the Board is a fully government owned enterprise, it acts as a relatively independent agent. It has its own board of directors and a London office, which is charged with negotiating the sale of groundnuts to international clients. The GPMB has complete control of the groundnut trade, from the collection at the farm level, to the sale on the international market. The advantage to the farmer is that he receives a fixed price for his crop and has a guaranteed market. A similar organisation for other crops does not exist.

The GPMB has encouraged the Gambian producer to grow groundnuts, and by 1965, and The Gambia's independence from colonial rule, groundnut exports had reached a record high of 117,946 tons (119,833 metric tons), and seemed set to continue to rise, the following year reaching 126,385 tons (128,407 metric tons). The economy of the new nation was just as dependent on the groundnut as the colony had been 65 years earlier.

The continued importance of groundnut production since independence

With independence in 1965, the economy of The Gambia changed little and groundnuts remained the country's main export, although plans were discussed to diversify the economy and increase domestic production of food. In order to try to organise its finances and plan its progress, the new government put forward its objectives in the form of Five Year Plans.

The 1975-80 Five Year Plan was the first attempt to integrate national economic and social development planning in The Gambia. Earlier plans had been essentially public expenditure programmes. The first development plan (1963/4-1966/7) which had covered the transition to independence in 1965, was concerned primarily with administrative and social expenditure. In the second plan (1967/8-1970/1) about 39 per cent of the total planned investment was for transport and communications and 24 per cent for electricity and water supplies, which were almost entirely confined to the Banjul-Kombo St. Mary area. Less than 14 per cent was allocated to agriculture and most of that was aimed at increasing groundnut yields. The third plan (1971/2-1974/5), was intended to directly stimulate productive activities. Accordingly, 23 per cent of projected investment was allocated to agriculture, livestock, fishing and manufacturing. However, transport and communications were allocated 52 per cent, leaving 17 per cent to administrative and social services, and nine per cent to electricity and water supplies.

The present plan states that rural development is the government's first priority, and lists the strategies designed to promote rural development and balance the unequal growth of Banjul. These strategies include investment in rural road and river communications; the provision of incentives to farmers through pricing policies for agricultural inputs and produce; the improvement of the agricultural extension services and the introduction of a farmer functional literacy campaign; commercial and industrial development in rural areas; reorientation of the educational system towards the needs of the rural community; expansion of programmes for rural health, water and electricity services; the improvement of government administrative structures, training of personnel, including the decentralisation of government and its greater involvement in rural problems.

The plan recognises inequalities and states that the correction of disparities within rural areas will involve preference to the poorest members of the community with attention given to the smaller farmer rather than the progressive farmer. This is to be achieved by concentrating on three stated objectives:

a) to improve nutritional standards in rural areas
b) to eliminate bulk cereal imports, and in particular rice, by 1980
c) to diversify rural cash crop incomes.

The aim to eliminate cereal imports, which have been a feature of the economy since 1830 (see Figure 7:1), [10] was an attempt by the government to reduce its balance of payments deficit. This policy has to date failed. Most of the development schemes instigated since independence involve groundnuts to a varying degree, and the new methods of credit allocation introduced by the government, definitely favour the groundnut farmer rather than the producer of food crops.

The effect of credit allocation on food crop production

The government's stated objectives with regard to credit is to phase out pure subsistence credit and to encourage the commercial banks, in particular the publically owned Commercial and Development Bank to assist creditable indigenous entrepreneurs in establishing or expanding commercial or production activities in rural areas. Branches of these banks have been established outside the capital, in Bakau, Serrekunda, Farafenni and Basse. But they have not assisted farmers to the extent that the government would have liked. Of course, there are still the village 'big men' who may lend out money to needy farmers, particularly during the 'hungry season' [11] to buy food, but most major agricultural inputs such as ploughs, seeds and fertilisers must be obtained through the local cooperative union. In order to understand the present system of credit allocation, it is necessary to trace the history and activities of the cooperative movement in The Gambia.

The history of the Gambian Cooperative Movement dates back to the early 1920s when the late Mr. E. Small, a Gambian reformer, made attempts at organising farmers into a countrywide marketing association. By June 1930 over 2,000 farmers had registered as members of the association. (BA3/131) The association was instrumental in holding up groundnut sales in the 1930/1 season as a protest against low prices. This led a colonial officer to write of him,

one might term him an isolated malcontent. There is not the slightest doubt he is not to be trusted, he works behind the scenes and is responsible for the discontent and unrest in Bathurst. (BA 4/42)

But Small was obviously not 'isolated'; there was general support for the cooperative movement and in 1948 the Colonial Council in Bathurst agreed to the formation of a Cooperative

Department and the appointment of a registrar. (BA 2/3293)
Already farmers in Brikama in Western Division, had taken action:

> A group of eleven villages has grown crops communally, sold
> them and lodged the proceeds with the Commissioner, Western
> Division. The long term aim is to build up a substantial
> amount which may be utilised for some worthwhile cooperative
> project. The short term aim is to use the initial proceeds
> for loans to buy food during the 'hungry season'. (BA 2/3293)

Even at this early date, the Gambian farmer had realised the
advantages that lie with cooperative societies, particularly in
providing their members with credit. Previously, credit had been
supplied by the local money lenders and by the agents of the
European firms at the wharf towns.

The Cooperative Societies Ordinance was ratified in May 1950,
but no societies were registered until 1954. (BA 16/1) In
October 1955 when a qualified cooperative officer was appointed,
there were only four small registered societies of the credit and
supply type. In January 1956 the cooperative officer took over
responsibility as registrar from the Financial Secretary and a
programme of development was commenced, directed chiefly at the
organisation of groundnut farmers. The cooperative society
quickly grew. In the 1955/56 season, four experimental groups of
twenty members were in operation. By the 1956/7 season there were
13 registered societies and by August 1957, nine registered
village marketing societies with 357 members. Thirty-six
societies were registered in the 1958/9 season and the palm kernal
trade entered the register for the first time.

In 1960 the objectives of the Produce Marketing Society (as the
cooperative had become known) was stated:

a) to secure for the farmer a larger share of the final value
   of his crop
b) to encourage collective saving by allocation from profits
   to reserve and individual savings by members
c) to extend, control and cheapen agricultural credit by
   borrowing on the security of those savings
d) to encourage farmers to invest in agricultural
   improvements and provide the credit facilities essential
   for such improvement by means of a), b) and c) above.

To help achieve these objectives, five district marketing
unions, and an Apex Banking and Marketing Union were set up in
1961. [12]

After Independence in 1965, the Produce Marketing Society became
known as the Gambia Cooperative Union (GCU) and is the only
registered apex society in the country. Its membership consists
of 62 marketing societies and 32 thrift and credit societies,
representing the two main functions of the Union, marketing
produce and lending money.

<u>Marketing activities of the GCU</u>   The GCU is a licenced buyer for the GPMB, and the 62 marketing societies serve as field agents. The location of these marketing cooperatives offer a good overall coverage of the country, the numbers are shown on Table 3:1.

Table 3:1
The location of marketing cooperatives in The Gambia, 1980

Brikama Circle	11 societies
Mansakonko Circle	9 societies
Georgetown Circle	12 societies
Basse Circle	12 societies
Kerewan Circle	9 societies
Barra Circle	9 societies
Total	62 societies

Source: Department of Cooperatives, 1980

Each society has a single buying point (secco), but the tonnages handled vary considerably. The larger societies may purchase over 2,000 metric tons, whilst the smaller ones may handle as little as 400 metric tons.

Members of the cooperative society sell their groundnut crop to the society and in return receive the government stated price. The society then delivers the produce to the GPMB depots at Kaur, Kuntaur, Basse or Denton Bridge. It is paid the value of the produce delivered plus an allowance to cover handling costs. Cash for the purchase of members' produce is provided interest free by the GCU. At the end of the financial year (30th June), any society with a surplus on trading and a favourable balance with the GCU, pays part of the surplus as a 'bonus' to its members. This is based on the volume of produce that each member has sold to the society, after allocating reserves.

Some societies purchase rice from their members, but the amount is small. The main volume in trade is groundnuts, and the cooperative share in this trade has been increasing steadily: in 1977/8, the GCU increased their share to over 50 per cent for the first time. Table 3:2 shows how the proportion of the trade undertaken by the cooperatives has grown since 1975/6. The government plans to phase out other buying agents, such as traders, making the cooperative societies the sole agents for the GPMB. So far these plans have not been implemented.

Table 3:2
Share of the groundnut trade taken by traders and cooperatives

	1975/6	1976/7	1977/8
	%	%	%
Cooperatives	40.68	43.58	51
Traders	59.32	56.42	48

Source: Rural Development Paper No.12, 1978

<u>Credit facilties offered by the GCU</u>   Apart from selling the groundnut crop to the GPMB, the GCU also provides credit facilities to its members. At the start of the planting season, most farmers are in need of cash.   The GCU, through government guarantee, secures loans from banks for onward lending to its member societies.   At the marketing society level, farmer members are issued cash, based on a percentage value of produce sold to the society the previous season, with a credit limit.   The credit is repaid with interest during the next buying season.   However, many loans are not fully recovered as the figures in Table 3:3 demonstrate.   Due to the increasing incidence of defaulted payments, an enquiry was set up in 1975.   Part of its recommendations were as follows:

> we recommend that part of the annual subsistence credit be issued in the form of farm inputs and materials, if possible, and that the ultimate objective should be to phase out the blanket issue of cash subsistence credit altogether. (Gambia Government 1975, p.15)

In 1976 under a Pilot Project, production credit was made available for the first time. The project was undertaken in three marketing societies, Sankwia, Faraba Banta and Farafenni. Credit was provided in the form of seeds, fertilisers and ox-drawn equipment. This was a supervised credit project and the amount of credit advanced and recovered at 30.6.77 is shown in Table 3:4. There is not enough data available to judge if production credit is more favourable to the farmer than subsistence credit.

Although women are not restricted from becoming cooperative members, the structure and functions of present marketing societies do not facilitate their membership. Since subsistence and production credit is distributed through marketing societies, women are not eligible to receive loans in their own right (they may receive a loan via their husbands). In order to overcome this handicap many women and non-farming men have formed thrift and credit societies. In September 1980 there were 32 thift and credit societies in operation, distributed as follows:

```
Banjul              12 societies
Brikama Circle      14 societies
Barra Circle         2 societies
Georgetown Circle    2 societies
Basse Circle         2 societies
TOTAL               32 societies
```

Source: Authors's fieldwork 1980.

They encompass many professions including the Soldier Town Dyers, the Brikama Artisans and Wood Carvers, the Banjul Seamstresses, the Serrekunda Market Gardeners, the Kombo Fishermen, the Georgetown Rice Growers and general groups known as the Bansang Women, the Kaur Women and the Basse Women.

Table 3:3
Figures of subsistence credit allocated and subsistence credit recovered, 1956 to 1977

	Subsistence credit issued	Subsistence credit outstanding	Subsistence credit recovered
	D,000	D,000	%
1956/69	10,783	36	99.7
1970/1	1,356	90	93.4
1971/2	1,648	120	92.7
1972/3	2,839	575	79.75
1973/4	2,697	250	90.75
1974/5	4,016	318	92.1
1975/6	5,137	456	91.1
1976/7	5,700	311	94.6

Source: Department of Cooperatives, 1977.

Table 3:4
Amount of credit advanced and recovered by the production credit
pilot scheme for the 1976/7 financial year

Name of Society	Number of Loanees	Loan Advanced	Loan Recovered	Recovery
	D	D	%	
Sankwia	622	31,146	29,417	95
Faraba Banta	549	35,674	33,420	94
Farafenni	931	65,979	55,387	84*
TOTAL	2,142	132,799	118,224	89

* Due to crop failure in this area.

Source: Department of Cooperatives, 1977.

Each week, members subscribe an amount of money decided upon by the society as a whole. This is usually in the range of 5-25 bututs. [13] This is deposited with the GCU, which operates a deposit account for every thrift and credit society. Cooperative law states that a registered society is eligible to take a loan not exceeding twice its savings. Since members can only save a small amount each week, its credit allowance is correspondingly small. This situation means that access to inputs and credit is difficult for women, who grow most of the country's rice. The credit system is very obviously biased towards the men who cultivate the groundnut crop, so in effect and indirectly, the government is encouraging the production of groundnuts.

The effect of agricultural development schemes on food crop production

Apart from affecting subsistence credit allocation, cooperative membership can also affect a farmer's chance of participating in one of the government sponsored development projects, in effect barring women from taking part. The case in point is the oxenisation scheme. The majority of Gambian farmers do not own improved farming implements or use animal traction. In 1974/5 only 30 per cent of farming units owned oxen and bulls, whilst only 11 per cent owned horses and 24 per cent donkeys (see Table 3:5). From Table 3:5 it is clear that in some areas farmers are opting for horses and donkeys in preference to oxen. In Western Division, very few units own either horses or donkeys. In contrast in the north bank districts there are more units with donkeys than bulls or oxen, in fact there are three times as many units in the north bank owning donkeys as there are owning oxen.

Oxen are used principally for ploughing, whereas horses and donkeys are used for planting and mechanised hoeing. The advantages of horses and donkeys is that they walk faster and straighter than oxen. However, they do not have the strength or stamina that oxen have.

Table 3:5
Farming units owning tractable livestock

% of units owning

Census District	oxen/bulls	horses	donkeys
Brikama	28	0	3
Mansa Konko	24	2	18
Kerewan	17	11	48
Kuntaur	22	16	35
Georgetown	31	12	19
Basse*	61	22	13
TOTAL	30	11	24

* Based only on 7 enumeration areas

Source: Agricultural Census, 1974/5

At the present time, the Department of Agriculture has no policy on the role of horses and donkeys in cultivation, but it does have a policy of oxenisation which is disseminated through the Mixed Farming Centres and is funded by the Rural Development Project and the European Economic Community. The criteria on which participants are accepted onto the programme are as follows:

a) the participant must be a cooperative member with a satisfactory repayment record
b) he must cultivate rice or groundnuts
c) he must possess a pair of oxen or purchase one and receive the second on credit
d) he must have access to a minimum labour force of six adults to make the project economically viable for him.

These stipulations obviously exclude a majority of the farming population from the scheme, particularly the women. As Mettrick states in his evaluation of the oxenisation programme, "Half the agricultural labour force responsible for a large part of the food supply is ignored by the extension service". (Mettrick 1978, p.35) The programme once again favours the male farmers who tend to cultivate groundnuts, and enables those with already high incomes to generate even higher incomes, whilst ignoring the small farmer that the government stipulates should be helped.

The oxenisation project covers 79 villages (total population of 47,148) in Lower River Division, North Bank Division and MacCarthy Island Division. This area was chosen as it had the least coverage of existing development projects, the rice and cotton schemes being undertaken in MacCarthy Island Division and Upper River Division. All the selected villages farmed colluvial slopes and cultivated some rice.

It is still too early to evaluate the impact of the project on crop production. Figures for rice production are not available, but Rural Development Project figures for the groundnut output suggest an average yield increase of 366 kg/ha, that is 28 per cent. This looks good on paper but has some hidden implications. With the introduction of oxenisation along with improved implements, such as ploughs and seeders, one would expect an increase in the area farmed assuming the same labour input. But no change in the absolute area under cultivation was registered; however, there were changes in the crop mix. The share of groundnuts increased by 40 per cent at the expense of rice and to a lesser extent of maize. This seems odd, as rice and groundnuts do not compete directly for either land or labour, particularly as rainfed rice is the women's responsibility. [14] The implication is that despite inputs of oxen, implements and fertiliser, farmers had sufficient seed to maintain their groundnut area, but not enough rice seed after the bad drought season the year before. As women are the principal rice cultivators this shows the need to incorporate them into a system whereby they can obtain inputs such as rice seed on credit and in their own right.

Since independence the government's stated aim is to diversify the agricultural economy and increase the output of food crops, but this has not occurred. In 1973 and 1974, the Department of Agriculture, advised by the FAO, undertook two sample surveys designed to cover 75 per cent of the rural population. [15] In both years all but a few of the enumerated units grew groundnuts. Cropping patterns in the average sampled farming unit are shown in Table 3:6.

In 1973, the average farmer decided to plant 63.5 per cent of his cultivated area with groundnuts. Although drawn from a sample, this figure seems to be representative. In 1976/7, of the total cultivated area in The Gambia, 61 per cent was devoted to the production of groundnuts, and from Table 3:7 the dominance of the groundnut crop becomes fully evident. Concentration is greatest in North Bank Division, with only 33 per cent of cultivable land not under groundnut cultivation. The smallest proportion of land under groundnuts is in Western Division, but even here the figure is 53 per cent.

Table 3:6

Mean crop area, per sampled farming unit, 1973/4

Crop	1973	1974
	ha	ha
Groundnuts	2.6	3.2
Millet	1.0	1.0
Rice, Swamp	0.8	0.9
Rice, Upland	0.6	0.0
Sorghum	1.0	1.0

Source: Dunsmore, 1976

This quite staggering specialisation in groundnut production has been at the expense of the traditional cereals, [16] with only nine per cent of cultivated land in 1976/7 being planted with late millet, seven per cent with sorghum, five per cent with early millet, two and a half per cent with findo (digitaria exilis), and also only two and a half per cent with maize. Although there is occasionally some intercropping, areas tend to be small and the general practice is for pure stand cultivation.

Economic considerations of the producer in the cultivation of groundnuts

Since 1975, the Gambian Government has tried to encourage the cultivation of foodcrops, particularly millet, sorghum and irrigated rice. The 1975-80 Development Plan called for a 25-30 per cent increase in the production of both millet and sorghum. This, it was stated, could be accomplished partly by a two per cent increase in acreage devoted to the two crops, but would also require a substantial increase in productivity. This has not occurred and there is strong evidence to suggest that the Gambian farmer is both unwilling and unable to increase production of cereals. As these crops are ecologically suited to the environment, and the government is actively encouraging their cultivation, there must be important reasons why the farmer has not responded. One reason is that the Gambian farmer, who has been performing in a monetary economy for 150 years or more, does not find it economic to produce more food.

54

Since 1974 the actual tonnage of domestically produced cereals appears to have declined. Of course, it is difficult to state exactly the annual production of these crops, as most of the production does not enter the market but is consumed by the farming family. However, the FAO tries to make estimates which are printed annually in the 'FAO Production Yearbook'. These figures are reproduced in Table 3:8 and although they should be viewed sceptically as actual production figures, they do give some idea as to the trend in millet, sorghum and irrigated rice production in the country as a whole. Because there has been this apparent drop in production, it has been claimed that the acreage devoted to each of these crops has declined. (CILSS, 1977) This is extremely dificult to substantiate, but can perhaps be seen as part of the process that Haswell (1975) noticed in her study of Genieri. In her three successive surveys of Genieri, which spanned a period of twenty-four years (1949-73), Haswell found that there had been a substantial increase in rice cultivation by women, which in turn permitted a reduction in the production of the food crops of millet and sorghum by the men. The men were able to turn this released labour to the cultivation of groundnuts to increase their case income. In the period 1949-73, the percentage of total production contributed by groundnuts in the village of Genieri rose from 31.5 per cent to 46 per cent whereas the production of foodcrops decreased from 68.5 per cent to 54 per cent. A similar situation was found by Weil (1973) in his study village, Bumari. It was discovered that the village had physically moved nearer the swamps in the 1950s and 1960s in order to increase rice production. The men's responsibility for food production was thus reduced, and they were consequently able to concentrate on the production of groundnuts. The process of releasing men from foodcrop production, compounded by the poor millet and sorghum harvests of recent years has led to an increase in the production of groundnuts (see Table 3:8) and the consequential decline in the acreage under the traditional cereal crops. This expansion of the area devoted to groundnut cultivation does not reflect any irrational behaviour on the part of the producer, since there are four very sound economic reasons why the farmer has continued to grow groundnuts at the expense of foodcrops.

Access to cheap imported rice

One very important reason why the Gambian farmer at an early date was able to neglect his foodcrops in favour of the groundnut crop, was that The Gambia has traditionally had access to imported rice at a reasonable cost, not only to the urban consumer but also to the rural consumer. This was helped by the efficient and cheap transport link with the interior provided by the River Gambia. This eliminated the necessity for the Gambian farmer to supply the urban food market and reduced his own need for self-sufficiency. An interesting confirmation of this lack of self-sufficiency is provided by the '1974-75 Agricultural Sample Survey'. In this

Table 3:7

Area under each major crop by division, 1976/7

Crop	Western Division		North Bank Division		Lower River Division	
	Area under cultivation ha	% Gambian total	Area under cultivation ha	% Gambian total	Area under cultivation ha	% Gambian total
Groundnuts	14,387	13	38,575	35	11,778	11
Early millet	539	6	4,099	45	700	8
Late millet	6,552	41	2,927	18	1,282	8
Sorghum	2,050	16	1,393	11	398	3
Maize	719	18	473	12	420	10
Findo	408	9	2,406	54	392	9
Upland rice	956	13	2,354	31	1,974	26
Swamp rice	1,315	10	5,295	39	2,565	19
Irrigated rice	–	–	–	–	–	–
TOTAL	26,926	15	57,522	32	19,509	11

Crop	MacCarthy Island Division		Upper River Division		Gambia Total	
	Area under cultivation ha	% Gambian total	Area under cultivation ha	% Gambian total	Area under cultivation ha	% Gambian total
Groundnuts	26,726	25	17,144	16	108,610	61
Early millet	2,705	29	1,122	12	9,165	5
Late millet	2,088	13	3,295	20	16,145	9
Sorghum	4,528	36	4,147	33	12,516	7
Maize	901	22	1,528	38	4,042	2.25
Findo	528	12	730	16	4,465	2.5
Upland rice	1,965	26	374	5	7,623	4.25
Swamp rice	3,097	23	1,450	11	13,722	8
Irrigated rice	1,012	52	931	48	1,943	1
TOTAL	43,550	24	30,721	17	178,231	100

Source: compiled from Rice, 1979

57

survey of 1,382 randomly selected farmers, it was found that less than half the farmers were self-sufficient with one crop, and that only 25 per cent of the farmers interviewed were self-sufficient in two crops, and these were mainly millet and sorghum.

Table 3:8
Production of millet, sorghum, irrigated rice and groundnuts in The Gambia, 1969-79

	1969	1970	1971	1972	1973	1974	1975	1976	1977	1978	1979
					metric tons						
Millet and Sorghum	45	30	45	35	35	47	45	22	19	25	25
Irrigated Rice	66	50	60	53	55	23	60	35	18	30	35
Groundnuts	114	117	117	115	137	142	137	157	145	105	150

Source: FAO Production Yearbooks, 1970-1979

Imported rice competes quite favourably with the traditional cereals in price and does not involve all the lengthy preparation that traditional cereals need before they can be cooked.   More important is that they have already been husked and cleaned, which reduces meal preparation time.   This is a very important consideration when it is remembered that the role of the Gambian woman is not confined to the raising of children and other household tasks, she is also an active participant in farming activities, particularly in the production of rice.

The price of rice in The Gambia is fixed by the government, at a subsidised rate. [17]   In May 1980 the price was fixed at D0.70 per kilogram.   The consumer subsidy of approximately 50 per cent (D0.32 per kg) is financed from the accumulated 'Farmers Fund' of the GPMB (comprising profits made on groundnut sales).   So, the groundnut farmer is subsidising the rice consumer.   Thus while both urban and rural consumers benefit from the subsidy it has done nothing to stimulate rice production.   This can be partly attributed to the pricing policy, despite the fact that the price paid for imported rice by the consumer is lower than the price paid for the equivalent amount of paddy to the Gambian rice producer by the GPMB.   The implication of this pricing policy for rice production will be dealt with below in Chapter Seven.

Pricing system favours the production of groundnuts

Table 3:9 is an attempt to explain why the farmer prefers to grow groundnuts, rather than increase his production of other crops which are just as suited to the conditions in the area. The table shows that in terms of return per hectare, the monetary benefits from growing groundnuts is high, at an estimated D755 per hectare. Irrigated rice is also very profitable per hectare, but its further development is hindered by difficulties in developing the rather special environments involved (see Chapter Seven).

Of all the crops grown in The Gambia in May 1980, groundnuts were the most profitable per hectare, apart from maize. In fact, the benefits from growing maize is much more attractive at D1,025 per hectare. The labour days spent on one hectare of groundnuts could theoretically be shifted towards the cultivation of approximately two hectares of maize (see Table 3:9). Such a shift could make the benefit from maize 270 per cent higher than from one hectare of groundnuts (the gross return being D2,050 for maize as opposed to D755 for groundnuts, for the same labour and input at prevailing prices). However, the more extensive cultivation of maize has been hindered by a number of factors. Firstly, consumers have a definite preference for (imported) rice, which is also available at a government fixed consumer price. In May 1980, this was 12 bututs (20 per cent) dearer than the market price for maize, which is not controlled. Secondly, the average housewife does not know how to process and cook maize, as it is usually just roasted on the cob as a 'snack' rather than forming part of the main meal. Thirdly, the production of maize is also hindered by the lack of developed marketing arrangements and the lack of any organised extension programmes to increase yields. Only a very small proportion of the maize harvest enters the market. It is brought directly by the producer or is collected from the farm by the small trader, who then sells it in one of the larger markets. It is an economically risky business, the producer or trader not knowing what demand or supply will be, hence not knowing what the market price will be. So, although the gross return on maize may be higher than for groundnuts, the farmer still prefers to grow groundnuts, for which he knows that there is a reliable market and a fixed price.

When it comes to the cultivation of millet and sorghum, the farmer makes a totally rational economic decision in deciding to grow groundnuts. These crops compete directly for the same land, resources and labour, as groundnuts, but are not as profitable. They do, however, require fewer labour days per hectare, which means that the production of millet and sorghum could be more profitable if the same labour input was put into them as in the maize and groundnut crops. But, this is dependent on the availability of suitable land, a fixed price and a reliable market, which are absent. It is much more rational for the farmer to grow groundnuts and from the cash obtained buy in subsidised rice to make up his household's requirements.

Table 3:9

Relative profitability of various crops in The Gambia, 1980

Crop	Production/ha	Labour input/ha	Price/kg* May 1980	Gross return/ Labour input (day)	Gross return/ha
	kg	day	D	D	D
Groundnuts	1510	114	0.50	6.62	755
Irrigated rice	1604	291	0.46	2.53	737.8
Upland rice	730	122	0.46	2.75	335.8
Swamp rice	1230	101	0.46	5.60	565.8
Early millet	1200	101	0.58	6.89	696
Late millet	720	47	0.58	8.89	417.6
Maize	1767	55	0.58	18.63	1024.9
Sorghum	756	57	0.58	7.69	438.5
Findo	530	32	0.58	9.60	307.4

Source: Agricultural Survey 1973/4; Dunsmore, 1976; Retail Price Bulletin, Central Statistics.

* Prices for groundnuts and rice are guaranteed producer prices, the remaining cereals are prevailing prices received by farmers in the free market (Author's fieldwork, May, 1980) and are hence subject to fluctuation.

The effect of natural disasters on cropping patterns

The switch away from foodcrop production can also to a certain degree be explained by the recent natural disasters which have affected the region. These seem to have affected foodcrops relatively more intensely than the groundnut crop. The drought of 1971-74 was manifested in The Gambia primarily by an abrupt termination of the rains. Millet and sorghum yields depend on these late rains for a good harvest. Also, recent attacks by pests, for example birds and beetles, have damaged foodcrops while hardly affecting the groundnut crop. The production figures for millet, sorghum and irrigated rice were particularly low in 1976 and 1977 (see Table 3:8), a direct result of a severe drought that affected the region. It is interesting to note that in 1976 production of millet and sorghum was down 51 per cent on the previous year, irrigated rice was down 42 per cent, yet groundnut production was up by 14.5 per cent. This indicates perhaps why the Gambian farmer has not taken heed of the government's call to grow more food. There is much less risk to be taken in growing groundnuts.

Change in consumer preference away from millet and sorghum

Another reason for this move away from growing millet and sorghum can perhaps be put down to a change in demand. There has been a shift away from millet and sorghum as staples, to rice. This change may be partly due to the millet and sorghum shortages which resulted from two severe droughts within ten years, but may also be partly due to a change of taste and aspirations towards the consumption of a more 'desirable' food base such as rice. Although no statistical data is available to prove this point, many people have commented on this change. [18] Haswell (1975) in her studies of the village of Genieri notes that this shift has been occurring since the 1950s. Van der Plas states "From the beginning of 1954 Gambian rice has become an increasingly important factor in the diet and income of the Gambia". (1957, p.104)

The Medical Research Centre (MRC) at Fajara has been carrying out research into tropical diseases and nutrition in The Gambia for a number of decades and in 1977 made a detailed nutritional study of pregnant and lactating women in the village of Keneba (Paul, 1979). It was found that 58.5 per cent of the dry weight of cereals consumed in the village was rice, with late millet second (22 per cent), followed by findo (Digitaria exilis) at 17 per cent. In every month except April and October, rice consumption was above 50 per cent of all cereals consumed. The months of the highest rice consumption were May through to September, a period coinciding with the farming season, indicating perhaps that the women preferred the relatively easy preparation of rice meals during this very busy period. The rather large amount of findo consumed in Keneba in 1977 was the result of poor rains, which reduced the millet and sorghum harvests by an average of 50 per cent. Findo is regarded by the Gambian household as an emergency foodcrop, only harvested in times of shortage.

Although perhaps 1977 is not a totally representative year, the figures given by the MRC for Keneba do indicate the important place that rice has in the Gambian diet, not just in the urban centres, but also in such villages as Keneba.

Conclusion

Until the 1860s, Gambian farmers combined adequate food production with a partial commitment to groundnut production for export, and for this period the 'vent for surplus' theory can be applied. After this date there is evidence that Gambian farmers, especially along the north bank of the river, began to concentrate on groundnut production to the neglect of food crops. This was the case particularly after the imposition of taxes by the colonial government in the 1890s. This shift in emphasis necessitated importations of rice into the region, to make up the food deficit. It is a situation that continues today, despite the independent government's commitment on paper to self-sufficiency in rice production and a diversification of the agricultural economy. 'Vent for surplus' theory certainly does not explain the large amounts of groundnuts exported from The Gambia in the twentieth century.

Many scholars have argued that imperial governments imposed "capitalism" on the economies of their colonies (Frank 1969; Amin 1973), and it would appear that the Gambian farmer was forced to increase his participation in the monetary economy by the imposition of taxes by the colonial government. It is also argued that with the imposition of capitalism, a dependency situation developed, with specific metropolitan-satellite relations being formed. This is explained by Frank:

> . . . the metropolis destroyed and or totally transformed the earlier viable social and economic systems of these societies, incorporated them into the metropolitan dominated worldwide capitalist system and converted them into sources for its own metropolitan capital accumulation and development. (Frank 1969, p.225)

However, rather than 'transforming' traditional structures, the British Government in The Gambia utilised them, to produce agricultural goods for the world market.

Whatever theoretical viewpoint one takes to explain the Gambian situation, the fact is that both colonial and independent governments have directly and indirectly encouraged the production of groundnuts. As a consequence the producer has neglected his food crops, which has resulted in rice having to be imported into the region in increasing quantities, this has forced the Gambian farmer to participate in the market economy – not only to sell his cash crop, but also to buy food. This has resulted in the factors of production acquiring an economic value they previously did not have, the implications of which will be discussed in the following chapter.

Notes

[1] In the 1978/79 season, groundnut exports were 90.5 per cent of the total exports of The Gambia, by value (excluding re-exports). Africa South of the Sahara, 1980, p.419

[2] Under the 1894 Protectorate Ordinance the Travelling Commissioner could withdraw powers from headmen or chiefs and appoint successors to dead or incapacitated chiefs. For a fuller discussion see M. Crowder, 1968.

[3] In the UK demand rose from 50,000 to 100,000 tons (50,800 to 101,600 metric tons), in Germany it rose from 80,000 to 200,000 tons (81,280 to 203,200 metric tons) (Hogendorn 1966).

[4] Strange farmers are dealt with in more detail in Chapter Four. They are migrants who come to a village and live under a landlord, for the express purpose of growing groundnuts.

[5] The rate was 4s for a yard containing no more than four huts with an additional payment for extra huts at the rate of 1s if the hut was inhabited by a member of the family and 2s if it was inhabited by a stranger.

[6] Taken over by Lever Brothers in 1917.

[7] Prior to this, produce had been exported by private merchant firms mostly run by Europeans.

[8] These may be defined as public bodies set up by government action and delegated legal powers of compulsion over producers and handlers of primary or processed agricultural products. The distinction between a board and a cooperative lies in the powers of compulsion that are vested in the former.

[9] See Chapter Eight.

[10] See Chapter Seven.

[11] For a fuller discussion of this period and its implications for the rural population see Thomson, 1970.

[12] Apex meaning the head office and main coordinating body for the cooperative unions.

[13] Exchange rates in April 1980 were as follows:
100 bututs = 1 dalasi (D)
D1 = £0.25 (£1 = D4)
D1 = $0.55 ($1 = D1.80)
D1 = CFA120
Since 1980 there has been a series of devaluations of the dalasi and the dalasi was floated in January 1987.

[14] Sexual division of labour in the River Gambia region was first noted by Moore (1738), an employee of the United

Africa Company. He commented that "The men work the corn ground [upland cereals], and the women and girls the rice ground". (Moore 1738, p.127) Moore also states quite clearly that women owned the rice which they cultivated ...

> and the women busy in cutting their rice; which I must remark is their own property; for, after they have set by a sufficient quantity for family use, they sell the remainder, and take the money themselves, the husband not interfering. (Moore 1738, p.139-40)

[15] In 1973, 620 farming units were enumerated and in 1974 2,284 units.

[16] The 'traditional' cereals are the upland crops of millet, sorghum, findi, maize and rice. Irrigated rice is excluded from this category since it is a relatively recent crop, and does not compete for the same land.

[17] In January 1986, the government de-regulated the rice market and withdrew subsidies.

[18] CILSS, 1977, M.R.C. reports, also personal communications with Gebre-Mariam, FAO marketing advisor, Banjul, April 1980.

4 The effects of groundnut specialisation on the Gambian economy

Introduction

The specialisation in groundnut production of The Gambia, described in the previous chapter, has had three major effects on the country's economy. Firstly it has meant that the factors of production have taken up added importance and economic value, which has resulted in their being put to more economically productive uses particularly the cultivation of groundnuts. Secondly, it has resulted in a marked seasonality of the money supply which has important implications for the marketing structure. Thirdly, two separate and very different marketing systems have developed within The Gambia. These are the government controlled Groundnut Produce Market Board (GPMB) and the local 'subsistence' marketing system. In order that the present system of marketing locally produced foodcrops can be more fully understood and placed in perspective, each of these effects will be discussed in turn.

The conflict between various crops for the factors of production

As a result of the increased specialisation in groundnut production, the factors of production assumed a monetary value which they had not previously possessed. A conflict therefore developed in the allocation of resources between foodcrops and

65

groundnuts, leading eventually to a decline in foodcrop production, millet and sorghum in particular. One consequence is the amount of food, mainly rice, imported into the country. At the present time, imported rice satisfies approximately 30 per cent of Gambian cereal requirements. This does not necessarily reflect a shortfall in domestic rice production, but rather an overall cereal deficit, resulting from reduced production of upland foodcrops.

Competition for land

An idealised diagram of the landuse of a typical Gambian village is shown in Figure 4:1. The upland crops, including groundnuts, are produced on the plateau and colluvial soils, under a bush fallow system. Intercropping is common and mixed cropping is sometimes practiced. Closer to the village, land is often under annual cultivation, the nutrient levels being maintained by the dumping of household waste. Here the crops are commonly grown as pure stands. Small areas within or near the compound may be used for fruit or vegetable production. Where salinity and soil reaction are within acceptable limits, alluvial areas are used for rice and for the dry season grazing of cattle. The result of increased groundnut cultivation has been to increase pressure on this system, particularly access to the uplands where groundnuts and upland crops compete for the same land.

To some extent the growing value attached to commercial farming has accentuated problems of access to land as a resource. This is not a generalised pressure on community resources; it operates differentially in its impact on different elements of the rural community. These reflect social stratification, with freeborn classes getting preferential access. This is achieved very subtly within existing land tenure systems, which are overtly egalitarian. Difficulties have only become obvious to the outside observer in cases where development projects have been investigated. [1] The land tenure situation is complex. Weil (1971) describes a fairly rigid system, where ownership is communal and individuals have rights of usage which may be inherited. On the other hand, Gamble (1955) endorsed by Haswell (1975) drew attention to the fluidity of the different forms of customary tenure which exist side by side.

> It is not by any means a straightforward matter to generalise about customary land tenure in The Gambia. In the past when land was abundant, rights were often not clearly defined. There was still plenty of unclaimed "bush" which anyone in need of land could clear and acquire. At the present day, with an increasing population, there is less unclaimed land and permanent rights over farms are acquired chiefly through inheritance. In some areas good land is scarce, and consequently disputes are becoming more frequent. Rights are therefore tending to be formulated, but the resulting decisions may differ from district to district, the north

Kombo area, for instance, being much more affected by European concepts of land ownership. (Gamble 1955, p.39)

Dey (1980) has studied the situation in more depth, and states that there is no simple, easily definable set of principles regulating land tenure in The Gambia. What is clear is that ultimately all land is deemed to belong to the government and that in the provinces control is vested in the District Authorities. Customary rights of tenure that have evolved historically are protected under the 1966 Land (Provinces) Act, this being the major form of land access.

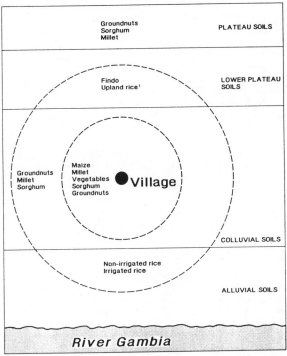

1. Upland rice: this category of rice has been greatly affected in recent years by poor harvests and has largely been abandoned on colluvial and plateau soils.

Figure 4:1   Idealised land-use pattern of a typical Gambian village

Before the land allocation system is described, the distinction between maruo and kamanyango fields must be explained. A maruo field is where foodcrops are grown. In principle, the crop cannot be sold but must be used for feeding sinkiro (literally those who eat from the same pot) members. The men cultivate sorghum, millet, maize and irrigated rice on such fields, whilst the women grow rainfed or swamp rice. The men's maruolu crop is controlled by the dabada (farming unit) head, who allocates to the sinkiro within the dabada. Women's rice is either controlled by the senior woman in the sinkiro, or by the individual women of a sinkiro who cultivate their own maruolu. All sinkiro members have a duty to work on a maruo. On the other hand, all men and women have a right to cultivate a crop of their own, over which they have disposal rights. The independent field of each sinkiro member is called a kamanyango. These are used primarily for cash crops, although a portion may be used at various socio-religious ceremonies, providing food for work parties or for cooking at social events. How these fields are allocated within the community is complex.

Within The Gambia both communal and individual forms of tenure exist under certain conditions and for specific types of land. Some land is owned communally and people have various types of hereditary or temporary rights to use it. Other land is owned by individuals who have the right to pass it on to their heirs or give it away if they wish. The system is based on three major principles:

i)   Uncleared land within village boundaries is communally owned in that anyone in the village has the right to clear a portion of this land with the permission of the village head.

ii)   Ownership rights are established by clearing and cultivation. These rights can be transferred or inherited.

iii) There is a prohibition on the sale or renting of land. [2]

There are four types of ownership of cleared land that cut across the distinction between maruo and kamanyango, which may be cultivated on land owned in any of these ways, or on land that has been borrowed or rented. Firstly, land can be owned by the compound, and will be administered by the compound head, on behalf of its members, each of whom has a right to a share of the land to cultivate his or her own crops, as well as a crop for the sinkiro. Certain fields are reserved for maruolu or kamanyangalu. Compound land in theory should not be alienated from the compound, nor should it pass into private ownership. Secondly, an individual can establish personal ownership rights to a piece of land by the act of clearing it for cultivation. Thirdly, some land is attached to certain offices, for example the village head and compound head. It cannot be alienated from the office to which it belongs, and is usually cultivated as maruo. Fourthly, there is leaseland. This is land that has been acquired by the government from farmers under the Lands (Provinces) Act 1946. The most important area of leaseland is Jahali swamp, which was taken over in 1950 and leased to the Gambia Rice Farm. Following the

68

collapse of the farm in 1954 a large part was lent to women tenant farmers living in nearby villages, who had originally cultivated the land. Since 1965 these women have not been charged any rent.

The system described so far neglects the problem of access by women to rice land which is somewhat different from that described above. There are three ways by which a woman can obtain rice land. The most important is through her husband, who allocates to her fields which had previously been worked by his mother. This keeps the fields in the same patrilineal compound. Secondly, women may cultivate fields previously cultivated by their own mothers. This land would then be passed on to the woman's daughter when she marries, thus passing into a different compound. Thirdly, a woman may borrow land from friends in other compounds. This land would have to be returned when asked for.

Although the customary land tenure system appears to be successful in performing its minimal task of providing a suitable resource base for the consumption requirements of the compound, it does not achieve equitable distribution throughout the community. With increasing scarcity of land and commercialisation of farming, high status compounds are able to influence distribution. The main social cleavages handed down from pre-colonial society still persist. Klein (1977) recognises four major societal groupings in pre-colonial Gambia:

a) __garmi__   Lineages who are eligible to provide rulers.

b) __jaambuur__   'Freemen', who are the largest social group. They are politically important as __jaambuur__ chiefs generally select the __garmi__ ruler.

c) __nyenyo__   Consists of the artisan and griot castes.

d) __jaam__   Slaves

In 1895 the domestic trade in slaves was abolished in The Gambia, although slave holding was not. Mistreatment became grounds for liberation, but automatic freedom only occurred on the death of the master. After emancipation, former slaves were partially integrated into village society, but found themselves with limited access to land. This has resulted in the contemporary situation where differences in income and income generating potentials are clearly associated with ancestral status. In a study of Koina in Upper River Division, Benini (1980) shows this disparity. (Table 4:1).

Koina is basically a Serahuli village. [3] The Serahulis were important in the trans-Sudan trade. Through this trade they acquired slaves, some of whom were settled in the village to grow food. Differences among the freeborn and the special status of artisans and liberated slaves have generated several levels of

Table 4:1

Income and income generating potentials as allocated between
Freeborn and other groups within the village of Koina, URD,
in 1980.

Ancestral Status	Owns a Plough	Owns a Cart	Hires Labour	Draws non-village income
Freeborn	70%	35%	55%	65%
Artisan/Slave	53%	13%	35%	53%

Source: Benini, 1980

social stratification at Koina. These minutely graded status and
wealth differences are illustrated in Figure 4:2 in the form of a
model. The founding lineage of the village of Koina, are the
Gumaneh. Their settlement was followed by that of the Ture
lineage and other freeborn families, each with its dependent
slaves. Today, 31 per cent of the population of the village are
descended from the Gumaneh lineage, 14 per cent from the Ture
lineage, 21 per cent are descended from the other freeborn
families, 11 per cent are descended from artisans and the
remaining 23 per cent are the descendants of slaves.

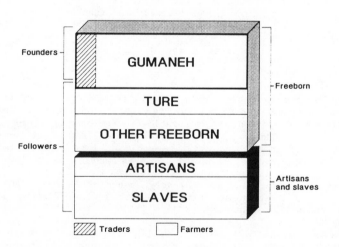

Figure 4:2 Social stratification at Koina, URD

Adapted from Benini, 1980

In 1970 the Community Development Agency sponsored a rice project in Koina. The importance of social standing in relation to access to land can be demonstrated by observing events during the operation of this project. The project lasted only four years: by 1974 it had collapsed. There were many technical problems, mainly pump breakdowns, but the main reason for the failure of the project was that it undermined the traditional power of the Gumaneh lineage within the village, who in 1974 withdrew their support for the project. The project gave the poorer members of the village the chance to grow enough rice to last out the year. This threatened the income of the Gumaneh traders who were also the village money lenders. [4] But this was only part of the problem. The president of the project appointed by the Community Development team was a Ture, and he made sure that Ture compounds were given a higher proportion of rice plots than the Gumanehs. Land being an economic asset, the economic superiority of the Gumaneh lineage was thereby threatened and this could not be tolerated. When the pump broke down at a critical period during the 1974 crop season, the Gumaneh money lenders saw their opportunity, refused to lend the money necessary for its repair, the crop was lost and the project collapsed. This example demonstrates the importance of lineage in the access to land, which leaves the less influential members of the village community with the poorer quality land as well as smaller quantities of land.

The problem of access to suitable fields is compounded by an increase in demand for these limited resources. The general problem was discussed in the previous chapter, but aggravating the shortage of land is the introduction of intermediate technology, namely the ox-plough, into the traditional hand-and-hoe culture. With this new equipment, farmers are able to cultivate more land with the same labour inputs. Between 1971/2 and 1972/3 the area under groundnut cultivation increased by 18 per cent [5] in areas where the ox-plough had been adopted. But this new technology can generate land tenure problems. Haswell (1975) discussed problems created by the introduction of tractor mechanisation in Genieri in 1948-9. The experiment was not successful. The disruption of the traditional landuse pattern was tolerated,

> . . . so long as they could assess the whereabouts of their particular plot in relation to economic trees left standing in the field, and other trees of very large diameter which it was not possible to fell with the equipment used. (Haswell 1975, p.48)

This toleration broke down when the expansion of the pilot scheme was proposed. A lesson was learnt, and when in 1969 cotton was introduced into Upper River Division, this was done as part of a crop improvement programme. The cotton project is still being undertaken today. The technology used is simple, with the Department of Agriculture promoting a package of inputs which includes seed, fertilisers and a spraying regime. In this case, land has been allocated as part of the normal cropping range, so that existing land tenure problems were not disturbed.

The specialisation in groundnut cultivation since 1830 has resulted in subtle changes that have enabled the richer, influential members of the village more ready access to better land. This has left poorer plots for the other members of the village to grow their food on. This could be one explanation of the poor yields of upland cereals over the last decade. Unable to meet subsistence needs the less influential farmers have therefore been pushed into growing larger areas of groundnuts to raise cash to buy food. The process of overall commercialisation is in this way accelerating. If increased commercialisation of production is linked to access to land, perhaps the decisive factor in determining a farmer's choice of crop is the resultant labour problem associated with a five month growing season. The constraints imposed upon the farmer by this short growing season are critical and emphasise the competition that exists between groundnuts and foodcrops, for the available resources.

Shortages of labour

Not only do groundnuts and foodcrops compete directly for suitable land, they also have almost identical labour/time requirements. They are all planted, need weeding and are harvested at about the same time, creating a potential bottleneck in agricultural production. If labour is limited, the farmer has to make a decision upon which crop to concentrate. In the rural parts of The Gambia, economic activity is centred around the village, with the village comprising a series of farming units, known as dabadas. The main source of labour for the farming unit is the family, but there are times when this is not enough and family labour is then supplemented by other forms of labour. These fall mainly into three groups of varying importance.

Kafu labour [6] One of the most important forms of labour is the kafu. The kafu is an age set to which almost every rural Gambian belongs. Generally there are three age categories, although Weil (1971) has identified only two. [7] The first kafu is that of the young boys (before they are circumcised). The second consists of young men aged between 13-40. Men over 40 belong to a third kafu of elders. Women have two kafus, the first consisting of girls and unmarried women, with the second consisting of married and older women.

Kafu labour is extremely important and efficient and can be called in times of emergency, but male kafu labour has to be paid for either in cash or kind. Male kafus are called, usually for the tasks of hoeing and weeding the groundnut and millet or sorghum fields, prior to planting. Once called, the crop owner must provide the kafu (which may number as many as sixty) with a good breakfast and lunch, as well as kolanuts, tobacco and often drummers. In the village of Sabi in 1976 the payment for one day's work (approximately 8 hours) ranged from D3.50 to D13.00 depending on the age of the group, with the 10-27 year olds receiving the largest fee. It is also customary to give money or a bull worth about D100, which the kafu will keep and use at a future social event, such as a dance, drumming or a feast. So the total expenses of a kafu may be high. Dey (1980) estimates that it could cost as much as £100. In contrast, the female kafu system works on a reciprocal basis. A woman cultivator simply requests help from members of her kafu, and she is expected to return such assistance when required by other members. Such labour is used by the women mainly for rice cultivation. Groups vary from five to ten women, who work each other's fields in turn. The crop owner usually provides lunch and kolanuts. Theoretically, the women are not gaining additional labour, but they enjoy working in groups and feel that they work more efficiently than as individuals.

It is interesting to note that the kafu system was used in 1946 as the basis for a colonial experiment in communal farm organisation in the Kantora district. The setting up of this farm emphasised the importance of this type of labour in the rural economy. The problems and ultimate failure of the farm are documented by Little (1949).

Strange Farmers   The second type of labour often used to supplement family labour is that of migrants. It is important to distinguish between 'strange farmers' (navetanes) and 'strangers' (lungtango). 'Strange farmers' are taken into the compound by the compound head, and given a portion of compound land to farm for themselves, (usually growing groundnuts), in return for an agreed number of labour days on the compound's fields. The lungtango, in contrast, are permanent migrants who settle and are given land by the village head (alkalo). All compound heads can take in strange farmers and provide them with land, but only the alkalo has the right to grant land to new permanent settlers. However, it is the navetanes who provide additional labour to the village.

The mechanics of the strange farmer system has been described by various writers [8] since the phenomenon was first noted in a government report of 1851:

> A great change has already taken place in the river. The Tilliebunkas (that is, men from the east) and Serahulies and other labourers, who now periodically visit the Gambia for the purpose of farming and selling their agricultural produce; and who pay the proprietors of the soil a share of the proceeds of their speculation, create thereby a new interest. (CO 87/50, 1851)

These migrants played a vital role in the development of the groundnut trade, finding it more economic to transport themselves to the coastal areas, than to transport their produce from the interior. Swindell (1979,1982) has looked at the historical impact of the strange farmer on the Gambian economy in some detail, and sees it as a response to the decline of domestic slavery in the nineteenth century. [9]

> The strange farmer system provided Gambian hosts (as it still does) with an ideal mechanism for obtaining extra labour without recourse to the payment of either cash wages, or a share of the crop. (Swindell 1979, p.101)

This was a logical step as it was the shortage of labour, not land, which was causing the bottleneck in groundnut production. As Swindell states:

> . . . the need for extra labour inputs was a function of pre-industrial agricultural techniques in an area of low population density, and the resultant movements of labour from potential groundnut areas in the interior were a function of transport systems which made coastal locations more economic. (Swindell 1979, p.104)

This mutually beneficial situation still continues, and its survival is a product of low population densities, the labour requirements of groundnut production, and the political economies of the neighbouring states. In 1974-5, an estimated 33,000 strange farmers were operating in the country. [10] Of these 24 per cent were Gambian, 21 per cent came from Senegal, 21 per cent were from Mali and 31 per cent from Guinea, the remainder were mainly from Guinea Bissau. From these figures it can be seen that although 45 per cent of the migrants can be classified as short distance migrants, many travel up to 800 kilometres.

The strange farmer usually leaves his own village at the end of the dry season in order to look for land on which he can grow groundnuts. In many instances he already has contacts and has established a pattern of lodging with one particular compound each season, who will provide him with food and some land. In return, the stranger will work up to four days a week on compound fields and will sometimes be rewarded with 10 per cent of the compound crop for his services. The rest of the time the stranger cultivates his 'borrowed' fields. At the end of the season the stranger sells his own crop and will either return home, or will look for dry season employment in neighbouring villages or towns.

The importance of the strange farmer is that he provides, throughout the agricultural season, a reliable source of labour to the compound on the agreed number of days per week. This labour is vital at critical periods of land clearing, weeding and harvesting and is economically attractive in that it enables the compound to avoid paying out any wages.

Koranic students The third type of labour available to certain members of the village is that of Koranic students. The availability of this labour is a direct result of the Sonike-Marabout wars. In the second half of the nineteenth century, Fode Kabba had formed a confederacy exercising paramount authority in Niamina, Jarra, Kiang and Foni, as well as on the south bank. It

74

was here that Koranic students gathered in considerable numbers. Park described these Islamic work groups, where boys were given instruction in the reading of the Koran; they were taught early in the morning and late in the evening, and

> . . . being considered, during their scholarship, as the domestic slaves of their master, they were employed in planting corn, bringing firewood and in other servile offices during the day. (Park 1878, p.240)

With the commercial success of the groundnut, the Koranic students' labour was directed by the marabouts, towards the cultivation of the cash crop. As a result marabout teachers usually sell large quantities of groundnuts to the traders. As Jeng sums it up:

> Marabout teachers had swiftly acquired a substantial, disciplined and committed labour force held together by economic appeals based on spiritual rationalisations. (Jeng 1978, p.173)

In Senegal, Cruise O'Brien (1971) discussed the cultivation of what has become known as the 'Wednesday' field, which is worked by Islamic adults, the produce being given to the local marabout. He describes the system:

> The extent of the individual fields varies of course very widely, and in a few cases they may go up to thirty acres or more, but most fields seem to be of the order of five to ten acres; size is limited by the amount of seed available, and land. A general average of productivity could hardly be estimated; two fields at Missirah, for different marabouts, produced eight tons of groundnuts in one case, ten tons of groundnuts and four of millet in the other. The Wednesday fields of Amsatou Mbacke of Daron Monsty, on the other hand, had an average production (in 1966) of less than one and a half tons of groundnuts. (Cruise O'Brien 1971, p.211)

By this means, a significant amount of young male labour is withdrawn from the family farming unit (and is utilised mainly for groundnut cultivation) by the marabout which means that they are not available to the dabada at critical times in the agricultural cycle.

The availability of labour to the farming unit at certain times in the agricultural cycle is crucial to get maximum production. Of course, agricultural production is also related to soil resources and climatic variables as well as human resources, but in an economy which is as labour intensive as The Gambia, where certain tasks have to be performed quickly at set times (dictated by climatic variables), labour availability is vital. As Jeng states:

> The evidence suggests that, although in specific years excessive or insufficient rainfall wrought havoc, migration of labour was more crucial than rainfall in determining the size of the export crop. (Jeng 1978, p.215)

Allocation of capital

The principal form of agricultural production practised in The
Gambia today is what Morgan and Pugh (1969) have termed
'rotational bush fallow'. It is a system which involves little
use of capital inputs. The settlement is fixed and the land under
cultivation rotates over a defined area of fallow grass or
woodland. Cleared land is usually cropped for between three and
six years and the period of fallow ranges from four to ten years.
This system has been carefully adapted by Gambian farmers to suit
local conditions. It involves the rotation of plots and includes
techniques such as intercropping which ensures a varied cycling of
plant nutrients. Very few farmers can see the need for, or can
afford, chemical fertilisers, but try to restore fertility by
rotating their crops. Rotations, including fallow periods, are
practised on the plateau and colluvial soils. No rotations are
used on the alluvial areas which are planted only with rice.

The common rotation is basically an alternation of groundnuts
and cereals. Near villages this may be almost continuous.
Elsewhere, when cattle are not tethered in the dry season, fallow
periods are introduced. Rotating groundnuts with other crops has
some specific benefits. It reduces the incidence of rosette
disease and counters the edaphic effects of successive crops of
groundnuts, which would cause accelerated breakdown of the soil
structure and a consequent decrease in permeability and increase
in runoff and erosion. For sorghum, rotations are needed to
reduce the build-up of the weed striga spp. [11] The Department
of Agriculture recommends the following rotation: groundnuts or
cotton/cereal (millet, sorghum, maize)/groundnuts/fallow. The
length of fallow required to re-establish fertility has not been
determined for The Gambia, but on comparable ferruginous soils at
Daron, in Senegal, it has been demonstrated that over a period of
twenty years, a rotation of groundnuts/cereals/groundnuts/fallow/
fallow, was satisfactory in maintaining soil fertility. This was
confirmed in wider-scale trials in southern Senegal over a period
of fifteen years. It is thought that a single year's fallow could
be adequate if combined with deep ploughing (20-25 cm) together
with the use of fertilisers, organic manures and green manures.
[12] However, the majority of Gambian farmers do not own improved
farming implements and animal traction is not widely used.
Production inputs such as fertilisers, selected improved varieties
of seed and pesticides are used by only a few farmers taking part
in development schemes. Even basic cultural practices such as
timely planting, weeding and harvesting are not strictly adhered
to, usually because there is a shortage of available labour at
these times. If a farmer wishes to improve his capital inputs he
must be in a position to borrow money, usually in the form of
credit.

As we saw in the last chapter, the main source of credit for the
small farmer is the Cooperative Society. This takes the form of

seasonal credit which is used mainly for subsistence purposes.
However, some is used to purchase inputs (Table 4:2). The biased
distribution of credit towards the groundnut crop is evident. In
1979, which can be regarded as a representative year, the amount
of improved groundnut seed bought on credit was 85 per cent
greater than that of rice seed. Similarly there was a marked
preference to purchase fertiliser for the groundnut crop (95 per
cent) than for the rice crop. Reasons for this preference to
invest capital in the groundnut crop were discussed in the
previous chapter. What is clear is that the Gambian farmer does
not have easy access to capital inputs, but what inputs he is able
to acquire tend to be aimed at the improvement of the groundnut
crop. Little capital investment has as yet been made in the
foodcrop sector of the economy.

The effect of the seasonal nature of groundnut production on the volume of the money supply in the economy

The marked seasonal nature of groundnut production has a profound
effect on the whole economy and in particular on the marketing
system. The reason for this is the large amount of money that
comes into circulation after the groundnut crop has been sold.
Groundnuts are usually harvested in October, and left on the
ground to dry for a time before being gathered into a heap for
further drying. In December, the plants are threshed on a hard
piece of ground, they are then winnowed and sacked ready for sale.
The government determines when the groundnut crop can be sold by
fixing the opening and closing dates of the buying season. This
period is known as the 'trade season' and usually stretches from
December to February/March. Officially, groundnuts cannot be sold
in bulk at any other time of the year. As groundnuts are the main
source of cash income for the majority of the population and there
is little resort to the banking system, this period obviously
necessitates relatively large payments of money. The seasonal
nature of the money supply can be seen on Figure 4:3 which shows
clearly the peak in the money supply during the trade season. The
secular trend probably owes as much to inflation as to any real
economic expansion. In the early 1970s the money supply doubled
at the beginning of the trade season. In November 1972, the total
money supply was D13,168,000. This had reached D22,931,000 by
December and in Januuary 1973 had reached D27,215,000. A similar
picture emerges in 1973/4 with the money supply jumping from
D14,532,000 in November 1973 to D35,075,000 in January 1974. Bad
harvests occurred in 1977/8 and the rise in the money supply,
although still very pronounced, was not as dramatic. In fact, in
December 1977 the money supply had fallen by almost D2,000,000
over the previous month although it perked up in the January. The
1978/9 season was a better one, probably because farmers increased
their output by planting more acreage in order to counteract the
poor weather conditions of the previous year, and January 1979 saw
the largest money supply figures of the decade, reaching a record

Table 4:2

Seasonal credit and the distribution of inputs, 1977-78, in Rural Development Project Areas

Cooperative Society	Groundnut Seed		Fertiliser (Single Super-Phosphate)		Rice Seed		Rice Fertiliser	
	Quantity (tons)	Value (D)	Quantity (tons)	Value (D)	Quantity (tons)	Value (D)	Quantity (tons)	Value (D)
Farafenni	38.40	19660.80	36.80	4195.20	2	900.00	0.09	614.72
Illiassa	72.35	37043.20	68.20	7774.80	16.58	7460.88	0.81	5487.30
Mo-Kunda	54.30	27801.60	47.95	5466.30	8.96	4031.10	4.65	3112.15
N.B.D.	165.05	84505.60	152.95	17436.30	27.54	12391.98	5.55	9214.17
Genieri	52.15	26700.80	72.60	8276.40	7.54	3391.76	0.34	4432.05
Sankwia	72.55	37144.60	74.75	8521.50	14.65	6591.94	0.66	876.02
Jappine	22.95	11750.40	30.30	2454.00	2.53	1138.50	0.13	6658.12
Dasilami	79.60	40755.20	79.50	9063.00	20.80	9361.12	0.99	
U.R.D.	277.25	116352.20	257.15	29314.90	45.52	20483.32	2.12	11966.29
Kaur	95.75	49024.00	40.65	4634.10	–	–	–	–
Njau	56.60	28979.20	53.15	6059.10	–	–	–	–
M.I.D. North	152.35	78003.20	93.80	10693.20	–	–	–	–
TOTAL	544.65	278860.80	503.90	57444.40	73.06	32875.30	7.67	21180.46

Source: Rural Development Project, Working Paper No.14, 1978, Annex I

78

D80,275,000. This was to be an exceptional season, in the next year the money supply rose only to D36,801,000 in January 1980, the lowest January figure since 1977. This was a direct result of weather conditions. The rains had come late and were shortlived; then, just as the groundnuts were drying in November and December 1979, it rained again, causing tons of groundnuts to rot in the field and others to be too infected with toxic fungi to be sold.

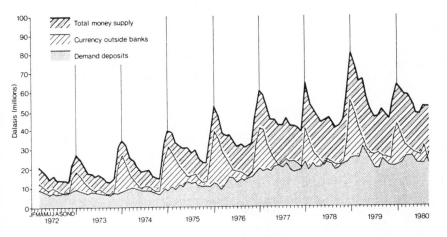

Figure 4:3   Money supply in The Gambia, March 1972 - September 1980

Source: Central Bank Reports

As quickly as the money supply rises in December, it declines in February and March each year as groundnut buying falls off and the trade season comes to an end. This is clearly shown on Figure 4:3. Money supply reaches its lowest levels in November. In 1980, because the groundnut harvest had been so poor, money supply did not decline as sharply as in other years. Perhaps this indicates, as well as any other measure, just how dependent the economy is upon the groundnut crop.

This seasonality of purchasing power is reflected in merchandise sales which reach a peak in the trade season. A demand generated for imported goods was allegedly one of the early incentives for the Gambian farmer to grow groundnuts as a cash crop. Up to date figures are not available, but in 1953 the United Africa Company (UAC) published some figures which clearly show the seasonal nature of the retail trade. In the 1950s UAC brought into The Gambia between 24 - 31 per cent of total commercial imports, and purchased 40 per cent of the total groundnut exports. The firm

79

had retail outlets in all major settlements and wharf-towns.
Table 4:3 shows the average monthly distribution of payments and
receipts by the UAC in The Gambia, from 1943-53, and from the
table it can be seen that merchandise sales each month never fall
below four and half per cent of the total. This gives a general
indicator of the background level of regular trade. Aggregating
over twelve months the percentage of the total is 54 per cent
which means that roughly half of the merchandise trade is
seasonal. Although very crude, this is sufficient to indicate the
strong relationship between the sale of the groundnut crop and the
increase in the amount of merchandise marketed.

Today, retailing is out of the hands of the large European
firms, many of whom no longer trade in The Gambia at all. Those
that do, such as Compagnie Francaise d'Afrique Occidental (CFAO)
and Maurel et Prom, now only have retail outlets in the Banjul-
Kombo St. Mary region. [13] There is only one chain of retailing
stores that operates throughout the country and that is the
government controlled National Trading Corporation (NTC).

The NTC was set up by Act of Parliament in 1973, to replace the
withdrawing European firms, such as the UAC and Morel et Freres.
It controls a large chain of stores. It has ten branches in the
provinces and nine in Banjul and the Kombos, which gives an even
coverage of the country. The location of these stores is shown in
Figure 4:4. All the stores are supplied from Banjul by road and
river. The NTC is a major supplier of basic commodities and until
1986 had a statutory monopoly to distribute imported rice. [14]
It also supplies cooking oil,soap and sugar and is a major
importer of building materials and electrical goods. The
corporation deals only in imported goods, except cooking oil which
is purchased from the GPMB mill at Denton Bridge. One of its
chief aims is to keep prices to a minimum, in order to be highly
competitive with other importers, and thus keep the price of these
goods at a reasonable level. However, most retailing of imported
goods is undertaken by individual businessmen in small canteens or
market stores around the local markets (see Chapter Six).
Retailing is therefore very much associated with local markets
rather than with the trading 'factories' as was the case twenty
or thirty years ago, when producers pledged crops to the firms in
order to obtain urgently required foodstuffs and consumer
durables. This has brought a very strong seasonal element into
the local marketing system, a very good example of which is the
market at Basse in Upper River Division.

Basse is the divisional headquarters of the Upper River Division,
the most easterly administrative area in The Gambia. It is
located 390 kilometres east of Banjul on the south bank of the
River Gambia, and until the end of 1981 was connected to the
capital either by vehicle over badly repaired laterite roads (a
journey which rarely took less than six hours and which usually
took over eight hours), or by river boat, a journey taking two

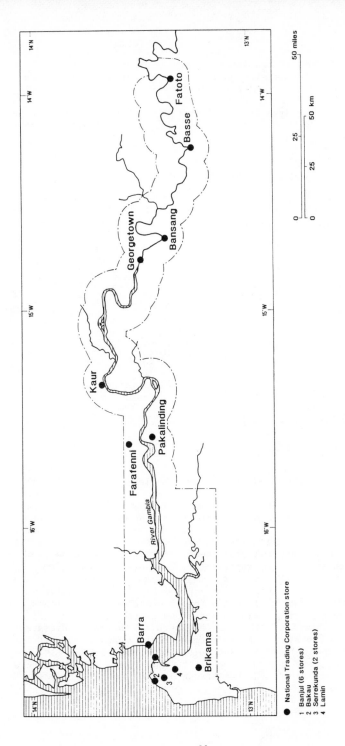

● National Trading Corporation store

1 Banjul (6 stores)
2 Bakau
3 Serrekunda (2 stores)
4 Lamin

Figure 4:4 The distribution of National Trading Corporation stores in The Gambia, 1980

Source: Author's fieldwork

Table 4:3
United Africa Company activity in The Gambia.
Monthly distribution of payments and receipts averaged over
the period 1943-53

Month	Receipts from merchandise Sales	Payments for groundnut Purchases
	%	%
September	4.7	-
October	4.5	-
November	9.5	0.1
December	13.5	29.6
January	16.7	46.4
February	10.5	19.1
March	8.6	3.7
April	7.2	0.9
May	6.8	0.2
June	6.3	-
July	5.8	-
August	5.9	-

Source: UAC, Statistical and Economic Review, No.11, p.10. 1953

days. Due to its role as an administrative centre, Basse has a
number of facilities not available in neighbouring settlements of
similar size. Basse houses the personnel and offices of most of
the government departments which assign personnel to the
provinces: the Education Department, the Public Works Department
amongst others are all represented in Basse. Court cases are
heard at the Court House, with only the more serious cases being
referred to Banjul. There is a well equipped health centre which
attracts large numbers of people from the surrounding villages, as
well as a number of schools, a mosque, a church and a post office.
Although similar facilities can be found at the other divisional
headquarters the sign of Basse's commercial importance is the fact
that it is the only settlement outside the Banjul-Kombo St. Mary
region that there are banking facilities. Both the 'Commercial
and Development Bank' and the 'Standard Bank' have branches in

Basse. [15] Basse's commercial importance is due to the location
of the GPMB's buying station in Basse Wharftown. In the groundnut
trading season the population of the town [16] is estimated to
more than double as people from a very large area come into the
town to sell their groundnut crop and purchase consumer goods.

The town of Basse is divided into two distinct areas, separated
by swampy rice fields. Basse Wharftown is immediately adjacent to
the river, while Basse Santa Su lies on higher ground about two
kilometres south of the river. All of Basse's permanent populace
live in Santa Su as the Wharftown is a seasonal trading town. It
is an area of empty corrugated iron shelters, inhabited only by
dogs, except during the trade season, when it becomes a hive of
activity, with every building transformed into a retail store.
This can be explained by the fact that most businessmen in Basse
own or rent two premises, one in Santa Su and the other in the
Wharftown. For nine months of the year only the Santa Su stores
operate, but during December through to February all business is
transferred to the Wharftown to take advantage of the groundnut
trade.

The reason for this shift in the economic nucleus of the town is
historical. Prior to the dry years of the 1970s, Basse used to
suffer severe flooding during and just after the rainy season,
[17] so much so that the Wharftown was often six feet under water,
and the only method of transportation was by canoe. For this
reason the town was shifted onto higher ground, about two
kilometres from the river and became known as Basse Santa Su. But
during the trade season, groundnuts still had to be taken to the
Wharftown for sale to the agents and to be loaded onto the river
cutters, which were the primary means of transporting the
groundnuts downstream to the oilmills. The traders followed suit
and so for three months of the year the Wharftown became the
centre of commercial activity. Although the river has not flooded
for about twenty years, this pattern is still adhered to.

This shift in the commercial centre of the town makes Basse
unique within The Gambia. Not only do retail stores move, but so
does the daily market. For most of the year only one market
operates in Basse, and that is in the centre of Santa Su. In the
market one can purchase virtually everything, from food to
imported consumer goods. However, during the trade season this is
not the case, as two markets operate simultaneously. The market
in Santa Su shrinks and only stocks foodstuffs, whilst another
market comes into existence in the Wharftown. The Wharftown
market sells only consumer goods (particularly cloth and enamelled
kitchen ware) aimed obviously at the groundnut farmer who has just
sold his harvest at the GPMB buying station 200 metres away. At
the end of the trade season, this market and all the retail
establishments close, and the Santa Su market resumes its role as
supplier of both food and consumer goods.

Another sign of the increased commercial activity of the trade season in Basse is the influx of lorries into the town and the trade brought by the visits of the Lady Chilel Jawara, the Gambian river boat. [18]   The Lady Chilel Jawara was The Gambia's only sizeable river boat, and made the two day journey to Basse, its upriver terminus, once a week during the trade season, but only fortnightly for the rest of the year.   This boat provided an important life line and link with Banjul.   Apart from bringing the mail, the Lady Chilel was the only source in Upper River Division of salt, smoked and dried fish, as well as fresh (but refrigerated) sea fish.   Her visits created a great deal of excitement, and many local people assembled on the quayside creating an informal marketplace offering cooked food, fruit and clay pots for sale to the ship's passengers.   Lorries create less excitement, but in terms of trade are more important for the commercial activity of the town than the river boat.   Basse is the first stopping point for lorries entering The Gambia from Guinea Conakry, Guinea Bissau, Sierra Leone and Senegal, before proceeding to Banjul.   These lorries come laden with oranges, coconuts, kolanuts and a few bananas and pineapples, which they unload in Basse and sell there in the market.   This may take a few weeks, but once the loads are sold the lorries reload with passengers and continue their journey to Banjul.   Once in Banjul, they are loaded with rice, sugar, flour and laundry soap.   They then return to their starting points, with only a brief night stop in Basse.   As far as could be ascertained there was no intra national lorry trade in The Gambia.   During the trade season, 10-12 lorries each week stop in Basse on their way from Guinea Conakry to Banjul; three each week from Freetown, Sierra Leone; three from Senegal and one each week from Guinea Bissau.   (During the rainy season this number is much reduced).   This generates considerable trade for Basse, and during the trade season the market is busy and bustling, the same range of goods being available in Basse as in Banjul.   This is not necessarily the case during the remainder of the year.

Although this is perhaps an extreme example of how the increase in the money supply during the trade season affects the commercial activity of a town, it is by no means an isolated occurrence.   In the trade season, all market towns experience an increase in sales.   The market at Kossemar, for example, is only open in the trade season and the luma markets of the north bank (which will be discussed in Chapter Six), also operate only in the trade season. The sale of groundnuts and the attendant increase in the money supply therefore have a very important effect upon the Gambian economy and in particular on the marketing system.

The development of a 'pluralistic' marketing economy

As a result of the specialisation in groundnut cultivation and its importance to the Gambian economy, two separate and very different marketing systems have developed. One is for the evacuation of the groundnut crop itself and the other for the sale of subsistence items. Although very different in character the two systems complement each other, and any change within one can have an effect on the other.

The sale of the groundnut crop is in the hands of the government through the operations of a marketing board, but this has not always been the case. The Gambia Oilseeds Marketing Board (GOMB) was not set up until 1949. Before this, the groundnut trade was in the hands of the large European companies, such as UAC, CFAO and Maurel et Prom. However, the Second World War brought about quite radical changes in the trade, with the setting up of the West African Products Control Board in 1942. This Board remained in existence until 1949 when, in The Gambia, it was replaced by the GOMB. The GOMB was created to facilitate the collection and export of groundnuts. It functioned by purchasing the nuts through its nine Authorised Buying Agents, at specified buying points. For example, in the 1950-51 season, the GOMB approved the purchase of groundnuts at seventy-two different points and authorised their agents to employ 330 buyers for the purchase of the crop. The GOMB fixed the price to be paid by agents at Bathurst "naked ex-scale" [19] with a lower minimum price set at all the other buying stations. A flat allowance was also added for the cost of transport from any buying point either to Bathurst, Balingho, Kaur or Kuntaur (the four main shipping points). The method of purchasing is still much the same today.

One of the reasons put forward for setting up the GOMB was to stabilise prices to the farmer, by fixing them in advance for each season. It was helped in this respect by the setting up in 1951 of the Farmers' Fund which it was claimed was for "the benefit and prosperity of the farming community of The Gambia". (BA 7/53, 1953) The fund was established with £1,725,000 which was transferred from the reserves of the GOMB with the intended function of subsidising producer prices in years when the world price was poor and accumulating in other years. Such profits as might accrue were to be used to finance community projects in the rural areas to the direct benefit of the agricultural population there. Projects such as mangrove clearance, pest destruction (especially baboons and wild pigs), improving village water supplies and ferries, setting up tractor teams and a pilot scheme for tsetse control in Upper River Division were proposed. The results were disappointing as very few projects came to fruition. The fund just became a compulsory savings scheme for groundnut farmers, which removed a large amount of spending power from the Gambian economy. This led the Gambian government in 1972 to insist that the fund be put to productive use, and resulted in the passing of the GPMB Act in 1973. With the implementation of this Act the Farmers' Fund, which had previously been administered by the government, was transferred to the marketing board. But just prior to the transfer, the government borrowed D1,829,000 in order to set up the Fish Marketing Corporation and the Livestock Marketing Board, both of which will be discussed in Chapter Eight. At the same time, the Act reconstituted the GOMB as the Groundnut Produce Marketing Board (GPMB), but retaining its essential functions.

The GPMB has complete control of the groundut trade, from the collection at farm level to sale on the the international market. It is a fully government owned enterprise, although it acts as a relatively independent agent. It has its own board of directors and a London office. The crop is bought through the Licenced Buying Agents and the Cooperative, and is transported by the GPMB's subsidiary, the Gambia River Transport Company (GRTC). The GPMB also operates its own crushing and milling operations to produce oil. These are located at Denton Bridge just outside Banjul, and at Kaur. The Board exports groundnuts both in the form of oil and also as raw nuts. A London-based office negotiates the sale of groundnuts directly in the world market. Sales go primarily to France, Holland and Portugal. In addition, the GPMB has a legal monopoly for the distribution of groundnut oil for local consumption.

The whole sequence of the marketing of groundnuts is shown in Figure 4:5, and, as can be seen, it by-passes the local marketplace. The producer brings his crop to the buying station by donkey or pick-up truck. Here it is passed through a rotary screen to remove dust and dirt. The nuts are then resacked and weighed, and the farmer paid in cash. After weighing, the nuts are deposited in the buyer's secco. [20] The buyer adds to his secco until he has sufficient to transport to one of the GPMB depots. The depots in operation in 1979-80 were at Banjul, Kaur, Kuntaur, Basse (south), Basse (north), Barra, Bansang and Kudang. The Board has plans to set up depots to cover the whole country, and there are plans to open depots at Tendeba and Kerewan in the near future. (See Figure 4:6).

Evacuation of the crop to the depots has never posed so severe a problem in The Gambia as it has in northern Nigeria or Senegal, due to the excellent routeway provided by the River Gambia. Very few areas of the country are more than seven miles away from the river and most of the buying points are located on its banks. This leaves the farmer with the problem of transporting his groundnuts to the river, which is normally done by donkey cart. Until independence in February 1965, the colonial government actively discouraged the development of the road network and discouraged the use of lorries for the movement of groundnuts to the depots. Evacuation from the buying points in the upper reaches of the river, (in effect the stretch from Koina to Kuntaur) was mostly by lighters towed by power craft. In the lower reaches, locally built sailing cutters were used for transporting a large part of the crop from buying station to shipping point. The cutters were owned by private individuals and

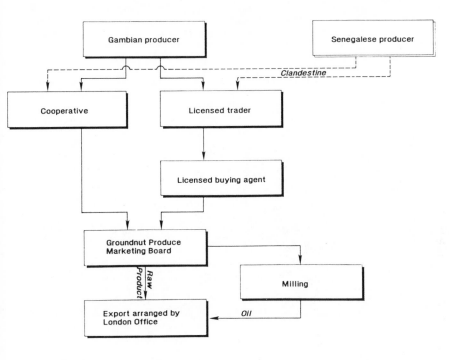

Figure 4:5 The system for marketing groundnuts, post 1973

were chartered by the buying agents. The craft also carried merchandise in the reverse direction whenever practicable. In the 1952-3 season the river fleet consisted of five motor tugs, one motor vessel, forty-two lighters and twenty-one sailing cutters; a total of sixty-nine vessels with a capacity of 2,765 metric tons. The average capacity of the lighters was about fifty-three metric tons and of the sailing cutters about twenty-three metric tons. Dependence on river transportation diminished as the road system developed and after independence the new government actively encouraged the use of lorry transportation. By 1981 a hard-surfaced road had been built as far as Basse on the south bank, but the north bank was still served only by a badly maintained laterite road (see figure 4:7). The major crossing point on the river until 1980 was at Farafenni, where the Trans-Gambian highway links Casamance with the rest of Senegal. The crossing is by two old ferry boats and the waiting time to get onto the ferry can be anything up to three days, especially if one of the ferries breaks down. In 1980, to try to help with this congestion, two new ferry boats were given by the West German Government to be used at the Banjul-Barra crossing point and this has meant that a lot more traffic is now using the western part of the north bank road.

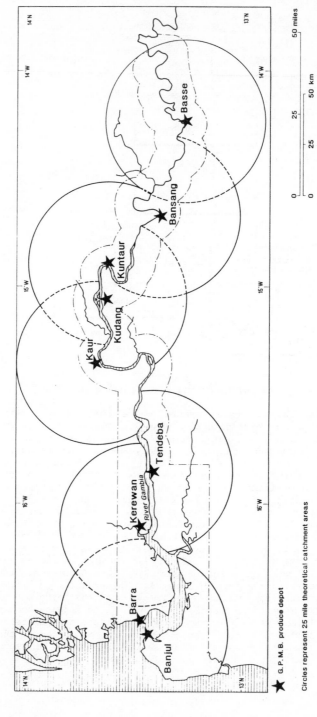

Circles represent 25 mile theoretical catchment areas

★ G. P. M. B. produce depot

Figure 4:6 The location of GPMB produce depots, 1979/80

Source: GPMB Report

It is in the western half of the country that the road network has been developed, and the buying agents have taken advantage of it. Apart from the greater convenience of moving groundnuts by lorry, which gives almost door to door service, for short distances it is also much cheaper. In the 1976/7 season, the cheapest freight rate for produce transported by the GRTC was D11.15 per metric ton. This was a flat rate charged to transport groundnuts a distance less than 40 km; it increased to D15.38 per metric ton for any distance between 40-79 km and D20.52 per metric ton for distances of between 79-145 km. In the same season, the road charge was D1.10 per metric ton for any distance up to 1.5 km, from 1.5-8 km it increased to D1.76, for 8-14.5 km was D4.18, 14.5-21 km was D6.38 and for any distance over 21 km the freight charge was D8.80 per metric ton. As no buying station is more than 40 km from a produce depot (see Figure 4:6) then it certainly works out much cheaper to use lorry transportation rather than the GRTC.

After the groundnuts reach the produce depots, they are stored until they can either be processed or exported. The Board has two processing plants, one at Kaur and the other at Denton Bridge, Banjul. At both plants, groundnuts can be directly loaded into seagoing vessels for export. As most buying points are more than 40 km from the processing plants, about 70 per cent of the groundnut crop is transported to the processing plants by river, the remainder being transported by road. Most of the groundnuts transported by road were from the Western Division and went directly to Banjul.

Of the crop purchased by the GPMB, approximately 51 per cent is crushed for oil in The Gambia, 43 per cent is exported after it has been decorticated and three per cent is confectionary nuts. The remaining three per cent is accounted for by experiments, spillages, and as seed nuts. Of the oil produced in 1977 about 2,023 metric tons were kept for sale locally, the rest was exported. The UK took 7,954 metric tons, 7,630 metric tons was exported to France, and 509 metric tons went to Belgium. Of the decorticated nuts sold in 1977, over half (that is 20,402 metric tons) went to Holland, 10,102 metric tons to Portugal, 5,043 metric tons to France, 2,540 metric tons to Italy, 1,320 metric tons to Ghana, with only 1,002 metric tons going to UK. These are all shipped by chartered vessels in bulk except for the confectionary nuts (Hand Picked Selected) which were sold to Holland and UK in 72 kilogram bags.

This completes the marketing procedure for groundnuts. It is a system which is efficient and appears profitable for all concerned, and contrasts markedly with the subsistence marketing sector.

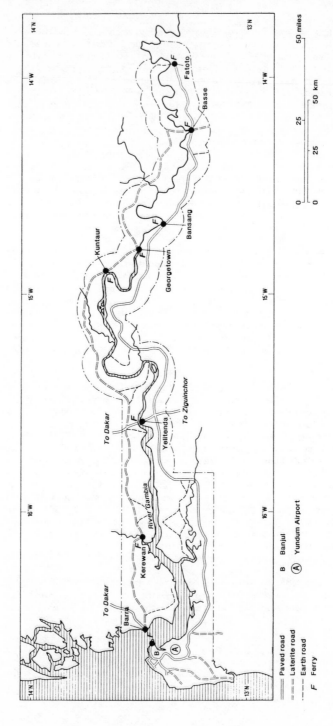

Figure 4:7 Road communications in The Gambia, 1980

Source: Author's fieldwork

Conclusion

Increased groundnut cultivation has had three very important effects on the economy, which in turn affect the marketing system. Firstly, land, labour and capital have taken up added importance which has resulted in competition developing for these factors of production between foodcrops and the cash crop, with groundnut cultivation ultimately benefiting. Secondly, the dominance of the economy by the sale of groundnuts has resulted in a marked seasonality of the money supply, which in turn directly affects purchases in the marketplace, stimulating demand in the groundnut buying period. Thirdly, to accommodate the efficient purchase of the cash crop, a government controlled marketing system for groundnuts has been developed. This system totally circumvents the traditional marketing network and has resulted in the evolution of a dualistic marketing economy in The Gambia. It is the neglected subsistence marketing sector which will be discussed in the following chapters.

Notes

[1] Benini, 1980
[2] In the last 20-30 years this position has been crumbling, an important symptom being the covert sale or renting of land. With regard to the special case of irrigated rice land, an open rental market is developing (Dey 1980, p.221). There are also many instances of farmland being publically sold in the Kombos, largely for construction purposes. In 1980, the government, alarmed at the number of sales, banned the selling of farmland in the Kombos.
[3] "To sum up, the distinct identity of the Serahuli diaspora essentially rests on their preponderance in rural trade, the concomitant wealth of traders, high individual mobility, devout adherence to Islam and isolation from modern administration and education in large remote villages". (Benini 1980, p.7)
[4] The interest charged by the money lender is not known, but is usually considerable. Haswell (1975) noted effective interest rates varying between 39-157 per cent for subsistence credit provided by the money lender in Genieri village, in the 1973-74 season.
[5] Dunsmore 1976, p.298
[6] The kafo, "This is an informal organisation having neither election nor initiation to membership, which includes most adult men . . . and cutting across the system of social stratification". (Gamble 1955, p.53)
[7] Weil (1971) identifies two, whereas Dey (1980) and Dunsmore (1976) identify three groups.
[8] See, Palmer, 1946; Jarrett, 1949; Gamble, 1958; Swindell, 1979, 1982.
[9] The Slave Trade Abolition Ordinance was passed in 1894.

[10] Swindell 1982, p.96
[11] <u>Striga</u> spp. is a semi parasitic weed. Only S. hermontheca
      and S.<u>senegalensis</u> have been reported in West Africa (Kowal
      and Kassam 1978, p.248)
[12] Dunsmore 1976, p.177
[13] UAC ceased trading in The Gambia in 1972, most of the other
      expatriate firms followed suit; Maurel et Prom closed most
      of its stations in 1977 but retained a store in Banjul, as
      did CFAO.
[14] Rice de-regulation took place in January 1986.
[15] The only places where one can find a bank in The Gambia are
      Banjul, Bakau, Serrekunda and Basse.
[16] In the 1973 census Basse is recorded as having a population
      of 2,899 and was the tenth largest settlement, in terms of
      population, in the country.
[17] "During the rains the upper River rises some 30 feet. This
      year when the floods were exceptionally heavy the buildings
      at Basse, the largest market in the Protectorate in the dry
      season, were 12 feet under water" (Annual Colonial Report,
      1927, p.4) According to the report of 1961, there was also
      a severe flood in Basse in that year.
[18] Lady Chilel Jawara sank in early 1985.
[19] In 1951 the "ex-scale" price was £41.16s a ton, at all other
      buying stations it was fixed at £40 a ton.
[20] A <u>secco</u> is a fenced off plot of ground, usually flat and
      dry, and is named after the French word <u>sec</u>, meaning dry.

5　The evolution of the marketing network in the twentieth century

Introduction [1]

With colonial domination of The Gambia at the turn of the twentieth century, a new period in Gambian marketplace development occurs. Marketplaces which had 'disappeared' in the second half of the nineteenth century re-emerge to become one of the most important institutions of the country. This chapter examines the development of the present-day marketing system in The Gambia, using central place and diffusion theory.

Theoretical Background

The fact that the principles of central place theory are dependent on economic characteristics has meant that it has been used extensively in the study of marketplace development. Since Christaller's (1966) study of central place systems in Southern Germany, first published in 1933, many studies have followed, investigating marketing systems as central place phenomena. (Hodder 1961; Hill 1966a) But central place theory is basically an inflexible static, hierarchical model (Beavon and Mabin 1975) and it is only recently that geographers are beginning to deal with the problem of the evolution of central place patterns. (Bromley 1978)

Skinner (1964) proposed one of the earliest models of central place development to be found in the literature, with his study of trade and marketing structures in rural China prior to the communist takeover in 1949. Using central place theory as a base, he was able to identify 'systems' of market towns, connected together by a series of 'spatial linkages', including the flow of goods and services, the travel patterns of traders and consumer movement. Perhaps the most striking aspect of the Chinese marketing system is the regular hexagonal and hierarchical distribution of market centres, which so resemble those described by Christaller. Such spatial regularity of periodic markets is not unique to traditional China and similar hexagonal marketing areas have been identified by Eighmy (1972) in western Nigeria and by McKim (1972) in north-east Ghana. According to Skinner, marketing first takes place between small peasant centres; an articulated system evolves with population increase, a growing division of labour, the development of modern forms of transportation and 'commercialisation'. Specifically he proposes the following sequence: thinly populated regions have few, small, widely but evenly spaced marketplaces; as the above factors come into play, these centres enlarge; finally new and smaller marketplaces locate between the old ones, while these take on higher level functions to service the new group. Thus by using the system perspective provided by central place theory, Skinner was able to move to a general model of market process.

Berry (1967), taking Skinner's analysis a stage further, has divided the growth of central place systems into two basic categories, that is those experiencing 'traditional' change and those experiencing 'modern' change. Traditional change is likely to occur under conditions of population growth, without transport improvements or more general socio-economic modernisation, and results in the addition of new, lower order market centres. Modern change normally occurs because of transport improvements and is usually accompanied by population growth. This type of change involves a decrease in the total number of centres, with fewer lower order centres being added to the system. In spatial terms, it is clear that the process of modern change occurs initially around the larger urban centres and that it gradually diffuses from the more urbanised core areas towards the less urbanised and more peripheral areas. Thus as modern change takes over from traditional change and the market system is increasingly affected by demographic, economic, social and technological changes, diffusion theory becomes applicable.

The pioneering work in the field of diffusion studies has been that of Hagerstrand (1952). From a detailed study of historical records in Sweden, Hagerstrand derived a three stage empirical model of the diffusion process: a primary stage, where centres of multiple adoptions quickly emerge; a diffusion stage, where the primary centres experience some retardation as new centres grow up in an attempt to surpass the initial points of growth; a saturation stage, where additional increments are not feasible under the given conditions. He concludes that the probability of a new adoption is greatest in the vicinity of an earlier one and lessens with increasing distance, subsequent diffusion depending on the location of earlier adoptions according to a principle termed the 'neighbourhood effect'. Adopting the basic terminology of Hagerstrand, Good (1970) in his study of markets in the Ankole region of Uganda, has interpreted the growth of a Ugandan market system in terms of diffusion processes, following the typical s-shaped cumulative growth curve. Good suggests that there are four major stages in the evolution of a marketing system, analogous to the stages identified by Hagerstrand. Eighmy (1972) has gone a step further by using diffusion principles to simulate the sequential location of markets on a rectangular grid of potential market sites. His model assumes that potential market sites nearest to an existing market site are more likely to have a market founded than potential sites located further away.

At first it would appear that the central place and diffusionist approaches are diametrically opposed. The Skinner/Berry model predicts that marketing evolves from horizontal peasant-to-peasant exchange to vertical rural-urban exchange, accompanied by simple intensification. As a contrast, the proponents of the diffusion theory of market system evolution, favour an intensification process through 'top-down' penetration. The sequence assumes that commercialisation 'diffuses' through the rural area, via the stimulus of the urban centres. A closer examination, however, reveals that the two approaches might in fact complement each other. In studies where the diffusion model has been successfully used to describe the development of marketing systems, the growth of marketplaces has been of recent origin. For example in the case of the Ankole region of Uganda, where Good applied the diffusion model, the first market was established in 1902. This was followed by a rapid growth in the number of markets operating, resulting in saturation and rationalisation, with today a tendency towards uniform spacing of markets, as one would expect from the operation of central place principles. This system has developed concurrently with transportation and general socio-economic improvements, as well as being accompanied by population growth. It is interesting to note that these are all conditions identified by Berry as necessary for modern change to take place. In other words, diffusion theory can be seen as the expression of or the mechanism behind modern change and not as a conflicting theory.

Bromley (1978) appreciated the usefulness of both central place and diffusion theory in providing an evolutionary model for his data from highland Ecuador and has produced a simplified six stage developmental model, drawing from both Berry's and Hagerstrand's work. The first three stages are characterised by traditional change, the fourth and fifth stages being a mixture of traditional and modern change, with the last stage being that of modern change only. Within the model, market foundations take place by outward

95

spatial trend diffusion from the centre of the basin towards the periphery. In stages four to six, modern change, involving the gradual decline and extinction of small market centres, gradually diffuses outwards towards the edge of the basin. Change first develops around the larger urban centres, from where it gradually diffuses towards the less urbanised and peripheral area.

All these models stress the importance of population growth and transportation improvements to marketplace evolution, which takes the form of a diffusion process from the urban centre to the rural periphery. This would appear to be the norm, but overlooks one very important factor, the purchasing power of the population. Far more significant than population and transportation characteristics which have affected the evolution of the marketing system in The Gambia is the peculiar distribution of purchasing power, associated with the spread of the cash crop groundnuts in the twentieth century. This has produced a situation where marketplace development takes place three hundred miles away from the primary urban centre and diffuses towards it, meeting up with the kind of diffusion of marketplaces described by Bromley which began to occur around the capital, Bathurst, by about 1935. The next section describes and attempts to explain this odd Gambian situation.

Marketplace evolution in The Gambia

Prior to the period of colonial supremacy in the region, and even before the establishment in 1816 of the one large urban centre in the country, rural markets were operating in The Gambia. As discussed in Chapter Two, these markets had possessed elements of long term continuity, allowing them to be treated as one of the basic central place institutions throughout the history of the region, although they did temporarily 'disappear' in the eighteenth and nineteenth centuries. However, during the period of colonial administration and particularly in the twentieth century, the marketing system was considerably altered, directly affected by socio-economic changes. The evolution of marketplaces in The Gambia is shown on Figure 5:1.

Marketplace development: patterns

At the turn of the twentieth century marketplaces existed only in the eastern part of The Gambia, with the exception of the Albert Market in the capital, Bathurst. Even by 1920 there were only eight markets operating in the Protectorate and none of these were west of Kuntaur. (see Figure 5:1) By 1935 six new markets had been officially established by the colonial administration, but none of these were further west than Kaur. It was a spatial pattern shaped rather like a keyhole, with the eastern part of the country having markets which were linked by river to the economic centre (the capital, itself linked by sea to the metropolis). The intervening areas were devoid of marketplaces.

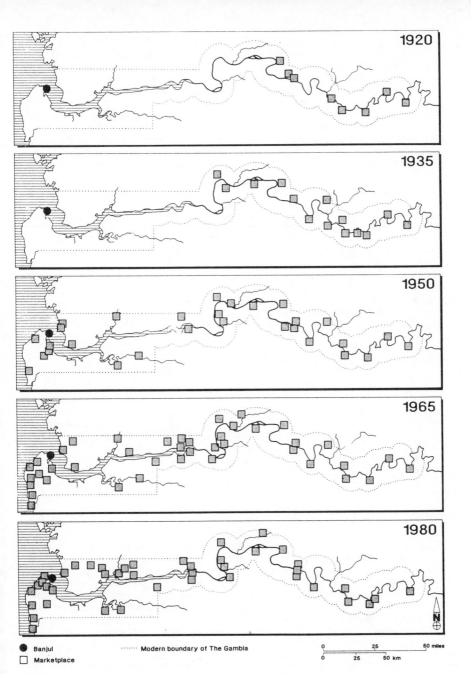

1920

1935

1950

1965

1980

● Banjul
□ Marketplace

······ Modern boundary of The Gambia

0   25   50 miles
0   25   50 km

N

Figure 5:1   The evolution of the marketplace network in The Gambia, 1920–1980

Source: Author's fieldwork

In 1933 a bill to provide for the establishment, control and management of markets in the Protectorate was passed although the establishment of marketplaces was still left to the initiative of the local people. The marketplace was becoming institutionalised and gradually coming under the control of the colonial administration. The 1933 bill recognised nine markets in the Protectorate: Basse, Fatoto, Kossemar, Bannatenda, Georgetown, Kuntaur, Kaur, Bansang and Jessadi. There were no markets registered in the North Bank or South Bank Provinces, as the Travelling Commissioner for the South Bank Province stated:

> As far as I am aware, there are as yet no markets established in this province. (BA 2/1344, 1933)

By 1939 still no markets were registered in the South Bank Province, but two had been registered in the North Bank. The total number in the Protectorate had risen to thirteen. The full list is as follows:

Upper River Province

Basse
Fatoto
Kossemar
Bannatenda
Kanube

MacCarthy Island Province

Georgetown
Kuntaur
Kaur
Bansang
Jessadi
Sankulikunda

North Bank Province

Jowara
Balingho

By 1950 it seems evident that the marketplace idea had been universally accepted and twenty-eight markets were operating in the Protectorate. This was more than double the pre-war number. Of these, more than half were located west of Kaur, with nine being established in Western Division alone. In 1955 Gamble states that the most flourishing markets - were at the administrative headquarters, particularly at Brikama, Georgetown and Basse. However, other centres were also important, including Kaur.

> The market at Kaur is an altogether different category from other markets in the division. Its revenue from fees during 1945 amounted to £171, which was more than four times the revenue derived from Jowara and Barra markets together. (BA 9/489, 1946)

During this period markets were constantly being opened and closed, as the colonial government tried to encourage trading. The Travelling Commissioners were always making recommendations for the establishment of new markets and the revival of old ones.

I visited Jessadi this morning and suggest that consideration should be given to the question of reviving the market there. People were seen selling fish on the ground and a cow had been slaughtered. It might be advisable to keep this market open during the trade season only.

On the other hand, the Sefu is anxious to build a market at Dankunku which would be open the whole year and when necessary could be used as a meeting house. (BA 9/632, 1948)

Other suggestions were:

Mbollet market has never been profitable and will probably never be so. It is hoped to try a market at Fass during the next financial year to take its place. (BA 9/818, 1952)

Because markets were set up in such 'ad hoc' conditions with very little planning and forethought the buildings themselves were not very secure and during this period many accidents occurred. In 1947 the Senior Commissioner reported:

The market house at Lamin is in a disgraceful state of repair and should be entirely rebuilt. A shed similar to those at Brikama or Gunjur is required.

The same remarks apply [to Bwiam market] as in the case of Lamin. (BA 9/746, 1947)

In 1951 the Travelling Commissioner of MacCarthy Island Province wrote to the Senior Commissioner:

It is with regret that I have to inform you that on Thursday 5th July, the Bansang market sheds collapsed under the strain of a high wind. (BA 9/551, 1951)

The next year

Yundum market was partly damaged in a storm during the rains. The salvaged material has been used elsewhere and it is not intended to rebuild this year. (BA 9/818, 1952)

It is interesting to note that in 1953 out of the twenty-eight markets operating, twenty were located near groundnut buying stations, or in the same villages as the buying stations. Of these, seven were only open during the trade season, indicating their dependence on the groundnut trade.

After 1965, the growth of the marketing network slowed down and the number of marketplaces in operation stabilised at around forty-five. Since 1965 adjustments have taken place within the system to take advantage of socio-economic and technological changes within the country.

Marketplace development: process

The process underlying the twentieth century evolution of marketplaces in The Gambia is difficult to isolate. If a central place mechanism is at work, as identified by Skinner in China, then we would expect there to be a system of small market centres which evolve into larger centres that are evenly distributed over the landscape. The use of the nearest neighbour statistic confirms what figure 5:1 shows, that this is not the case. Because of the peculiar size and shape of the country and the importance of the river as a means of transportation, Dacey's (1960) adaptation of nearest neighbour analysis was used. [2] Linear nearest neighbour analysis as formulated by Dacey was carried out on the Gambian data for five separate years, at fifteen year intervals, to test if there was any uniformity of the spacing of markets along the river, as would be expected if central place principles were in operation. The results are given in Table 5:1. A figure of 0.66 indicates random spacing, a figure of less than 0.66 indicates a tendency towards clustering, whilst a figure greater than 0.66 indicates uniformity of spacing. From the table it becomes clear that in 1920 and 1935 markets were randomly spaced, but with a marked tendency towards a clustered pattern as figure 5:1 shows. In 1950 the pattern is still random but with an underlying grouped element. In 1965 first order market neighbours are tending towards uniformity, a pattern that by 1980 has reverted back to randomness. It can be concluded therefore that there is no uniformity in the spacing of marketplaces along the River Gambia, and this indicates that the principles of central place theory are not important components in the Gambian situation.

Table 5:1
Linear nearest neighbour analysis on marketplaces in
The Gambia, 1920 – 1980

	First order neighbours	Second order neighbours	Third order neighbours
1920	0.66	0.44	0.00
1935	0.66	0.66	0.20
1950	0.60	0.60	0.46
1965	0.76	0.62	0.52
1980	0.65	0.60	0.37

Source: Author's fieldwork

However, the pattern of twentieth century marketplace development in The Gambia does conform to diffusion theory, with the system having experienced the three stages of diffusion identified by Hagerstrand, i.e., the primary, diffusion and saturation stages. The period prior to 1935, when all markets operating in the Protectorate were located east of Kuntaur and connected to the commercial centre of the region, Bathurst, by the river, can be regarded as the primary stage. The diffusion stage can be tentatively put between 1935 and 1950. During this period marketplaces diffused westwards from Basse and eastwards from the capital simultaneously, covering the whole country by 1950. By 1965 The Gambia had entered the saturation stage with markets such as Panchang, Illiasa, Jowara, Bondali and Balanfa closing down. In total, between 1960 and 1980 fourteen markets closed down and fifteen new markets were opened. It is a period of rationalisation, with many uneconomic riverside markets such as Fattatenda, Karantaba and Jappeni closing, to be replaced by markets located on the main east-west roads such as Niani Bantang, Soma and Sibanor. A good example of how the development of road transportation since independence [3] has affected markets is that of Farafenni. Farafenni has boasted a market since 1945, but it was not until 1957, with the opening of the Trans-Gambian Highway that it reached any great size. The market there is now one of the largest on the north bank and a large variety of goods can be purchased there, many items coming from across the border via the Highway. So important has Farafenni grown that in the 1975-80 Development Plan, Farafenni was designated an official growth centre (along with Basse). After 1965 the number of marketplaces in operation in The Gambia stabilised at around forty-five. Therefore, since 1920 the number of markets operating in The Gambia has formed an s-shaped cumulative growth curve, as diffusion theory predicts.

Although the use of diffusion theory describes the growth of the Gambian marketing network, it does not explain why marketplaces developed in an area three hundred miles east of the only economic urban centre (Bathurst, now Banjul) and gradually spread towards it - quite the opposite to what one would expect. It is suggested that the reason for this anomaly is the imposition of a cash crop economy by the colonial government on a previously subsistence - communalist society. So successful was the introduction of the cash crop that by 1857 food crop cultivation was being neglected in favour of the new cash crop. This trend has continued, with increasing tonnages of groundnuts being exported from the region, accompanied by increasing imports of food, mainly rice. (See Figure 5:2) It is the spread of a monetary economy and the growing demand for imported foodstuffs that has been responsible for the peculiar pattern of marketplace development in The Gambia during this century.

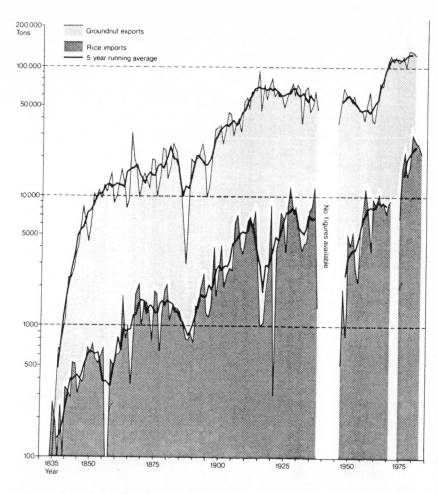

Figure 5:2 Groundnut exports from and rice imports to The Gambia,
1835–1978

Source: Blue Books, GPMB reports

Recent studies on the sporadic nature of the marketing structure
in Sierra Leone do not shed any light on the reasons for the
evolution of the marketing network as found in The Gambia. For
instance Riddell's (1974) analysis of marketing in Sierra Leone,
where periodic markets do not appear until late in this century,
argues that Sierra Leonean villages were very close to the pure

102

model of subsistence, and that this inhibited the growth of a regular periodic marketing system. Similarly Van der Laan (1975), in his study of Lebanese traders in Sierra Leone, ignores indigenous exchange in inland regions of the country. Howard (1981) however, shows that internal and overseas trade in Sierra Leone was far greater than these authors suggest. He argues that one reason why marketplaces did not develop in the north-western region was that historically much of the local exchange had occurred in households, caravans, shops and other institutions rather than marketplaces. Such explanations cannot be easily transferred to the Gambian case. Inter-regional trade was occurring even before the first Europeans sailed up the river and there is historical documentary evidence to show that self-sufficiency was not the norm, particularly after the introduction of the groundnut as a cash crop in the 1830s.

So why did markets not develop in the western part of the country? Perhaps small scale traders - African, Afro-European and later Lebanese - filled this economic vacuum, as Howard suggests they did in the north-western part of Sierra Leone, at about the same time. For the nineteenth century there is little evidence of this activity, but in the early twentieth century Lebanese trading interest was strong. If these interests were located in marketless areas, this might have inhibited the growth of regular market meetings. In fact this did not occur - Lebanese interests were attracted to the eastern provinces, where marketplaces were operating. Lebanese immigration into The Gambia began around 1912. The colonial government disapproved, especially at Lebanese settlement in Bathurst.

> I am of the opinion that Syrians should be discouraged from settling in Bathurst. They are quite as susceptible as Europeans to various tropical diseases and are frequently of poor physique and would therefore require as good, if not better sanitary surroundings as considered necessary for average Europeans. These conditions cannot be offered in Bathurst at present. (BA 2/172 303/12, 1912)

But settlement did take place in Bathurst, where the Lebanese later proved to be serious competition for the European firms, with companies such as S. Madi becoming very active and successful in the groundnut trade. As well as settling in the capital, Lebanese immigrants began to move out into the Protectorate, obtaining leases to hold land. This also worried the colonial government.

> I am directed by HE the Governor to inform you that this government does not approve of Syrians holding land in the Protectorate, as it is considered to be contrary to public policy. (BA 2/172 303/12, 1912)

The memo does not go on to explain what is meant by "public policy", but it is suspected that the government was worried by the competition to European trade that the Lebanese represented. In November 1923, twenty-seven land leases were in Lebanese names, in December 1924 this had risen to forty-three. But after the above memo had been circulated, the number had dropped to twenty-two (November 1926). The numbers then began to creep up, reaching fifty-two in December 1929, the last available figures. The Lebanese by this time were (and still are) an important part of the trading network of The Gambia and the colonial government had to accept them.

These early Lebanese immigrants concentrated themselves in the eastern part of the country. All the land leases taken out up until 1929 were in Upper River Province and MacCarthy Island Province. By 1929, Lebanese had settled in sixteen villages, which included Kuntaur, Kaur, Basse Wharftown, Basse Santa Su, Fatoto, Jessadi Wharftown, Bansang Wharftown and Kossemar Tenda, all well established trading centres, with thriving markets. The Lebanese have thus followed the pattern of marketplace development, by settling in Bathurst and the eastern part of the country, and avoiding the intervening territory. It could be that they were attracted by the trade that was already occurring in these areas, but being astute businessmen it must be assumed that they did not settle in the western districts because purchasing power in these areas was not high enough to make trading there profitable.

It is impossible to provide data showing that purchasing power was greater in the eastern part of The Gambia; one can only hypothesize. Purchasing power for the Gambian producer comes from the sale of his groundnut crop. Therefore one can assume that in areas of greatest groundnut cultivation, the amount of money the producer has to spend is greater, and his demand for imported food is higher. Although there is no concrete data, the historical evidence indicates that groundnut production was much more intense in the eastern half of the country. One of the prime reasons for this was the increased accessibility of the river upstream, which facilitated easier exports of groundnuts and imports of food. East of Kuntaur there were fewer mangrove swamps, which meant that cutters could load up with groundnuts directly for shipment to Bathurst. Downstream of Kuntaur, mangrove swamps, which extend quite some distance inland, hindered the building of wharfs, particularly on the north bank. In a period where communications by land were entirely based on animal and human power, accessibility to a buying station was paramount in the producer's decision to grow a cash crop. This was particularly the case in the early years of the twentieth century when, with the operation of the Merchants' Combine, traders refused to buy nuts at the farm gate and would only buy nuts in the wharftowns. This meant that trade was centralised in factories under European management, that the price paid for groundnuts was kept low and that the responsibility for transporting nuts from the farm gate to the trading station was the producers'. This in effect meant that only in areas within a day's travelling distance from the trading station was groundnut cultivation a profitable venture.

the new arrangements have been rather a sudden blow to the
Natives . . . Now not only has the Native been deprived of the
presents of goods that used to accompany a sale, but if he
wants the best price he has to transport his nuts to the
wharf, at a cost in some instances of 6d a measure. In the
past the traders ventured into all parts of the interior,
bought nuts and undertook themselves the responsibility for
transporting nuts to the wharves. (CO 87/163, 1901)

The combine was effective from 1900 to 1909, after which
conditions of free competition were allowed to operate. However,
after this date the farmer was still left with the problem of
transporting his own nuts to the wharftown buying stations. It
was a situation which did not help stimulate groundnut cultivation
in the areas to the west of Kuntaur, where access to buying
stations was much more difficult.

At an early date it is evident that in the eastern provinces of
The Gambia food crop production was being neglected in favour of
groundnut cultivation and this necessitated the importation and
purchasing of food. It is suggested that this is one reason why
marketplaces developed more rapidly in the east. It was this
area, with its advantages in terms of accessibility and which had
not been so badly affected by the destruction caused by the
Soninke-Marabout wars in the second half of the nineteenth
century, that found it so easy to respond to the European demand
for groundnuts, but at the same time neglecting food production.
This balance was redressed by the growth of local marketplaces.
By the same argument, it is possible to suggest that because
marketplaces did not spring up west of Kuntaur until after 1935,
that up until that date groundnut production in these areas was
not hindering food production. So as purchasing power was low
and sufficient food was being grown, marketplaces were not needed
and any exchange that did take place occurred through other
mechanisms.

With this relatively high purchasing power in the east, markets
were flourishing. Of these markets, Basse was by far the biggest
and most important. In 1921 the Travelling Commissioner wrote:

In Basse market during the trade season some thousands of
pounds change hands daily – hundreds of grass huts are put up
by all kinds of traders, without any sort of order – usually
several fires occur during the season and practically wipe out
the market each time, and make a great danger to the European
firms' buildings. (BA 331/20, 1921)

In 1927 the Travelling Commissioner wrote to the Senior
Commissioner:

I have the honour to inform you that I have received a
deputation from the Native traders in Basse Santa Su market
requesting that a permanent shelter be erected in the Santa Su
market for use in the Rainy Season. There is quite a big
trade done in the market during the Rains and at present when
it rains the unfortunate traders have to pack up and run to

105

the nearest shelter, not only this, but the ground becomes a quagmire and it is sometimes unfit to be used for days. Basse is the biggest market town in the Protectorate and the government could well afford the expenditure. (BA 2/610, 1927)

Again in 1928, the Travelling Commissioner had the same petition:

A permanent market shed is very badly needed at Basse Santa Su market . . . As regards market dues, I think Basse can claim the biggest revenue from this source in the Protectorate. (BA 2/610, 1928)

In April 1930 work was completed on a permanent market shelter at Basse Santa Su. This was ten years after the Governor had approved the imposition of fees in the markets and twelve years after the Commissioners had made this very valid point:

It was pointed out by H.E. that if market dues were instituted it would be only reasonable to provide a proper market or some facilities for the traders. (BA 207/19, 1918)

By the 1950s groundnut cultivation was taking place in all parts of the country and by this date markets were also widespread institutions. In 1950 there were twice the pre-war number of markets operating in the country. Of these more than half were located west of Kaur, with nine being established in Western Division alone. This dramatic increase in marketplace activity in Western Division cannot wholly be seen as a response to increased spending power generated by the cultivation of the cash crop as it was in other parts of the Protectorate, because this area was not a big groundnut producing region. Instead it can be seen as part of a 'diffusion process' associated with transport improvements and population growth; two conditions that were met in this region during this latter period. From 1911 until 1944 the population of Bathurst more than tripled. Even more dramatic, the population of Kombo St. Mary increased six times between 1911 and 1963. In addition to this dramatic increase in population growth, the road network of the area was much improved. So what may tentatively be termed 'modern change' was beginning to occur around Bathurst from about 1935 and was diffusing from the urban centre at the same time. With the diffusion of this 'modern change' south and eastwards away from the capital, markets began to be established and to flourish. These markets, facilitated by the improved road communications, satisfied the growing demands of the ever increasing Bathurst-Kombo St. Mary population and have continued to do so since. The diffusion of markets away from Bathurst had by 1950 met up with the growth of markets westwards, which was associated with the spread of groundnut cultivation. Markets had therefore by this time become common institutions in all parts of the country and by 1960 the total number of markets operating had stabilised. In the late 1960s drought hit The Gambia, and was to continue, in varying degrees of severity, into the 1980s. As a consequence groundnut production fluctuated. This obviously affected markets that were only just profitable; markets such as Panchang, Illiasa, Jowara, Bondali and Balanfa closed down. During this period the system underwent a period of adjustment and rationalisation, and the system reacted to such factors as the increased use of road transportation.

Conclusion

Central place theory, but more especially diffusion theory, help describe the pattern of marketplace development in The Gambia in the twentieth century. It is a pattern where in the early decades of this century marketplaces develop three hundred miles east of the primary urban centre and diffuse towards it, whilst from about 1935, a secondary area of marketplace development occurs, associated with 'modern change' around the capital. By 1950 both these waves of marketplace diffusion have met up and markets become common institutions over all the country. The number of markets operating in the country reached a peak in the 1960s, a period that can be equated with Hagerstrand's saturation stage. Since then, the number of markets has stabilised at about forty-five, and there has been a rationalisation of the system. The Gambian situation is quite different from that described by Good or Bromley, which none of the models can adequately explain. Population characteristics and transportation improvements, although influencing the system, do not appear as key factors in the evolution of Gambian marketplaces. It is suggested that purchasing power potentials associated with groundnut cultivation are much more important.

Notes

[1] A revised version of this chapter has been published in *Tijdschrift voor economische sociale geografie* (1986) entitled 'The evolution of the marketing network in The Gambia, in the twentieth century'.

[2] Dacey (1960) has analysed the spacing of river towns in the central lowlands of the USA. He identified 'reflexive nearest neighbours' for the first, second, third, etc. nearest neighbours, and by dividing the number of reflexive towns by the total number of towns he derived a linear nearest neighbour statistic. A random pattern was represented by a statistic of 0.66, a statistic less than this indicates a clustered grouping and a figure greater than 0.66 indicated uniformity.

[3] Unlike other areas of Africa, transportation has never been a problem in The Gambia. Traditionally, the major internal communication in the country has been by means of the river. The colonial government realised the importance of the river and actively discouraged the development of road transportation. It was not until the period of independence that the emphasis changed and road communications were extended.

6 The present-day marketing network in The Gambia

Introduction

In the last chapter the effect that groundnut cultivation has had on the marketing system was discussed. This specialisation produced two distinct networks, one for the groundnut and the other for subsistence goods. The government controlled cash crop sector was briefly described and in this chapter the focus will be on the subsistence sector, particularly that of locally produced foodstuffs. The various markets within this system will be examined, using two classifications which emphasis the many common characteristics that these markets have. Firstly, markets will be considered as either official or unofficial and secondly, to aid the discussion of market inter-relationships, they will be classified as either urban, peri-urban or rural in nature. An indepth examination of the network reveals that although market inter-relationships are poorly developed in the rural areas, a primitive system of distribution is beginning to take shape between the peri-urban and urban markets.

Official Markets

In 1979/80 there were forty-three official markets operating within The Gambia. They are listed in Table 6:1 and are shown on Figure 6:1. These markets are recognised by both the Provinces

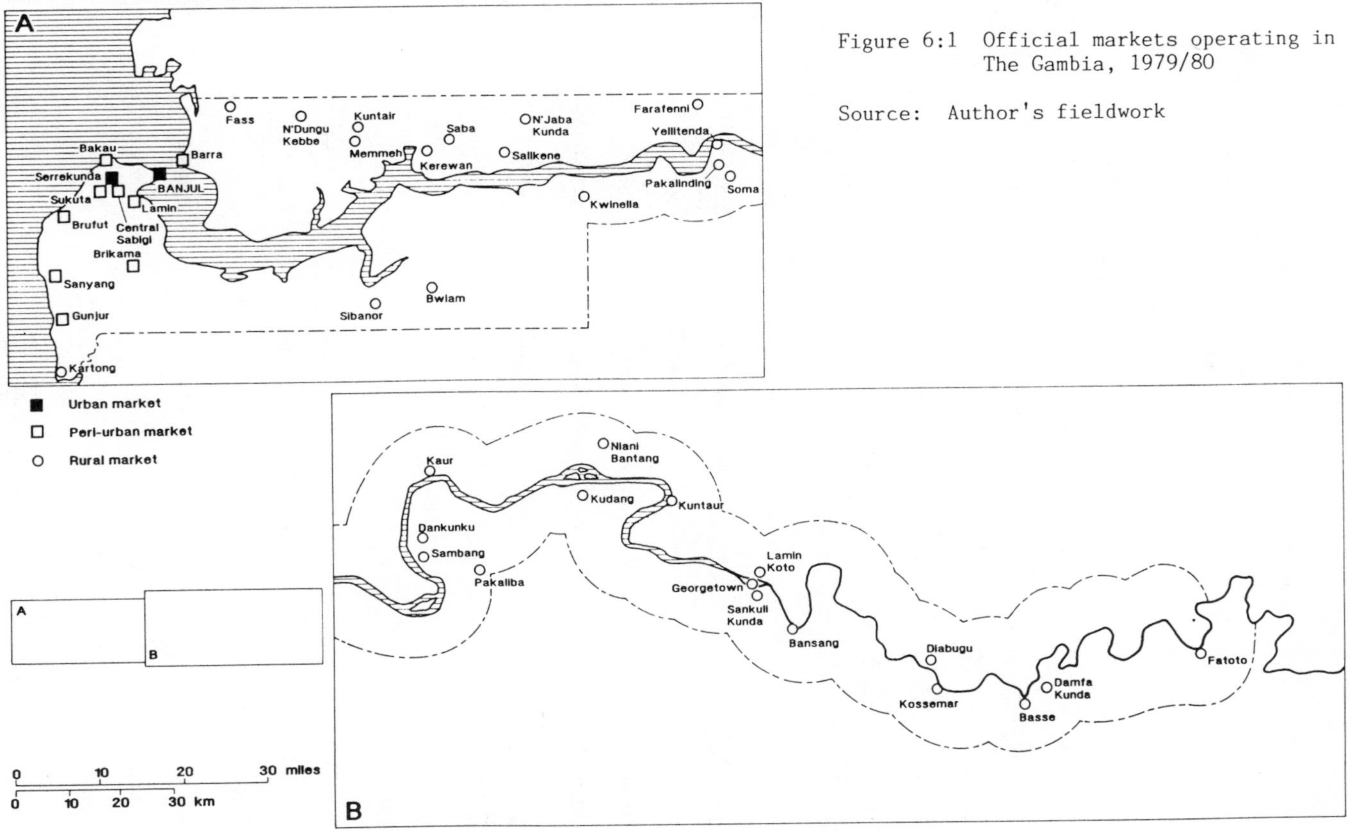

Figure 6:1 Official markets operating in The Gambia, 1979/80

Source: Author's fieldwork

A

Fass
N'Dungu Kebbe
Kuntair
Memmeh
Saba
Kerewan
Farafenni
N'Jaba Kunda
Salikene
Yellitenda
Soma
Pakalinding
Kwinella
Bwiam
Sibanor

Barra
Bakau
BANJUL
Lamin
Serrekunda
Sukuta
Brufut Central Sabigi
Brikama
Sanyang
Gunjur
Kartong

Urban market
Peri-urban market
Rural market

B

Kaur
Nianl Bantang
Kudang
Dankunku
Sambang
Pakaliba
Kuntaur
Georgetown
Lamin Koto
Sankull Kunda
Bansang
Diabugu
Kossemar
Damfa Kunda
Basse
Fatoto

0   10   20   30 miles
0   10   20   30 km

A
B

Table 6:1
Official markets operating in The Gambia, 1979/80

Market Site	Local Council Area	Category of Market
Banjul*	Banjul City Council	Urban
Bakau*	Kanifing City Council	Peri-urban
Central Sabigi*	Kanifing City Council	Peri-urban
Serrekunda*	Kanifing City Council	Urban
Basse*	Basse Area Council	Rural
Damfa Kunda[t]	Basse Area Council	Rural
Diabugu	Basse Area Council	Rural
Fatoto	Basse Area Council	Rural
Kossemar[t]	Basse Area Council	Rural
Brikama*	Brikama Area Council	Peri-urban
Brufut	Brikama Area Council	Peri-urban
Bwiam	Brikama Area Council	Rural
Gunjur*	Brikama Area Council	Peri-urban
Kartong	Brikama Area Council	Rural
Lamin	Brikama Area Council	Peri-urban
Sanyang	Brikama Area Council	Peri-urban
Sibanor	Brikama Area Council	Rural
Sukuta*[e]	Brikama Area Council	Peri-urban
Bansang	Georgetown Area Council	Rural
Dankunku[t]	Georgetown Area Council	Rural
Georgetown*	Georgetown Area Council	Rural
Kudang[t]	Georgetown Area Council	Rural
Sambang	Georgetown Area Council	Rural

Market Site	Local Council Area	Category of Market
Sankuli Kunda[t]	Georgetown Area Council	Rural
Barra*	Kerewan Area Council	Peri-urban
Farafenni*	Kerewan Area Council	Rural
Fass	Kerewan Area Council	Rural
Kerewan*	Kerewan Area Council	Rural
Kuntair	Kerewan Area Council	Rural
Memmeh	Kerewan Area Council	Rural
N'Dungu Kebbe	Kerewan Area Council	Rural
N'Jaba Kunda	Kerewan Area Council	Rural
Saba	Kerewan Area Council	Rural
Salikene	Kerewan Area Council	Rural
Kaur*	Kuntaur Area Council	Rural
Kuntaur*	Kuntaur Area Council	Rural
Lamin Koto[t]	Kuntaur Area Council	Rural
Niani Bantang[t]	Kuntaur Area Council	Rural
Kwinella	Mansa Konko Area Cou.	Rural
Pakaliba	Mansa Konko Area Cou.	Rural
Pakalinding	Mansa Konko Area Cou.	Rural
Soma	Mansa Konko Area Cou.	Rural
Yellitenda[r]	Mansa Konko Area Cou.	Rural

* Markets where surveys were undertaken, 1979/80
t Markets that were open only in the trade season
e Markets that open in the evenings only
r Markets that sell only cooked food

Source: Author's fieldwork, 1979/80

Markets Rules (Cap. 109, 1967) and the Kombo St. Mary Market
Regulations (Cap. 109, 1967), by which they are governed. They
come under the direct control of the city or area councils in
whose area they are sited, who are by the Area Councils
(Additional Functions) Notice (Cap. 109, 1967) charged with "the
establishment and regulation of markets".

There are six area councils, Basse, Brikama, Georgetown,
Kerewan, Kuntaur and Mansa Konko, along with two city councils,
Banjul and Kanifing (which controls the Kombo St. Mary
conurbation). Their location and the divisional area they control
is shown in Figure 1:2. For each market under its jurisdiction,
the council appoints a market master, who is responsible for the
smooth running of the market, as well as the allocation of plots
and the collection of rents. The last function is his most
important and time consuming task. In most markets the market
master is able to perform his duties on his own, but in the larger
markets of Banjul and Serrekunda, rent collectors are employed to
help with the fee collections.

Market rents are fixed by central government and are consistent
throughout the country. The scale of fees in operation during the
1979/80 period is shown in Table 6:2. In each market there are
three categories of fees for vendors, plus an additional charge
for butchers on every animal offered for sale. This helps meet
the costs incurred by the health inspector, who has to examine
every carcass before it can be sold. The categories of market
vendors are, firstly, those who rent or have been permitted to
construct a "canteen". These are small sheds where the vendor is
able to store and lock up his stock. Secondly, there are a
limited number of tables in each market, on which a vendor may
display her wares, and thirdly, there are the vendors who display
their produce on a cloth on the floor. [1]   All official markets
have at least one kwiang. These are constructions erected by the
area council for the shelter and convenience of traders. These
are constructed from concrete with corrugated iron roofs, and
protect the traders from both sunshine and rain. They usually
contain concrete tables, and an area reserved for butchers. Many
of the busier markets also have local council constructed canteens
which are made from breeze blocks and are much more solid than the
corrugated structures found in most markets. The canteens are in
great demand and are rented out in a monthly basis. Because of
their secure nature they are often rented by two or more traders
as a store for their goods, which they sell in another part of the
market.

Markets in The Gambia, although government controlled, do not
follow any uniform plan. Plans of Basse and Banjul markets
(Figures 6:2 and 6:3) indicate the laissez-faire nature of
markets. The kwiang structures are indicated, but the rest of the
market is a chaotic mixture of corrugated iron canteens and
tables, with floor sellers fitting in between. However, there is

some order to the apparent choas, with vendors of particular goods seeming to congregate together. Of course there is much mixing, but in general, traders selling vegetables, for example, will sit in one part of the market, those selling dried fish in another. A rough indication of the location of various vendors in Basse and Banjul markets are shown on the plans.

Table 6:2
Fees charged in official markets, 1979/80

	Rent (dalasi)
Rent charged on canteen facilities	25.00 per month
Rent charged to hire table space	0.50 per day
Rent charged to hire floor space	0.25 per day
Fee charged per cow carcass	2.0
Fee charged per sheep or goat carcass	1.0

Source: Interviews by the author with traders and market masters, 1979/80

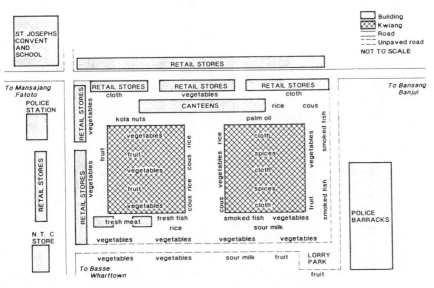

Figure 6:2 Plan of Basse rainy season market, 1980

Source: Author's fieldwork

113

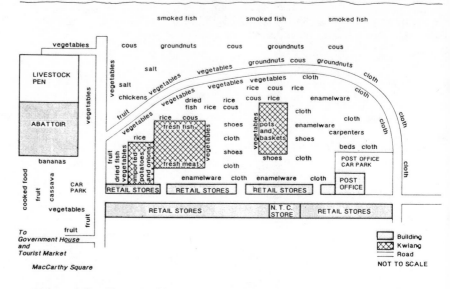

Figure 6:3   Plan of Albert Market, Banjul, 1980

Source: Author's fieldwork

   Although all markets offer canteen, table and floor facilities, the availability varies, as Table 6:3 demonstrates. In the more crowded markets, such as Banjul and Serrekunda, one finds a large percentage of floor sellers (67 per cent and 62 per cent respectively). In the less busy markets of Central Sabigi and Kerewan the numbers are well under 10 per cent, with over 70 per cent of the vendors renting tables (93 per cent and 95 per cent respectively). Canteens are the lowest category, due to the small numbers available. Only in Barra market were over eight per cent of the sellers renting canteens, here the figure was a surprising 45 per cent (due to the high number of restaurants serving travellers). In all markets there is a mixture of sex and nationality. Tables 6:4 and 6:5 give the results of the survey and show that in all official markets, women traders out number men. In the urban markets, 57 per cent of vendors interviewed were women and in the other official markets this figure was higher at 66 per cent. In terms of nationality, as would be expected, Gambians predominate, comprising 77 per cent of the traders interviewed in official markets. However there were a significant number of Senegalese nationals trading in the markets, comprising 13 per cent of those interviewed, with Guinea Comakry nationals making up six per cent of the sample.

Table 6:3
Percentages of traders selling their wares from canteens, tables or the floor, 1979/80

Markets in which a survey was undertaken   Averages

	Banjul	Serrekunda	Bakau	Central Sabigi	Gunjur	Sukuta	Brikama	Georgetown	Basse	Kuntaur	Kaur	Farafenni	Kerewan	Barra	Kaur Luma	Farafenni Luma	Urban Markets	Other Official Mkts	Luma Markets	All Markets
Floor	67	62	16	3	30	10	22	29	80	24	12	45	5	8	97	93	64.5	23.5	95.0	61.0
Table	25	30	82	93	70	85	71	64	17	76	80	53	95	47	3	7	27.5	69.5	5.0	34.0
Canteen	8	8	2	4	0	5	7	7	3	0	8	2	0	45	0	0	8.0	7.0	0	5.0
TOTAL	100	100	100	100	100	100	100	100	100	100	100	100	100	100	100	100	100	100	100	100

Source: Author's fieldwork 1979/80

Sex and nationality are reflected in the allocation of market space. Table 6:6 shows the cross-tabulation percentages for type of market space rented and the sex of the vendor, distinguishing between the urban markets of Banjul and Serrekunda, and the other official markets. From these figures it becomes clear that very few women rent canteens. In the urban markets where table facilities are very limited, most women rent floor space. In the other official markets, which are less crowded, more women rent tables. It would seem that those men who do trade in the markets have the capital behind them to either rent tables or canteens. Women do not have access to such capital. The renting of canteens is also dominated by three national groups, Gambians, Senegalese and Guinea Conakry nationals. Table 6:7 shows the percentages of floor, tables and canteen space, as it is rented by various nationals. In Banjul and Serrekunda, Gambians and Senegalese traders rent 85 per cent of the canteens and 94 per cent of tables. In the provinces, the Guinea Conakrians become more evident in trade, renting almost a third of the canteens. This is associated with their role in the butchering trade, with butchers by law having to transact their business in canteens. However these figures do show that large numbers of traders in the official markets do not have access to marketplace selling facilities and display their wares on the floor. This lack of facilities produces problems of storage. Most traders take home what goods they have left at the end of the day, as is shown in

115

Table 6:8, the figure being a high 83 per cent at Sukuta. In Banjul only 25 per cent of traders take their unsold produce home as here storage facilities are best developed, if a little primitive. Several traders get together and either rent a canteen to store their goods (15 per cent) or may jointly hire a nightwatchman to guard their wares which will have been boxed up and hidden under a table, usually in the kwiang (43 per cent). This is not satisfactory, but is perhaps better than carrying goods back and forth each day. In some markets, canteens are available for rent and traders use them as storage facilities. This occurs at Serrekunda, Barra, Farafenni, Brikama, Bakau, Kuntaur and Georgetown and, to a lesser extent, at Sukuta, Kaur, Basse and Kerewan. But most traders only have the option of storing their leftover goods at home, using them themselves, giving them away, or, if possible, drying the produce to sell at a future date (as can be done with peppers, cassava and fish).

MARKETS	Imported rice	Local rice	Cous	Fresh meat	Livestock	Fresh sea fish	Fresh river fish	Dried smoked fish	Imported potatoes	Imported onions	Vegetables	Fruit	Palm oil	Sour milk
Banjul	X		X	X		X		X	X	X	X	X	X	
Serrekunda	X		X	X		X		X	X	X	X	X	X	X
Bakau	X		X	X		X		X	X	X	X	X	X	X
Central Sabigi	X		X	X		X		X	X	X	X	X	X	X
Brikama	X		X	X		X		X	X	X	X	X	X	
Sukuta			X			X		X		X	X	X		
Gunjur				X		X		X		X	X	X		
Kerewan				X			X	X			X			
Barra	X			X		X		X	X	X	X	X	X	X
Farafenni	X			X				X	X	X	X	X	X	X
Kuntaur		X						X	X	X	X	X	X	
Kaur				X				X	X	X	X	X	X	
Georgetown		X		X				X	X	X	X	X	X	
Basse	X	X	X	X			X	X	X	X	X	X	X	X
Farafenni Luma		X	X	X	X			X	X	X	X	X		
Kaur Luma				X				X	X	X	X	X	X	

Figure 6:4   Matrix showing the categories of food available in the markets where surveys were undertaken, 1979/80

Source: Author's fieldwork

Table 6:4
Percentage of male/female traders in marketplaces
where surveys were undertaken, 1979/80

markets in which is survey was undertaken   Averages

	Banjul	Serrekunda	Bakau	Central Sabigt	Gunjur	Sukuta	Brikama	Georgetown	Basse	Kuntaur	Kaur	Farafenni	Kerewan	Barra	Kaur Luma	Farafenni Luma	Urban Markets	Other Official Mkts	Luma Markets	All Markets
Male	44	42	35	21	17	33	33	36	30	36	20	56	42	46	73	75	43	34	74	40
Female	56	58	65	79	83	67	67	64	70	64	80	44	58	54	27	25	57	66	26	60
TOTAL	100	100	100	100	100	100	100	100	100	100	100	100	100	100	100	100	100	100	100	100

Source: Author's fieldwork 1979/80

Table 6:5
Nationalities of traders interviewed in surveyed
marketplaces, as percentages, 1979/80

Markets in which a survey was undertaken   Averages

	Banjul	Serrekunda	Bakau	Central Sabigt	Gunjur	Sukuta	Brikama	Georgetown	Basse	Kuntaur	Kaur	Farafenni	Kerewan	Barra	Kaur Luma	Farafenni Luma	Urban Markets	Other Official Mkts	Luma Markets	All Markets
Gambian	73	86	91	90	69	98	86	79	84	60	68	50	84	47	67	37	79.5	75.5	52.0	69.0
Senegalese	18	8	5	7	14	2	9	11	4	20	20	38	6	17	30	55	13.0	13.0	42.5	23.0
Mauritanean	1	0	0	0	3	0	0	3	1	0	12	2	5	4	0	3	0.5	2.5	1.5	1.5
Guinea Conakry	6	4	2	3	7	0	4	7	7	12	0	9	0	31	0	2	5.0	6.5	1.0	4.0
Guinea Bissau	0	0	0	0	7	0	1	0	1	8	0	0	0	1	3	0	0	1.5	1.5	1.0
Malian	2	2	2	0	0	0	0	0	3	0	0	1	5	0	0	3	2.0	1.0	1.5	1.5
Other	0	0	0	0	0	0	0	0	0	0	0	0	0	0	0	0	0	0	0	0
TOTAL	100	100	100	100	100	100	100	100	100	100	100	100	100	100	100	100	100	100	100	100

Source: Author's fieldwork 1979/80

117

All official markets supply the same range of goods and services, but in varying quantities. The matrix in Figure 6:4 shows the main categories of food available in the markets where surveys were undertaken. From this it is evident that differences are minimal and usually based on environmental variations. For example, locally produced rice was only available at Kuntaur, Georgetown and Basse, where there are currently rice growing schemes. Fresh sea fish are available in the markets on the Atlantic seaboard, whilst from Kerewan eastwards, only fresh river fish are found in the markets. In most markets fresh meat and fish are available daily, vegetables and fruit are plentiful although seasonal, and other commonly used foodstuffs are available. Although the markets of Banjul and Serrekunda are larger than the other markets, the same choice of goods is available, even as far east as Basse. The excellent east-west communications, of both river and road is responsible for this lack of diversification between markets. However markets in the system do perform different functions in the chain of distribution, and this aspect will be discussed later in this chapter under the heading of market inter-relationships.

Table 6:6
The sex of traders and the type of market space rented in official markets where a survey was undertaken, 1979/80 (Percentages)

Official urban markets (Banjul and Serrekunda)

	Floor	Table	Canteen	Row Total
Male	18.9	17.4	6.5	42.9
Female	46.2	9.4	1.5	57.1
Column Total	65.1	26.9	8.0	100.0

Other official markets

	Floor	Table	Canteen	Row Total
Male	8.2	20.7	5.7	34.6
Female	26.3	32.2	2.9	65.4
Column Total	34.5	56.9	8.6	100.0

Source: Author's fieldwork, 1979/80

Unofficial markets

In 1979/80 there were fourteen unofficial markets operating in The Gambia which are listed in Table 6:9 and can be divided into two categories, based on periodicity, seven being open daily and seven weekly.

Unofficial daily markets

The daily unofficial markets are all located within the urban conglomeration, two being located in Banjul and the others in districts neighbouring Serrekunda. The markets that are situated in Banjul are not of recent origin. As far back as 1923 the Honourable Councillor Bottomley (BA Ref 2.559) had observed a great number of street markets operating in various parts of Bathurst, populated he claimed by people from the North Bank Province. In March 1940 (BA Ref 2.559) three sub-markets were identified as operating in Bathurst, one in the area behind the Albert Market and the Post Office, secondly, in the area between Cotton Street and Brown Street (Marche Santa), and thirdly, at Lasso Wharf between Allen Street and Grant Street. The first of these markets has become absorbed into the main Albert market, and is no longer separately distinguishable. However, the other two continue to function. These markets, one of which specialises entirely in cooked food and the other which opens only in the evening, are directly supplied from the main market. Many of the vendors trade in the main market during the day then sell or cook the produce they had not sold earlier in the day. Both Marche Santa and the Lasso Wharf markets supplement the services supplied by the main market, which closes at dusk (18.30 - 19.00 hours), but which is usually emptying from 15.00 hours onwards. All offices and most craft shops close at 15.00 hours for the day, so the Marche Santa provides food in the late afternoon and evening for the many single immigrant men living and working in Banjul. The Lasso Wharf market supplies fresh vegetables and fruit. Of course, these markets also provide a social venue for the district, and in the evening many people can be seen here just walking and greeting friends.

The other daily unofficial markets are of more recent origin, associated with the dramatic growth of population, due to large scale immigration into the Serrekunda conglomeration. New Jeswang, Latrikunda, Fagikunda and Talinding Kunjang are all small villages which have now been swallowed up by the expanding village of Serrekunda. The London Corner market is on the outskirts of Serrekunda, at the junction of the Brikama, Banjul and Latrikunda roads, on the opposite side of the village to the official market. The location of these markets are shown on Figure 6:5. These markets open daily from about 08.00 hours until 15.00 hours. They supply fruit and vegetables (but generally not fresh meat or fish) to the local populace who are not able to walk the three kilometres to the main market or who have not purchased enough supplies at the main market. They tend to be small neighbourhood markets and meet on public ground, usually at the side of the road, with no permanent constructions (a few traders may bring low stalls on which to advertise their wares). As these markets grow, they are gradually absorbed into the official system. When this occurs, the city or area council concerned take responsibility for the upkeep of the market, a market master is appointed, market

Table 6:7
The nationality of traders and the type of market space rented,
in official markets where a survey was undertaken, 1979/80
(percentages)

Official urban markets (Banjul and Serrekunda)

	Floor	Table	Canteen	Row Total
Gambian	53.2	19.7	5.3	78.2
Senegalese	6.8	5.6	1.5	13.8
Mauritanian	0.2	0.0	0.2	0.5
Guinea Conakry	3.2	1.5	0.7	5.3
Guinea Bissau	0.2	0.0	0.0	0.2
Malian	1.5	0.2	0.2	1.9
Column Total	65.0	26.9	8.0	100.0

Other official markets

	Floor	Table	Canteen	Row Total
Gambian	27.7	45.1	3.5	76.3
Senegalese	2.3	7.8	1.3	11.4
Mauritanian	0.3	0.7	0.6	1.6
Guinea Conakry	2.6	2.6	3.1	8.3
Guinea Bissau	1.0	0.0	0.1	1.2
Malian	0.4	0.7	0.0	1.2
Column Total	34.4	57.0	8.6	100.0

Source: Author's fieldwork, 1979/80

Table 6:8
Where traders interviewed stored their unsold produce, 1979/80
(percentages)

	Markets in which a survey was undertaken																Averages			
	Banjul	Serrekunda	Bakau	Central Sabigt	Gunjur	Sukuta	Brikama	Georgetown	Basse	Kuntaur	Kaur	Farafenni	Kerewan	Barra	Kaur Luma	Farafenni Luma	Urban Markets	Other Official Mkts	Luma Markets	All Markets
At home	25	43	63	82	80	83	64	63	81	71	72	46	74	32	80	96	34.0	67.5	88.0	63.0
In Market	43	17	7	4	3	2	4	19	7	0	8	13	0	0	3	2	30.0	6.0	2.5	13.0
In rented Canteen	15	21	19	0	0	5	19	15	8	17	12	20	5	42	7	2	18.0	13.0	5.0	12.0
Other	17	19	11	14	17	10	13	3	4	12	8	21	21	26	10	0	18.0	13.0	5.0	12.0
TOTAL	100	100	100	100	100	100	100	100	100	100	100	100	100	100	100	100	100	100	100	100

Source: Author's fieldwork 1979/80

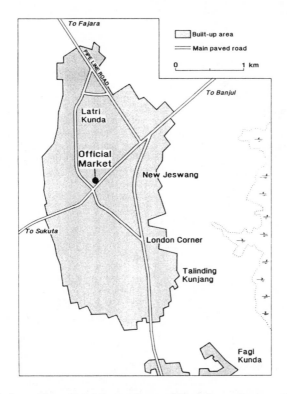

Figure 6:5   The location of unofficial markets within the
              Serrekunda conglomeration, 1980

Source: Author's fieldwork

dues are collected and butchering is permitted. One market which
has recently been taken over by an Area Council (Kanifing City
Council) is that at Central Sabigi.   Central Sabigi is a new
"suburb" of Serrekunda, which stretches either side of the main
Banjul-Brikama paved road, five kilometres outside Serrekunda. It
is hardly a village, just a linear pattern of compounds. Because
the village is some distance from Serrekunda and the bus service
is poor, and most of the taxis plying the main road are full, the
women of the neighbourhood opened their own unofficial market on a
vacant plot by the main road. In 1979 this market was officially
reorganised and a row of canteens were built, along with a few
rows of tables. It is a neat, well laid out, clean market and
even boasts a butcher, although by comparison to other official
markets it is small.

121

Table 6:9
Unofficial markets operating in The Gambia, 1979/80

Daily Markets

Market Site   Local Council Area

Lasso Wharf[e]   Banjul City Council
Marche Santa[r]   Banjul City Council
Fagikunda   Kanifing City Council
Latrikunda   Kanifing City Council
London Corner   Kanifing City Council
New Jeswang   Kanifing City Council
Talinding Kunjang   Kanifing City Council

Weekly Luma Markets**

Market Site   Local Council Area

Farafenni*   Kerewan Area Council
Ker Pate Kore   Kerewan Area Council
Minti Kunda[t]   Kerewan Area Council
N'Geyen Sanjal[t]   Kerewan Area Council
N'Jaba Kunda[t]   Kerewan Area Council
Kaur*   Kuntaur Area Council
Soma   Mansa Konko Area Council

* markets where surveys were undertaken in 1979/80
t markets open only in the trade season
e markets that open in the evenings only
r markets that sell only cooked foods

Source: Author's fieldwork, 1979/80

** This list may not be complete as these markets arise
spontaneously and may disappear as quickly. The author was
only able to find seven _luma_ markets operating in the 1979/80
season.

Central Sabigi is supplied with goods almost exclusively from
Serrekunda and Banjul markets. A few locally produced goods can
be bought. Palm kernels, okra, cashew fruit, peppers, tomatoes,
bitter tomatoes and sour milk from the neighbourhood were sold.
Traders from further afield were also found there. A woman from
Abuko was selling onions, and palm oil produced in Tujering was
also being sold. Fresh fish from Old Jeswang and Bakau were

plentiful, but the bulk of goods originated from Serrekunda market, with some from Banjul. Goods such as raw cous, shelled groundnuts, salt, dry fish and yaite (dried sea snail), onions, tomatoes, bitter tomatoes and cabbages had been purchased in Serrekunda market. Imported foodstuffs, such as Irish potatoes, tomato paste, Maggi Cubes, Blue Band margarine, macaroni, tea bags and kolanuts, originated mainly from Banjul market. The usual pattern is for a woman to go to either Banjul or Serrekunda market once to three times a week, to stock up on goods. These would then distributed among a number of friends to sell in the market. The main items for sale were vegetables, condiments and dried fish, with 58 per cent of those interviewed selling these goods; other classes of goods, namely, cereals and grain products, oilseeds and nuts, and fresh meat and fish, were each represented by ten per cent of sellers. It is therefore a well stocked market, with the same range of goods available as in the urban markets (see Figure 6:4). This seems to be the general case with all the unofficial daily markets, except that they lawfully cannot offer fresh meat or fish for sale.

Unofficial weekly markets

Of more recent origin are the unofficially recognised weekly markets, of which in the 1979/80 trade season there were seven. These lumas [2] as they are known by the local people, only began operating in the dry season of 1979/80. They appear to be a spontaneous gathering of people from a number of villages, usually near the border, who agree to meet on a certain day each week during the dry season to exchange goods. They meet on public ground and no rents are collected. However, four of the largest luma markets, Farafenni, Kaur, Soma and Ker Pate Kore proved to be so popular and successful that they remained open during the rainy season of 1980 also. Spatially these markets differ considerably from the daily ones (as can be seen from Figure 6:6). All but one of the luma markets operating in 1979/80 lie between Kerewan and Kaur on the north side of the river, the exception being Soma, on the south side. Soma luma is thought to be directly associated with the extension of good communications to the south bank, by way of the Trans-Gambian Highway. Why these markets occur in this geographically limited areas is not clear. One possibility is that this part of The Gambia, particularly the Baddibus, was until recently an area of rural in-migration associated with the spread and intensification of groundnut cultivation. Today the groundnut frontier has moved eastwards, and south into Casamance. A recent commentator states that: "Groundnut cropping is currently intensifying in the lower river north bank and western division, and there is a strong tendency towards immigration". She points out that: "Areas receiving migrants include Banjul-Kombo St. Mary first and foremost, but also the growing groundnut area in the Saloum districts, Niani and the expanding rice growing area in Niamina East". (Colvin 1982, p.299) The fact that this region attracts migrants and is principally a groundnut cultivating area,

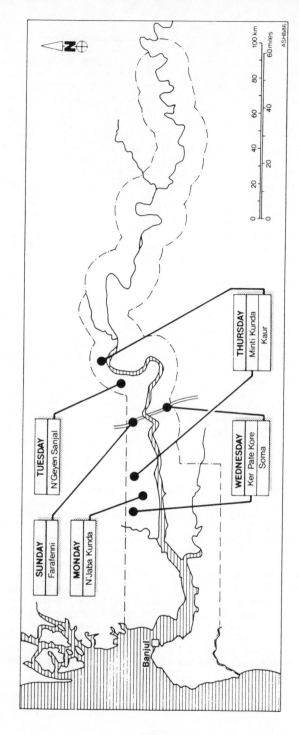

Figure 6:6 Luma markets in operation, 1979/80

Source: Author's fieldwork

124

Table 6:10
Distances travelled by traders to attend a marketplace in which a survey was undertaken, 1979/80

	Markets in which a survey was undertaken																Averages			
	Banjul	Serrekunda	Bakau	Central Sabigi	Gunjur	Sukuta	Brikama	Georgetown	Basse	Kuntaur	Kaur	Farafenni	Kerewan	Barra	Kaur Luma	Farafenni Luma	Urban Markets	Other Official Mkts	Luma Markets	All Markets
Market Village	45	25	83	72	100	98	85	79	30	64	88	98	68	86	10	32	35.0	79.5	21.0	66.5
Up to 4.9 km	0	50	0	28	0	2	2	7	14	20	4	0	11	13	0	15	25.0	8.5	7.5	10.5
5 - 9.9 km	2	4	9	0	0	0	2	7	49	0	0	2	5	0	13	3	3.0	6.0	8.0	6.0
10 - 19.9 km	26	12	4	0	0	0	7	7	5	4	0	0	0	0	41	13	19.0	2.0	27.0	7.5
20 - 39.9 km	22	6	4	0	0	0	2	0	1	4	4	0	16	1	13	15	14.0	2.5	14.0	5.5
40 - 59.9 km	4	2	0	0	0	0	0	0	0	0	0	0	0	0	3	2	3.0	0	2.5	0.5
60 - 100 km	0	1	0	0	0	0	2	0	0	0	4	0	0	0	3	15	0.5	0.5	9.0	1.5
100 - 150 km	0	0	0	0	0	0	0	0	0	0	0	0	0	0	7	3	0	0	5.0	0.5
150 km and over	1	0	0	0	0	0	0	0	1	8	0	0	0	0	10	2	0.5	1.0	6.0	1.5
TOTAL	100	100	100	100	100	100	100	100	100	100	100	100	100	100	100	100	100	100	100	100

Source: Author's fieldwork, 1979/80

Table 6:11
Form of transport used to get to market by traders interviewed in surveyed markets, 1979/80

	Markets in which a survey was undertaken																Averages			
	Banjul	Serrekunda	Bakau	Central Sabigi	Gunjur	Sukuta	Brikama	Georgetown	Basse	Kuntaur	Kaur	Farafenni	Kerewan	Barra	Kaur Luma	Farafenni Luma	Urban Markets	Other Official Mkts	Luma Markets	All Markets
By foot	30	60	65	86	100	72	70	100	73	84	92	95	63	96	17	35	45.0	83.0	26.0	51.5
Donkey	0	0	0	0	0	0	0	0	10	4	0	0	5	0	23	10	0	1.5	16.5	6.0
Cycle	0	1	0	4	0	7	4	0	6	4	4	2	21	0	0	0	0.5	4.5	0	1.5
Lorry	3	0	0	0	0	0	3	0	7	0	0	0	0	0	3	0	1.5	1.0	1.5	1.5
Bus	16	6	4	0	0	0	4	0	0	0	0	0	0	0	0	0	11.0	0.5	0	3.5
Taxi	50	33	31	10	0	21	19	0	4	8	4	3	11	4	57	55	41.0	9.5	56.0	35.5
Private car	1	1	0	0	0	0	0	0	0	0	0	0	0	0	0	0	1.0	0	0	0.5
TOTAL	100	100	100	100	100	100	100	100	100	100	100	100	100	100	100	100	100	100	100	100

Source: Author's fieldwork, 1979/80

has encouraged the establishment of lumas, which are basically a Senegalese phenomenon which has crossed into Gambian territory with the 'strange' farmers.

The lumas attract traders from a wide radius and the figures from Kaur and Farafenni shown in Table 6:10 confirm this. More than 20 per cent travel over 40 kilometres to attend. The greatest distance travelled was by a trader resident in Basse, who travelled the 250 kilometres to Farafenni luma every week to sell his wares. Other sellers travelled from Gunjur, Serrekunda and Jorunku in The Gambia, as well as M'Bar (130 kilometres from Farafenni), Kaolack (96 kilometres), and N'Gaba (85 kilometres), all in Senegal north of the Gambian border. Because such long distances were travelled it is not surprising that 56 per cent of sellers travelled to the lumas by taxi and 14 per cent by donkey as Table 6:11 shows. Also, perhaps related to the long distances involved, 74 per cent of the sellers were in fact men, which is a great contrast to other Gambian markets (see Table 6:4).

As has been stated, these markets are basically Senegalese phenomenon and the Senegalese influence is marked, with Senegalese traders representing over 40 per cent of sellers, nearly all of of whom crossed the border to attend the market (see Table 6:5). The amount of produce from Senegal for sale in these markets is also very noticeable. A large majority of goods had been purchased from the market in Kaolack (Senegal), this area of The Gambia being part of its natural hinterland. Foodstuffs such as onions, Irish potatoes, sweet potatoes, cabbages, tomatoes, bitter tomatoes and pumpkins, as well as spices and imported foodstuffs such as Maggi Cubes, macaroni and condensed milk, had all previously been purchased by traders in Kaolack before being offered for sale at the lumas. Foodstuffs such as shelled groundnuts, smoked-dried bonga fish and raw cous also originate in villages north of the border. An unlawful trade in livestock also takes place. In Kaur luma a goat from N'Ganda (Senegal) was for sale and in Farafenni luma, cows and sheep from Ker Aip, Medina and N'Goro (all in Senegal) were being marketed. One of the reasons that this trade is able to take place is that the luma markets either meet in villages where there is no customs post, or as in the case of Farafenni, the luma is held in a field on the Gambian side of the border but between the Senegalese and Gambian customs posts. (Customs officers, it was observed, wait at the post for lorries and taxis to pass, none were seen in the luma).

Apart from goods crossing the border, Gambian products are also sold in the luma markets. In Farafenni luma, palm oil from Sifoe and Somita, baobab fruit from M'Bap, mangoes from Tanji, dry fish from Gunjur, netetu (locust beans) from Brikama, as well as cassava and limes from Sukuta were being sold. In Kaur luma, palm oil from Banjul, netetu from Kuntaur, maize from Bantanto, mangoes from Gunjur, dry fish from N'Geyen Sanjal and Balanghar were for sale, along with shelled groundnuts from N'Gawarr. There is also

Table 6:12
Percentage of type of sale transacted by traders in the marketplaces in which a survey was undertaken in 1979/80

| | Markets in which a survey was undertaken | | | | | | | | | | | | | | | | Average | | | |
	Banjul	Serrekunda	Bakau	Central Sabigi	Gunjur	Sukuta	Brikama	Georgetown	Basse	Kuntaur	Kaur	Farafenni	Kerewan	Barra	Kaur Luma	Farafenni Luma	Urban Markets	Other Official Mkts	Luma Markets	All Markets
Retail	64	86	98	100	100	95	83	93	96	92	96	85	84	93	50	33	72	92	39	85
Wholesale	22	6	2	0	0	5	10	7	2	0	4	0	11	0	13	8	16	3	10	6
Both	13	8	0	0	0	0	7	0	2	8	0	15	5	7	37	58	11	5	51	9
TOTAL	100	100	100	100	100	100	100	100	100	100	100	100	100	100	100	100	100	100	100	100

Source: Author's fieldwork, 1979/80

Table 6:13
Percentage of customers in each surveyed marketplace who purchase some of their food requirements outside the marketplace 1979/80

| | Markets in which a survey was undertaken | | | | | | | | | | | | | | | | Average | | | |
	Banjul	Serrekunda	Bakau	Central Sabigi	Gunjur	Sukuta	Brikama	Georgetown	Basse	Kuntaur	Kaur	Farafenni	Kerewan	Barra	Kaur Luma	Farafenni Luma	Urban Markets	Other Official Mkts	Luma Markets	All Markets
Respondents occasionally using super-markets and retail stores to purchase food stuffs	18	0	1	0	0	2	1	0	0	0	0	0	0	3	0	0	9	1	0	4
Respondents who buy all their food requirements in the market-place	82	100	99	100	100	98	99	100	100	100	100	100	100	97	100	100	91	99	100	96
TOTAL	100	100	100	100	100	100	100	100	100	100	100	100	100	100	100	100	100	100	100	100

Source: Author's fieldwork, 1979/80

a healthy wholesale trade (see Table 6:12) in onions, Irish potatoes, cereals and dried fish, which will be discussed more fully later in this chapter in the section on market inter-relationships.

Not only are the number of Senegalese traders and amount of Senegalese produce noticeable in the lumas, but the proportion of Senegalese customers is significant. Of the customers interviewed, 18 per cent were Senegalese nationals, with a further 16 per cent comprising nationalities other than Gambian. This is a high proportion as compared with other markets in the country where the average number of non-Gambian customers is only ten per cent of the total. Of the customers interviewed, 21 per cent crossed the border in order to purchase goods in the luma, in no other markets had customers crossed the border. It would also appear that, like the traders, customers are prepared to travel long distances to attend a luma market. Of those interviewed 47 per cent had travelled over ten kilometres and 21 per cent had travelled over 20 kilometres to attend the market; in the official markets only one per cent of customers travelled such distances (see Table 6.14). The lumas also differ from the official markets in that 49 per cent of the customers interviewed were men, in other markets the average was one and a half per cent. This is difficult to explain except to say that in addition to foodstuffs, agricultural equipment, fertilisers and livestock were being displayed, and these are items that in general women cannot afford to purchase.

Luma markets meet once a week and on such days as not to compete with each other, as is shown on Figure 6:6, Soma and Ker Pate lumas meet on the same day, but are far apart, similarly Kaur and Minti Kunda. No luma meets on Friday due to mosque prayers, most people preferring to stay in their own village to pray. No luma meets on a Saturday either. This is because the largest luma at Farafenni meets on Sundays and people are busy on Saturday preparing for that market. This schedule fits well with periodic market cycle theory, which is succinctly put by Fagerlund and Smith: "Proximity in space implies separation in time". (1970, p.343) In other words, as Stine (1962) found in Korea, if a trader moves his place of business periodically, he could tap a wider area of demand. However, in the Gambian case, few traders participated in more than one luma with 78 per cent of respondents saying that they sold only in one luma, ten per cent in other lumas, seven per cent in nearby markets, with three per cent selling in non-Gambian markets. None of the customers interviewed attended any other luma than the one that they were interviewed in. Interaction is thus very limited, but to be expected with the relatively recent operation of these markets. What will happen to them in the future will be of great interest. In particular, the government's reaction will be important.

Other retail outlets

Apart from the market network, there are two other types of retail outlet, the supermarkets and the small store. It is only in the last couple of years that supermarkets have begun to develop in The Gambia. Apart from the outlets of the government controlled National Trading Company (NTC), which was discussed in Chapter Three, all supermarkets are concentrated in Banjul, with only the Compagnie Francais d'Afrique Occidentale (CFAO), opening a large supermarket in Bakau in the late 1970s to tap the expatriate demand there. The major supermarkets in Banjul are CFAO, Maurel et Prom and Sonner Stores. These supermarkets play an unimportant role in the marketing of local foodstuffs. Table 6:13 shows that in all the markets where interviews were undertaken, only four per cent of respondents occasionally used supermarkets or retail stores to purchase foodstuffs. The food sold in these establishments is mainly imported and hardly any locally produced goods can be found. These stores supply the relatively small high income group which can afford to enjoy western cuisine. However, basic ingredients for local dishes, such as tomato paste and tinned meat and fish are available, and perhaps help to explain why approximately nine per cent of consumers interviewed in Banjul and Serrekunda markets said that they occasionally used the supermarkets. In the rest of the country only one per cent of respondents said that they sometimes used the supermarkets.

In the provinces, a retail alternative to the market is offered in the form of the small family store, owned and operated in many instances by Mauritanians, Senegalese or native Serahulis. Most villages can boast at least one store. In many villages, these retail establishments are found adjacent to the market, but they form part of a separate system. The system of retail establishments is concerned mainly with the flow of urban-produced products and imported goods, from the coast to the interior. These stores tend to stock durable goods which have been imported. Apart from the usual trinkets, these stores sell tomato paste, sardines, Blue Band margarine, Ovaltine, soft drinks and powdered milk. Some more enterprising store keepers also offer for sale Irish potatoes, imported rice, onions, dried peppers and bread. Although certain goods are much more expensive in these stores than in the local markets, some items are only available there. Items such as margarine, sardines, flour, powdered milk, and locally baked bread are usually not offered for sale in the local marketplace. These stores have a virtual monopoly on such goods, and prices reflect this. However, the stores do offer the consumer one advantage over the market, which perhaps guarantees their continued existence - the availability of credit. For some compounds, extended credit from the store owners in the form of provisions is essential to survive the hungry season. In this respect these stores have taken over the role left vacant when the European firms, such as the United Africa Company (UAC) [3] and Maurel et Prom, [4] closed down their provincial factories in the late 1960s and early 1970s.

The existence of permanent retail establishments in rural areas implies a comparatively high, continuous density of local purchasing power. In most rural areas there is sufficient demand for low value imported goods, such as sugar, soap, matches and cigarettes, to maintain several general stores selling essentially these low value goods, but sometimes also stocking a few higher value goods, for example, cooking utensils, cloth, umbrellas and blankets.

Market Inter-relationships

In terms of retail trade, Gambian markets are much alike, but they do perform different functions in the chain of distribution and three types of market can be identified which cut across the official/non-official categorisation. These are the urban, peri-urban and rural markets, which all perform different wholesaling functions. In general the wholesale trade for foodstuffs in The Gambia is poorly developed and most producers themselves dispose of their surpluses in the marketplace. This is especially the case in the rural areas of the north bank and south bank, east of Brikama. But as one moves nearer the capital and the densely populated Kombo St. Mary district, the beginnings of a wholesaling network does become apparent.

Rural markets

The Gambia is well served with rural markets as Figure 6:1 demonstrates, the least well served area being the north bank of Upper River Division, the Wuli and Sandu districts, where there is only one market, Diabugu. This is partly due to very poor communications, low population density and the effects of the 1968-73 drought, which hit this area particularly hard. The rest of the country is reasonably well served with rural markets, which are usually located in major settlements and are open every day, with some only opening during the trade season. These trade season markets all lie east of the Trans-Gambian Highway and are located either in wharf towns, such as Kudang and Kossemar, or in small villages off the main roads, for example Dankunku and Damfa Kunda (for the location of the others see Table 6:1). Their seasonality is directly related to the groundnut buying season and the opening of buying stations in these rather remote villages.

Provincial rural markets serve a very limited area and are very loosely connected. Few sellers come more than forty kilometres to sell in a particular market, and in fact, more than 95 per cent of all sellers travel less than ten kilometres to market (see Table 6:10). Customers in these markets follow a similar pattern. Of the customers interviewed in the rural markets, 92 per cent resided in the market village, with none travelling further than twenty kilometres (see Table 6:14) to attend a market. These

Table 6:14
Distances travelled by customers to attend a marketplace
in which a survey was undertaken, 1979/80

	Banjul	Serrekunda	Bakau	Central Sabigi	Gunjur	Sukuta	Brikama	Georgetown	Basse	Kuntaur	Kaur	Farafenni	Kerewan	Barra	Kaur Luma	Farafenni Luma	Urban Markets	Other Official Mkts	Luma Markets	All Markets
Market Village	100	90	100	100	95	98	100	100	62	81	80	94	100	85	30	37	96	92	33	90
Up to 4.9 km	0	6	0	0	5	0	0	0	32	19	5	0	0	12	10	26	3	6	18	5
5 - 9.9 km	0	2	0	0	0	0	0	0	6	0	15	3	0	0	0	5	1	2	3	1
10 - 19 km	0	3	0	0	0	2	0	0	0	0	0	3	0	3	40	11	1	1	26	2
20 - 39 km	0	0	0	0	0	0	0	0	0	0	0	0	0	0	20	21	0	0	21	1
TOTAL	100	100	100	100	100	100	100	100	100	100	100	100	100	100	100	100	100	100	100	100

Markets in which a survey was undertaken / Averages

Source Author's fieldwork, 1979/80

Table 6:15
Percentages of farmers interviewed in the marketplace:
where they disposed of their surplus production 1979/80

	Banjul	Serrekunda	Bakau	Central Sabigi	Gunjur	Sukuta	Brikama	Georgetown	Basse	Kuntaur	Kaur	Farafenni	Kerewan	Barra	Kaur Luma	Farafenni Luma	Urban Markets	Other Official Mkts	Luma Markets	All Markets
Home Consumption	NA*	80	12	29	73	19	60	93	6	100	50	69	100	0	22	15	40	46	19	44
Local Market	NA	13	12	0	0	0	20	0	18	0	25	0	0	0	0	0	7	7	0	6
Nearby Market	NA	0	0	0	0	0	0	0	6	0	0	0	0	0	0	0	0	1	0	1
Urban Market	NA	7	76	71	18	69	5	0	0	0	0	0	0	0	0	0	4	28	0	22
Luma Market	NA	0	0	0	0	0	0	0	0	0	0	0	0	0	0	0	0	0	0	0
Cooperative	NA	0	0	0	9	12	15	7	71	0	25	31	0	100	78	85	0	19	81	27
TOTAL	NA	100	100	100	100	100	100	100	100	100	100	100	100	100	100	100	100	100	100	100

Markets in which a survey was undertaken / Averages

Source: Author's fieldwork, 1979/80

* Not Applicable

markets then serve and are served by a limited area of about fifteen kilometres in radius, there being virtually no interaction with other markets. Kerewan is one of the smallest and most poorly stocked markets in the provinces, despite its being the site of the local government headquarters (with a population of 2,166 in 1973). Fish is very plentiful here, being netted from the river at Kerewan beach and Jorunka, 32 kilometres away from where it is transported by canoe to Kerewan. However, a cow is slaughtered only twice a week, the animal coming from the nearby villages of Saba or Jowara. Stocks of food in the market are small, with the usual vegetables and dried fish available. Most of the produce for sale had been produced in the village itself, but some dried peppers and netetu (locust beans) had been brought in from surrounding villages. No goods entered the market from further afield than Jorunku, and certainly none came from the urban markets. Of the sellers interviewed in this market, 84 per cent lived within a ten kilometre radius (see Table 6:10), with 63 per cent of them walking to market and 21 per cent using a bicycle (see Table 6:11). Only 16 per cent of the respondents attended another market, which they all did once a week, suggesting that it was a nearby luma market.

Kerewan is perhaps an extreme example of the isolated rural Gambian market, but even Basse, the largest of the provincial markets, shows few signs of connectivity with other markets. Large quantities of produce enter Basse market, much of it coming from the surrounding villages of Giroba, Damfa Kunda, Alohungari and Chamoi, all on the south bank of the river, within five kilometres of Basse. Produce such as onions, okra, cassava, sweetcorn, tomatoes and other vegetables and fruit are all supplied by these villages. A large quantity of goods also come from the north bank, with 12 per cent of sellers crossing the river to sell in the market. [5] These producers come from as far afield as Jar Kunda, involving a walk of 21 kilometres. Other villages supplying goods are Madina Koto (8 kilometres from Basse), Taibutu (8 kilometres), Sutuko (9 kilometres), Tuba Wuli (16 kilometres) and Kerewan (16 kilometres). From these north bank villages a different kind of produce enters the market, the goods being more durable. For example large quantities of shelled groundnuts, maize, beans, groundnut oil, cous and eggs were carried across the river along with large quantities of sour milk [6] which is very abundant in this region. Partly this reflects the impact of the Rural Community Development Project's encouragement of market gardening in the Basse environs. Villages north of of Basse were excluded, perhaps because of the shortages of reliable deep wells there. Basse market is basically therefore a locally supplied market, with 93 per cent of sellers living within a 10 kilometre radius (see Table 6:10). Of these 73 per cent walked to market, with 10 per cent using donkeys (see Table 6:11) Only four per cent of the sellers interviewed said that they occasionally visited other markets. Basse is fortunate in being well served by distant suppliers in Guinea Conakry, Guinea

Bissau, Sierra Leone, Daker and Banjul. Supplies of oranges, coconuts, pineapples, kolanuts and palm oil come from these sources, via the lorry trade which passes through the village. For a further discussion of this lorry trade see Chapter Five.

Although most of Gambia's provincial markets are small, isolated and locally supplied, there are a few exceptions. These exceptions are on the north bank, in the same area where the luma markets have sprung up. These markets are not only supplied locally, but also receive supplies from across the border. For example, a large quantity of goods available in Farafenni market is acquired in Kaolack (Senegal). Goods such as onions, tomatoes, Irish potatoes, cassava, cabbage, dried-smoked fish, kolanuts and even fresh fish are brought to the market from Kaolack. This can be explained by the fact that in terms of time, Farafenni is nearer Kaolack than Banjul and does not include a time-consuming ferry crossing. Farafenni is located on the Trans-Gambian Highway, which crosses the paved south bank Basse-Banjul road at Soma (see Figure 4:7). However, palm oil from Gunjur and Somita, peppers from Sibanor and cassava from Brikama were all found in the market, indicating the importance of a good road network in encouraging inter-market activity. Forty-two kilometres to the east of Farafenni is the market at Kaur. Although further away from the Trans-Gambian Highway, Kaur receives more goods from Senegal (perhaps due to laxer customs controls) than its neighbour, Farafenni. In Kaur market, large amounts of fresh vegetables and spices from Kaolack were found. There were also large quantities of dried-smoked bonga fish and other dried fish from N'Jau and N'Ganda, both in Senegal. Kuntaur, a further 64 kilometres east of Kaur, also relies on markets across the border for supplies. Large quantities of goods enter the market here from Koungheul, 45 kilometres away. These goods tend to be imported foodstuffs and non-perishable foodstuffs, such as dry fish, dry pepper, macaroni, Maggi Cubes, pepper corns and Senegalese groundnut oil. [7] Most of the fresh vegetables available in the market were grown in Kuntaur itself, with fresh river fish coming from nearby Panchang.

These three markets, Farafenni, Kaur and Kuntaur, are unlike other rural daily markets in The Gambia, in that they rely heavily on supplies from across the border. It is therefore not surprising that they also have a larger proportion of Senegalese vendors in their markets than other daily markets. Farafenni has the highest proportion, with 38 per cent, Kaur and Kuntaur each have 20 per cent, the rest of the rural markets averaging 10 per cent (see Table 6:5). However these Senegalese supplies do not always come directly into the markets. All three markets rely on the lumas for supplies particularly those at Farafenni and Kaur, the majority of goods for sale in the lumas, as we have seen, coming from across the border.

The lumas perform a valuable wholesale function. Table 6:12 shows that of the traders interviewed in the luma market 61 per cent were engaged in wholesale activity of some kind which is very high when compared to other rural markets (8 per cent) and the urban markets (27 per cent). Traders from all over The Gambia travel to them to replenish their stocks. Even women from the local surrounding markets use the weekly luma as a source of supply. An important element in this trade are various cereals. All the cous that was for sale in these markets originated in Senegal, supplies coming from Ker Mamou N'Gatane, N'Geyen and Prohane. The grain arrives by the lorry load and in many cases was brought in such quantities by traders from Banjul and Serrekunda markets. Similarly shelled groundnuts from Ker Mamou N'Gatane and Dierry Cow, both in Senegal, were quickly snapped up by traders from the urban markets. The economic reasons for this will be discussed in the next chapter on cereal marketing, but the important role of the lumas in supplying urban markets with cous must be stressed here. Of the sixteen markets in which surveys were undertaken, cous from Farafenni luma was observed on sale in six: Banjul, Serrekunda, Brikama, Bakau, Sutuka and Central Sabigi. These are all urban or peri-urban markets. Other goods from the lumas, such as shelled groundnuts, white and black beans, dried-smoked fish, onions, dry peppers, as well as other spices and imported food items, were found on sale in Banjul, Serrekunda, Farafenni and Kaur markets. In fact the meat that was for sale in the latter two markets had been purchased on the hoof in the lumas earlier in the week.

Peri-Urban Markets

As one moves westwards towards the urban centres of Banjul and Serrekunda, market connectivity becomes more developed, being most advanced in the peri-urban markets. These markets are all located south of Banjul, and west of Brikama except Barra, which is located on the north bank of the river mouth, opposite Banjul (see Figure 6:1). These markets differ from the strictly rural markets, in that there is a direct link between them and the urban markets. Two types of peri-urban market can be identified, firstly, those that rely primarily on the urban markets for supplies, and secondly, those that supply the urban markets, these functions not being mutually exclusive.

Although all the peri-urban markets contain goods obtained in the urban markets, there are two markets in particular which are dependent on the urban markets for supplies of fresh vegetables and fruit, these are the markets at Central Sabigi and Bakau. The dependent nature of Central Sabigi market was discussed in the section on unofficial markets. A similar situation is found at Bakau. Most of the goods that are for sale in Bakau market, which is seven kilometres from Serrekunda, are bought in Banjul and Serrekunda markets, with a noticeable quantity of fresh vegetables, such as tomatoes, bitter tomatoes and sweet peppers coming from Lamin market. The usual procedure is for a consortium of three or more women to travel to the urban market and purchase one basket of produce between them. This transaction is usually finished by 10.00 hours, when dozens of taxis can be seen laden with baskets of fresh produce, travelling to surrounding markets. On arrival at the peri-urban market, the women split the contents of the basket evenly and go their separate ways into the market. The women go once to three times a week, either to Banjul or Serrekunda, to buy supplies. Goods that were purchased in the urban markets in this way were fresh vegetables and fruit (42 per cent of traders dealing in these commodities), groundnut oil, dry fish and imported foodstuffs, such as Maggi Cubes and tomato paste. Despite the import of large quantities of goods from the urban markets, a lot of goods for sale in Bakau market had been produced in the village, such as some fresh vegetables, sour milk and fresh fish, which are landed on Bakau beach. In fact of the farmers interviewed in the market 12 per cent disposed of their surplus production in Bakau market, with 76 per cent selling their surpluses in the urban markets. A similar pattern of trade occurs at all the peri-urban markets, although the volume of goods thus obtained is small. The other markets in this category, that is Brikama, Brufut, Gunjur, Lamin, Sanyang and Sukuta, tend to be net exporters of produce to the urban markets not net importers (see Table 6:15).

Gunjur is one of the most distant of the peri-urban markets, a distance of 32 kilometres from Serrekunda, but communications are good. Although the road is not paved, there is a busy taxi service all along the Atlantic seaboard, as far south as Kartong. As fares are government controlled, travelling is relatively cheap and easy. Producers from Gunjur sell their goods wholesale at both Banjul and Serrekunda markets. The main goods sold in this way are tomatoes, bitter tomatoes, shallots and palm oil. With the proceeds of these sales, some of the producers buy goods such as dry pepper, tomato paste, coconuts, limes, _yaite_ and other condiments which they in turn sell in the market at Gunjur. Sukuta, on the other hand, is one of the nearest peri-urban markets, being only four kilometres outside Serrekunda. It differs from the others in that it is an evening market. The village of Sukuta (population of 3,845 in 1973), is a village that depends upon horticulture for its income. Of all the farmers interviewed in this market, 69 per cent grew vegetables, a very high proportion indeed, in fact only in four other markets, Central Sabigi, Brikama, Basse and Gunjur did farmers grow vegetables (see Table 6:16). In Sutuka the water table is sufficiently high for water to be bucket-drawn by hand from shallow wells. This primitive irrigation allows the cultivation of tomatoes, onions and lettuce which are grown all year round. This produce is taken directly to the urban markets by the cultivators, where most is sold wholesale and some retailed. By mid-afternoon the women return to Sukuta, eat and rest before setting up stall in the market at around 16.00 - 18.00 hours.

Considering the horticultural emphasis of the village economy, few fresh vegetables were found in the market, but then, few local compounds need to purchase fresh fruit or vegetables. The market is not used by itinerant wholesalers, bulking for the urban market. Other goods found in the market were: fresh fruit from Brufut, palm oil from Kartong and Tujering, and many imported food items from the urban markets. As most women purchased their daily groceries from the urban market before returning home in the late afternoon, the market was not busy.

Table 6:16
Percentages of farmers interviewed in the marketplace: which crops they cultivated in 1979/80

| | Markets in which a survey was undertaken | | | | | | | | | | | | | | | | Averages | | | |
	Banjul	Serrekunda	Bakau	Central Sabigi	Gunjur	Sukuta	Brikama	Georgetown	Basse	Kuntaur	Kaur	Farafenni	Kerewan	Barra	Kaur Luma	Farafenni Luma	Urban Markets	Other Official Mkts	Luma Markets	All Markets
Cereals	NA*	67	12	14	73	19	55	100	0	100	75	69	100	0	22	15	34	45	19	42
Groundnuts	NA	13	0	29	9	12	10	0	76	0	25	31	0	100	78	85	7	19	81	29
Fruit	NA	20	88	0	0	0	0	0	0	0	0	0	0	0	0	0	10	7	0	7
Vegetables	NA	0	0	57	18	69	35	0	24	0	0	0	0	0	0	0	0	17	0	13
TOTAL	NA	100	100	100	100	100	100	100	100	100	100	100	100	100	100	100	100	100	100	100

Source: Author's fieldwork, 1979/80

*NA not applicable

The largest peri-urban market in the system is that of Brikama (population of 9,483 in 1973), the administrative centre for Western Division. Although 24 kilometres from Serrekunda, Brikama does have the advantage of being linked to both urban centres by a paved road, with a bus and frequent taxi service. There are two markets in Brikama. The larger and busier is also newer and near the carpark on the outskirts of town. The older is in the centre of the town and consists of a kwiang that shelters about thirty-five women vendors. It has no meat or fish sellers and consists of women reselling produce they had earlier purchased in the new market. The new market attracts produce from the surrounding villages, a great quantity of fresh vegetables coming from Sanyang and Basori, with dry fish from Brufut and Kartong. As this region is the major palm oil producing area in the country, there is always plenty for sale in the market, supplies coming from neighbouring villages such as Sifoe and Kaimbujae. Not all this produce enters the market at Brikama, but instead may be unloaded in the carpark from one taxi and reloaded into another one bound for Banjul or Serrekunda, without any commercial transaction taking place. The produce which is exported from Brikama consists mainly of vegetables such as tomatoes, onions, bitter tomatoes, okra and sweet pepper, as well as fruit - mangoes and oranges, depending on the season.

Producers from peri-urban settlements begin to arrive in the carparks of the urban markets between 06.30 and 07.30 hours. They arrive by taxi and taxi-bus, which are laden with baskets of vegetables and fruit. The usual method is for a buyer seeing a basket of produce (usually still tied to the roof of the taxi) that she wants, to throw her headscarf onto it. This gives her first refusal on the goods. Negotiation takes place when the basket has been brought down for closer inspection. The producer may however choose not to sell all her produce, keeping back a small proportion to sell herself in the urban market. Alternatively she may use some of the proceeds of the transaction to buy goods to take back and sell in her local market. In the urban markets, then, it is the grower herself who brings produce to market frequently travelling up to 40 kilometres in order to get a more lucrative sale (see Table 6:10). It can thus be seen as the beginnings of a rather primitive wholesale trade, which is only a stage further developed in the urban markets.

Peri-urban consumers also use the urban markets. In contrast to the rural markets, 52 per cent of the consumers interviewed in Bakau market, 51 per cent on Central Sabigi market and 22 per cent in Sukuta market, said that they attended urban markets one to three times a week. This is aided, no doubt, by the ease of transportation to the urban centres from these settlements.

Of the traders interviewed in the peri-urban markets, 10 per cent purchased supplies from the urban markets. Of these 33 per cent visited them daily, 43 per cent attended one to three times a week and 24 per cent said that they bought supplies there only occasionally. Urban markets therefore contribute to redistributing produce, from areas of plenty to those of demand, within the peri-urban region.

Urban markets

There are two urban markets in The Gambia, sited in the largest settlements, Banjul and Serrekunda (each with an estimated population of over 40,000 in 1979).[8] Of the two, Albert market in Banjul is by far the oldest, dating back to 1816 when the Colony of Bathurst was constructed on the then recently acquired Island of Banjul. In contrast, Serrekunda market is relatively recent. There is no mention of the market in the colonial reports, and it began operating only in the early 1970s.

While these are the largest, busiest and most important of Gambian markets, in terms of population served, the facilities which the market management provide to traders is no better than those provided in other smaller markets. Canteen and table availability is small and storage facilities non-existent. However, due to the higher prices prevailing in these markets, goods from a very wide radius are attracted. One group of women from Ziguinchor in Casamance, travel every week to Banjul market to sell bananas. They are middlewomen, buying the bananas from producers, hiring a taxi to bring the fruit to Banjul, returning to the Casamance after three to five days with soap and sugar or other items which are in demand there. But these are exceptions to the rule; most sellers are producers. The wholesale trade, as we will see in the Gambian urban markets, is in its infancy, with only 35 per cent of traders in Banjul and 14 per cent in Serrekunda engaged in some form of wholesaling (see Table 6:12).

Of all the sellers interviewed in the urban markets, only 35 per cent lived in Banjul or Serrekunda, which contrasts significantly with the other official markets, where 79 per cent of sellers live in the market settlement (see Table 6:10). Traders travel long distances to sell in these markets, with 18 per cent travelling over 40 kilometres and 19 per cent travelling between 20 and 40 kilometres. This explains why 41 per cent of sellers in urban markets had to travel to market by taxi and 11 per cent by bus (see Table 6:11).

As we have seen, the peri-urban area to the south of the urban areas is relatively well connected, with a steady flow of goods entering the urban markets, and either being sold there to final consumers, or redistributed to those peri-urban markets currently displaying shortages. By contrast, the north bank is not so integrated. Despite a new cheap and regular ferry service linking Banjul and Barra, only seven per cent of the sellers interviewed in Banjul market (none in Serrekunda) had crossed the river to sell. Goods that were brought over the river for sale consisted mainly of sacks of groundnuts and onions. The groundnuts were nearly all illegally imported from Senegal, a sample of sellers were found to have produced their groundnuts in Kess Aib Kass, Ker Ousaim and Passy. The onions, on the other hand, were produced mainly in Upper Niumi, notably the villages of Bakalarr, Bantang Killing and Lamin, with smaller quantities coming from Berending in Lower Niumi. These goods were all brought over from Barra in privately hired canoes. They were landed on the beach behind Banjul market where wholesalers waited to buy. As far as could be ascertained, no market dues were paid, the transactions observed were swiftly completed and the sacks quickly absorbed into the crowded market. Other goods from across the river, enter the market more legitimately. Tomatoes, okra (<u>Hibiscus esculentus</u> Linn.), bitter tomatoes (<u>Solanum incanum</u> Linn.), and sour leaves (<u>Hibiscus subdariffa</u> Linn.) from the Niumis are sold in the market by women producers, who headload their goods using the official ferry. They sell directly to consumers and pay the 25 butut floor market fee. The contribution made by the north bank to the urban market system is thus rather limited, but of interest.

138

When asked if they were selling their goods in small lots or in bulk, 16 per cent of respondents in the urban markets said they were selling strictly by the basket, with 11 per cent by both methods. The usual pattern for such operations is for a producer to dispose of most of her produce wholesale, keeping back one basket for personal retail throughout the day. This trade of selling whole baskets of produce is much more developed in Banjul than Serrekunda, with 35 per cent of sellers interviewed in Banjul operating in this way, but only 14 per cent in Serrekunda. Most vendors in the urban markets sell solely in the urban markets (94 per cent) with 69 per cent of them selling in the market daily, only five per cent said that they occasionally visited other markets nearby. When asked where they obtained their wares, 27 per cent had produced their own, but an astonishing 52 per cent had purchased their goods in the same market, indicating the importance of the "whole basket" sale approach. Apart from fruit and vegetables, a large quantity of dried fish are sold in this way, originating almost solely from Brufut, with smaller supplies coming from other Atlantic villages such as Gunjur and the estuarine village of Old Jeswang. Other aspects of the urban wholesale trade are more developed with most of the shelled groundnuts, raw cous, maize and black and white beans having been purchased by the lorry load at Farafenni luma. This trade will be discussed in the next chapter on cereal marketing. Perhaps the only wholesale trade proper, is that in imported 'Irish' potatoes (Solanum tuberosum Linn.) and onions. These come from The Netherlands and at present there are five import-wholesalers all operating from the Banjul market. Their turnover is approximately 250 x 50 kg bags per month. However, storage facilities are poor, and the sacks, although left piled up inside the kwiang, covered with tarpaulin and under the watchful eye of a night watchman, are still subject to attacks by insects, rodents and human theft. The wholesale structure in these markets is thus poorly developed, the majority of vendors being either producers themselves, or a member of a consortium that has purchased a basket of produce earlier in the day. It is only in the imported potato and onion trade that a true wholesale trade exists, but possibly the cous trade from Farafenni is developing in that direction.

The imported food items, such as tomato paste, Maggi Cubes, Margarine, tea, coffee, powdered milk and rice for sale in most Gambian markets have, in the majority of cases, been purchased from the NTC or other supermarkets. It is only in the area of the luma markets that such goods come from across the border. These commodities are bought usually by the carton, by male traders, most of whom are of Senegalese nationality and who rent or own canteens, in which they sell and store their stock. Occasionally one finds women in possession of large tins of tomato paste from which they are selling by the teaspoon. On closer examination it is revealed that the tin has in many cases been sold to the women on credit by a canteen trader. This trade is thus in the hands of a relatively few male Senegalese traders, who have the capital to buy the stock.

139

In general, credit facilities for petty traders are very
limited. In the urban markets, 52 per cent of vendors buy their
goods with cash, 27 per cent produce their own, and 21 per cent
sell the goods on credit from the producer, paying her either at
the end of the market day, but more usually the next morning, when
more goods will be handed over on credit. In the other daily
markets, such facilities were used by only 11 per cent, but three
per cent of vendors manage to obtain credit or loans from
relatives and friends. The general shortage of working capital
must be removed before a more organised wholesale trade can
develop.

Conclusion

In The Gambia, there is a loosely connected system of markets of
various categories, both official and unofficial. It is a system
that becomes more integrated in the western part of the country,
around the urban centres, with a wholesaling and bulking network
beginning to develop. However, in the centre of the country
another wholesale nucleus is growing in the form of the luma
markets, which are the distribution points in The Gambia of goods
which originate in the Kaolack region of Senegal. The rest of the
country is served by small rural markets which satisfy the
immediate subsistence needs of the local community. How these
needs are met by the system will be dealt with in the next three
chapters, the first dealing with the distribution of cereals
through the network of marketing types described here.

Notes

[1]   Against regulation 10 in the Provinces Markets Rules and
       regulation 14 of the Kombo St. Mary Market Regulations.
[2]   The word "luma" is thought to be of Senegalese origin, yet
       nobody interviewed knew its etymology or even exactly what
       the term implies.
[3]   United Africa Company ceased trading in The Gambia in 1972.
[4]   Maurel et Prom closed their provincial stores in 1977, when
       they decided to withdraw from the groundnut trade, instead
       concentrating on general trading in Banjul.
[5]   This figure is second only to Georgetown market (which is
       located on MacCarthy Island), where 21 per cent of traders
       cross the river.
[6]   Sour milk is prepared by leaving milk to go sour in a
       covered container (usually a calabash) with no starter, as
       the containers harbour the yoghurt bacillus. If the milk is
       not considered sour enough, baobab fruit juice may be added.
       For details of the marketing of sour milk see Chapter Eight.

[7]   Senegalese groundnut oil is bottled under the brand name
        <u>Niani</u>. In 1979/80 it was rumoured that Senegalese groundnut
        oil contained less toxin than Gambian produced oil, and so
        was in great demand in The Gambia.
[8]   Personal communication, M. Gibril, Director of Central
        Statistics, December 1979.

7 The marketing of cereals

Introduction

In the last chapter the structure of the Gambian marketing network was discussed, here the movement of cereals through that system will be described. Rice is the major staple food in The Gambia, with local and imported rice satisfying about half of Gambian cereal requirements. The deficit is made up by the 'upland' cereals of millet, sorghum, findo and maize. Most of the imported rice is consumed in the urban areas, in the rural areas the annual farming calendar determines seasonal eating patterns and demands for various cereals in the marketplace. Cereal crops are harvested between September and December, so food supplies are particularly plentiful in November and December, whilst in July and August shortages occur, a time traditionally known as 'the hungry season'. The annual pattern can best be considered in terms of dry season and wet season diets.

In the dry season, January to the end of June, the rural Gambian's diet consists mainly of rice interspersed with other cereals. These would all be eaten with groundnut sauce. There are few leaf vegetables available during this period except those grown in watered vegetable gardens, and these are not usually ready for consumption until April. Cassava leaves are available, but leaf sauces (jambo) are not frequently eaten during this period, chiefly because there are plenty of other food items

available. There is also money available for buying such items as
oil, meat and dried fish in the early part of the year. Shortages
begin to be felt in June.

The rural wet season diet varies considerably, month by month.
By June most people especially in rural areas would be eating late
millet or imported rice, and any groundnuts unsuitable for
planting would be used in sauces. July is a busy month for
planting groundnuts and millets. Late millet supplemented by
imported rice is the main staple. Leaf sauces (jambo) are the
main sauces, as leaves are plentiful. Nyankantango [1] made with
locust beans (Parkia biglosa. Benth, known locally as netetu) is
used at this time, as it is a convenient dish to take to the
fields. Occasionally people will resort to eating millet
porridge, made with only water and salt. August is the month when
the upland crops are weeded and rice is transplanted. During this
month the diet is much the same as July, but with more porridge
consumed, as stocks of food and money to supplement supplies run
out. These shortages continue until the maize crop is harvested
in the middle of September. Later in the same month findo is
ready. The maize is eaten on the cob, roasted or boiled or as
porridge, and findo becomes the staple. The sauces to eat with
the findo would still be mainly jambo, made from sour leaves. In
October early millet and some rice is ready for harvest, along
with some groundnuts, and the diet improves. November sees the
rice and groundnut harvests in full swing, by now there are no
food shortages and nearly everyone would be eating rice, with
meat, fish and various vegetables.

From this brief and simplified description of the diet of the
average rural Gambian, the importance of rice, particularly
imported rice, becomes evident. How this and any local cereal
surpluses are marketed will be discussed below under the headings
of "rice", which includes imported as well as domestically
produced rice, from both floodland and rainfed crops, and "upland
cereals", a term which embraces all the cereals grown on the
colluvial and plateau soils, except upland rice which is dealt
with in the previous section.

Rice

In 1976/77 only 23,288 ha of rice (Oryza Sativa Linn) was
cultivated in The Gambia, representing 13 per cent of total
cultivated area. The largest area of rice cultivation is in
MacCarthy Island Division and Upper River Division, where the
river is uncontaminated by the salinity of the lower estuary, but
it is also grown in suitable localities in other parts of the
country.

Rice is grown under three types of conditions in The Gambia:
rainfed, which accounts for 35 per cent of the total area under

rice cultivation; non-irrigated swamp rice that accounts for 60 per cent and irrigated rice which contributes five per cent of the total rice area. These can be categorised as follows:

1. ALLUVIAL AREAS

    A. Irrigated Rice

        (i)   Levees: areas which are naturally readily drained.
        (ii)   Sloughs: areas subject to drainage problems in the wet season.

    B. Non-irrigated Rice (Swamp Rice)

        (i)   Saline affected areas requiring leaching out of salt before use.
        (ii)   Ba-faro: areas subject to uncontrollable freshwater flooding from the river or one or its tributaries.
        (iii) Bantofaro: wetland areas not normally subject to flooding from the river.

2. UPLAND AREAS (Rainfed Rice)

    (i)   Tandako: upland depressions on plateau or colluvial areas.
    (ii)   Tributary valleys: gently sloping land usually not bunded or terraced, of alluvial/colluvial origin.

The authors of the 1974-76 Agricultural Census attribute more than half of the total area under rainfed rice (category 2) to the Jenoi 'circle', [2] evenly split between the North Bank Division and Lower River Division. This type of rice is sown in July and harvested in October, and thus clashes with the labour requirements of the groundnut crop. However, labour is not the largest constraint on the expansion of this crop, it is rainfall. In recent years, rainfed rice planted in the depressions on plateau and colluvial soils 2(i), has been almost abandoned because of poor harvests. This is the result of reduced rainfall, which has been below the FAO West Africa Rice Mission's recognised minimum requirement for rice cultivation of 1,200 mm. For the same reasons, yields have been reduced on the saline areas B(i), where planting has had to be put back to late September to ensure that the land has been washed free from salt. Similar consequences because of reduced rainfall have occurred in the bantofaro areas B(iii). However, in contrast, the yields in the ba-faro B(ii) areas appear satisfactory.

Out of the total area of 13,700 ha under swamp rice (category 1.B), that cleared from mangrove in North Bank Division, Lower River Division and Western Division accounts for around 10,000 ha. The balance has involved the development of the mainly freshwater

144

swamps of MacCarthy Island and Upper River Divisions. Swamp rice is sown in protected seed beds in July, is transplanted in September and harvested in January, avoiding the peak labour periods of the groundnut crop. The main problem with extending swamp rice acreage is the saline content of the river. The tidally flooded rice is centred around Lower River Division and North Bank Division, but an adverse level of salt is present as far up river as Kuntaur, [3] especially during the last three months of the year, after the fresh water rainy season flood has passed.

Irrigated rice (category 1.A) has largely been developed since 1966, when a Taiwanese mission arrived in The Gambia to supervise a 1,620 ha project in MacCarthy Island Division and Upper River Division. In both these areas fresh water from the river is available throughout the year. Currently the project is being run by representatives of the People's Republic of China, who replaced the Taiwanese in 1974. The project produces about 7,112 metric tons of paddy rice annually, with a yield of 4,390 kg per hectare. But this is only half the production that the Chinese expected from the project. The scheme was intended to involve double cropping, with a first crop (dry season) sown in January, transplanted in late February and harvested in June, with a second crop (wet season) to be sown in June, transplanted in July and harvested in October. But currently only one crop a year is realised. The reason is that many of the farmers involved are reluctant to attempt the second crop, due to other agricultural commitments in July, particularly the groundnut crop. Dey (1980) suggests that competition with the groundnut crop is only a partial explanation, claiming that the increasing participation of men in a women's production system is also to blame. Prior to the introduction of the Taiwanese project, she argues, the production of rice was solely the responsibility of women. The introduction of irrigated rice brought about new labour patterns, with both men and women working in the rice fields, although peforming different farming operations. The result has been that instead of the older women of the compound controlling operations, irrigated rice production has increasingly come under the supervision of the male head of the compound. This implied that women were not only losing control of their own labour, but also the right to dispose of the harvested crop. This gives the women little incentive to plant two crops a year, especially when the second crop would leave them short of male helpers, busy in the groundnut fields.

Traditionally rice has been grown using hand cultivation techniques. The seed is always sown in a nursery and later planted in the field. In the mid 1950s, the Tractor Ploughing Scheme was initiated to carry out pre-planting cultivation for rice on alluvial areas. In recent years the scheme has been based at Sapu in MacCarthy Island Division. The original objective was to cultivate 4,850 ha annually between December and July. The target was never met. In the period 1970 to 1973, an average of only 2,030 ha was ploughed and 1,935 ha harrowed. The probable cause for this is that the service has to be paid for by the cultivator, and as most of the rice grown in these fields is for subsistence purposes, the cultivator just does not have the cash to increase the areas to be ploughed. [4] Oxdrawn implements are not used in rice cultivation. However, trials in Casamance showed that the N'Dama ox was capable of doing the work, with suitable implements,if it was only worked for four hours a day and was given extra feed. (Dunsmore 1976, p.184) With improvements in methods of production and the introduction of improved strains, more uniform ripening of the crop is now being achieved. This enables harvesting to be done by sickle rather than harvesting the individual ears as had previously been the case. A pedal thresher has also successfully been introduced in the irrigated schemes. Drying of the grain is done entirely in the sun although the GPMB does have a drier attached to its mill at Kuntaur.

Rice marketing

With the introduction of groundnuts as a cash crop in the 1830s, food production in The Gambia began to suffer. As has been described in Chapter Three, men began to neglect their role as providers of upland cereals, in favour of cultivating the seemingly more profitable cash crop. This put the burden of food supply onto the women, traditionally rice growers. It was a burden they could not cope with and cereal deficits began to occur. 1857 was a critical year, and marks the point at which the majority of producers began to neglect food crop cultivation. A general shortage of food occurred in this year, a year in which an unprecedented 13,554 tons (13,771 metric tons) of groundnuts were exported from the river. The famine was reported by O'Connor:

> The natives have until the present year [1857], cultivated enough grain crops for their own sustenance – as indeed witness my former reports on the many villages and districts that I visited in 1854. But an alarming scarcity of foodstuffs have this year struck considerable parts of the river, including, alas, the very extensive places I visited three years ago. Though the groundnut crop exported was the highest on record viz – 13,554 tons – shipped mainly in French vessels to the French markets – the greater prosperity of trade was not felt by the natives on account of their neglect of the rice and corn fields and the consequent need for them to spend their groundnut income on imported food. (CO 87/64, 1857)

This was not, however, the first year in which rice had had to be imported. The first recorded imports of rice into the River Gambia region was in 1835 when 247 tons (251 metric tons) were imported. By 1863 imports had reached 1,714 tons (1,741 metric tons), in 1879 was 1,891 tons (1,921 metric tons), by 1893 was 2,537 tons (2,578 metric tons) and by 1937 had reached a record 11,470 tons (11,654 metric tons). (Blue Books) The amount of rice imported can be seen on Figure 7:1.

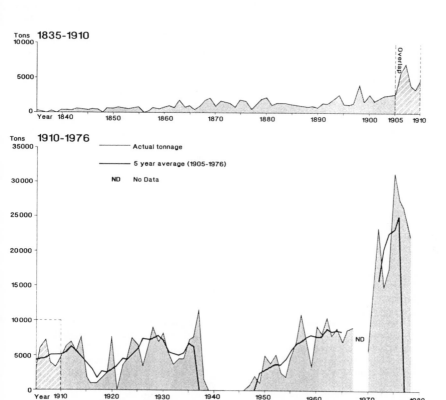

Figure 7:1   Tonnages of rice imported into The Gambia, 1835-1976

By 1939 the colonial government had begun to be concerned at
rising rice imports, but plans to develop domestic rice production
were hindered by the outbreak of World War Two. During the war no
rice was imported into the colony and the farmers responded by
producing more food. The Governor's report for 1946 states:

> The Protectorate no longer looked to government to import its
> rice; the farmers, men and women, by unremitting toil during
> the war years, had achieved self-sufficiency in food crops
> whilst maintaining high export figures for its valuable
> groundnut crop. (Governors Report 1946, p.3)

By 1947 rice was once again being imported into the country,
with initially only 500 tons (508 metric tons), but by 1950 this
had reached 4,750 tons (4,826 metric tons) and in 1957 was a post
war record of 11,100 tons (11,278 metric tons). But local rice
was being grown and sent down to Bathurst, where it was less

expensive than imported rice. This depressed the price of imported rice, which meant it had to be sold at a smaller profit. Traders put pressure on the colonial government, and the shipment of locally produced rice into the urban areas was actively discouraged by the colonial government. The situation came to a head in 1954 and is documented by van der Plas (1957) in a report to the Colonial Government. He explains how the rice reached urban markets.

> River rice in the trade season in 1954 came down almost exclusively by lorry or bus. Traders in the river sent it down. Bathurst traders, especially women who went up river to barter dried fish, peppers, tomatoes, sugar, flour, soap, sometimes kolanuts or textiles against rice, brought or sent rice to Bathurst. Cutter captains on the trip home at the end of the trade season brought more. (van der Plas 1957, p.14)

So much rice entered the market in Bathurst, that the price plummeted. The colonial administration reacted by prohibiting the export of rice from the Protectorate without a permit, and later, on 15th July 1954 they closed all the roads, stopping completely the flow of rice from the provinces. Later in the year however, this policy backfired when there was a rice shortage in Bathurst as a result of the delay in a shipment of rice from Indo-China. This made the need for river rice acute, and eventually rice was sent down from Sapu and obtained from Kaolack (Senegal).

This incident demonstrated to the government the need to control the marketing of rice within the colony in order to maintain supplies and stabilise prices. Between 1957 and 1962 rice import prices dropped substantially, falling as low as £32.15.3. per ton in 1960 (price was £44.12.8. per ton in 1963), but retail prices in The Gambia stayed at the same level. It seems clear then that the private trade realised high profits during this period without passing on any benefits to the consumer. An FAO report of 1964 recommended a revision of the system with the importation of rice and purchasing of local rice being handled by a "cooperative using the GPMB infrastructure". (Nasta 1964, p.23) This was not achieved until 1973. However, in 1965 the Gambian Government entered into the importing process with the creation of a licensed consortium of business people, authorised to import rice, and to resell at a fixed price which permitted a fair margin of profit. This was accompanied by a realisation that importing such large quantities of rice was a drain on the economy and led to calls by the government for greater efforts to attain rice self sufficiency. This resulted in the development of the irrigated rice schemes discussed above. Despite substantial investments in these rice schemes, which developed 2,706 ha for irrigation between 1966 and 1980, and produced an average of 10,000 metric tons per year between 1974/5 and 1978/9, rice imports into The Gambia have continued to grow. Clean rice imports averaged 8,700 metric tons from 1962-66 (see Table 7:1), the years immediately preceding the irrigated rice development programmes, but they rose to an average of over 20,000 metric tons between 1970/1 and 1978/9 (see Table 7:2), the period after the implementation of the schemes.

Table 7:1
Rice imports into The Gambia, 1962–1967

		Clean Rice Metric Tons	Value m$
1962		10,600	1.3
1963		8,200	1.0
1964		9,000	1.1
1965		6,800	1.0
1966		8,600	0.8
1967		9,000	1.3
	average	8,700	1.1

Source: US Department of Agriculture and Aid, Rice in West Africa 1968, p.18

With the growing importance of imported rice, the government decided in 1973 to give complete control of this operation to the GPMB, which until 1986 was the sole legal agent for the importation of rice. [5] After making monthly estimates of rice needs, the GPMB purchased rice on the international market, for delivery at Banjul. The imported rice was distributed by the GPMB to its licensed agents including the NTC. The NTC marketed more than 50 per cent of imported rice, selling directly to consumers, and also by the sack to petty traders, who then retailed it in the market. The prices for each transaction were controlled, with fixed margins for each market agent as shown on Table 7:3. The higher price outside Banjul was aimed at compensating the retailer for transport costs. A sufficient supply of imported rice, coupled with consumer awareness of the legal price, seemed to ensure that the controlled price was respected.

Table 7:2
Rice imports into The Gambia, 1970/1 to 1978/9

		Clean rice Metric Tons	Value D
1970/1		5,341	959,600
1971/2		14,907	2,412,852
1972/3		23,072	9,229,463
1973/4		14,946	8,981,407
1974/5		17,385	10,987,738
1975/6		31,066	14,021,965
1976/7		27,852	11,104,921
1977/8		26,191	10,167,135
1978/9		22,135	14,199,535
	average	20,322	9,117,290

Financial year runs from 1st October to 30th September.

Source: GPMB accounts.

149

Table 7:3

The price structure of imported rice, 1976/7

(Value on release from the store)

	Dalasis per 160 lb.* bag	
	Banjul Area	Other Area
GPMB store	41.26	41.26
Wholesale margin	1.40	1.40
Wholesale price	42.66	42.66
Retail margin	1.64	3.24
Retail price	44.30	45.90

* 72.5 kg bag

Source: CILSS, 1977

Of this imported rice, at least 50 per cent was consumed in the urban areas. In 1977/8, 11,666 metric tons of clean rice was sold in the provinces and, in the same year, 11,298 metric tons were sold in Banjul and Kombo St. Mary. In 1978/9 the figures were even more biased towards the urban areas with 8,470 metric tons being sold in the provinces and 12,126 metric tons in the urban areas. Thus although Banjul and Kombo St. Mary contain only 16 per cent of the total Gambian population, they consume over 70 per cent of the imported rice. It is not surprising then to find that all GPMB storage warehouses for imported rice are concentrated in the Banjul area. The GPMB released rice on demand, and as most imported rice was consumed in Banjul, extensive up country storage was not necessary.

Between 1973 and 1986 the GPMB also played an important role in the collection of locally grown rice. Prior to this date, the marketing of domestically produced rice was in the hands of private traders, and there were no price controls. If the producer wished to sell any rice she had a choice of three buyers: the Jula women; small traders from the towns; or local small traders, who in turn sold the rice to other larger traders who supplied urban consumers. (See Figure 7:2). The Jula women were mainly urban based women who received supplies from the coastal areas on the weekly river boat during the period immediately after the rice harvest, and exchanged these for rice which they in turn sent down river. Van der Plas described one such woman in 1955:

> At Sutukung, a woman (originally from Serrekunda) at the roadside, bartered mangoes, neto (locust beans) balls, red peppers, sour spinach, dried fish against paddy. By every ship she gets a consignment from Bathurst. In one hour she had obtained five bunches of rice in the ear and 1/9d in copper. (van der Plas 1957, p.14)

150

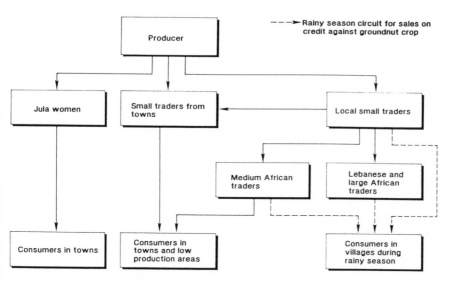

Figure 7:2   The marketing of domestically produced rice, before
             1973

Traders with shops also accepted rice as part payment for goods, usually using the coming groundnut crop as collateral. However, van der Plas notes the use of the price of imported rice by merchants to "beat down the price of rice in the hands of the farmers. These are handicapped, because they have to return to their villages . . ." (van der Plas 1957, p.16). A year later, Macluskie (1958), reporting on The Gambia Rice Farm Scheme, stated that in his opinion "the uncontrolled importation of cheap broken rice, would run counter to the development of a rice industry". (Macluskie 1958, p.30)   He held that the local producer required protection, which he recommended should take three forms:

a) A minimum price for paddy should be guaranteed to the producer.   This price should be related to the price of groundnuts.

b) The government should purchase excess paddy if the guaranteed price is not obtained through ordinary trading channels.

c) That shipments of imported rice should be controlled by import licence.

However, nothing was done and for the next fifteen years consumers continued to receive domestically produced rice through the same channels, the traders continued to make handsome profits, and the low prices paid to domestic producers, as Macluskie predicted, did not encourage the growth of a Gambian rice industry.

At the same time that the GPMB was given the sole legal right to import rice into The Gambia in 1973, it was also given the monopoly to buy locally produced rice. This it did through licenced buying agents. In the late 1970s there were eight cooperative societies and five private traders who performed this function (see Figure 7:3). These agents bought from the producers at the government's fixed price and delivered to the GPMB rice mill at Kuntaur, where they received payment on the basis of the weight and quality of the paddy rice. The amount of paddy rice bought by the GPMB was small, but as can be seen from Table 7:4 had been steadily increasing. This rice was milled at Kuntaur and was released with imported rice, the two often being mixed. The conversion rate for paddy to clean rice at the Kuntaur mill is poor, being between 57-59 per cent by weight (the FAO standard is 65-72 per cent). [6]

Table 7:4
Locally produced paddy rice purchased by the GPMB 1972/3 to 1978/9

	1972/3	1973/4	1974/5	1975/6	1976/7	1977/8	1978/9
Quantity metric tons	40	591	748	552	729	1,946	2,100

Source: GPMB accounts

However, not all domestically produced rice was sold to the GPMB, most was consumed by the producing family. The FAO has estimated that on average 25 per cent of locally grown rice is marketed, and that in the 1976/77 season the amount marketed was approximately 7,500 metric tons. In effect, this meant that 30,000 metric tons of paddy rice was produced in The Gambia in 1976/77. Of this 22,500 metric tons were consumed, 700 metric tons were sold to the GPMB (see Table 7:4), the rest approximately 6,800 metric tons, was marketed by the private sector. Figure 7:4 shows this sequence. Surveys carried out by the author indicated that traders paid a higher price for paddy rice than the GPMB, which explained why most commercial rice was marketed by them, despite the supposed GPMB monopoly, and may explain why that monopoly was withdrawn in 1986. Farmers going directly to the market in 1979/80, when questioned, said that the traders paid a higher price than the GPMB, one that was approaching the controlled consumer price. For obvious reasons, no hard data could be collected on this trade, but producers selling small quantities of clean rice (up to about 10 kg) were seen in Kuntaur market and the <u>lumas</u> at Farafenni and Kaur. The rice was being sold by volume and not weight as this circumvented the official price control on clean rice which was strictly adhered to.

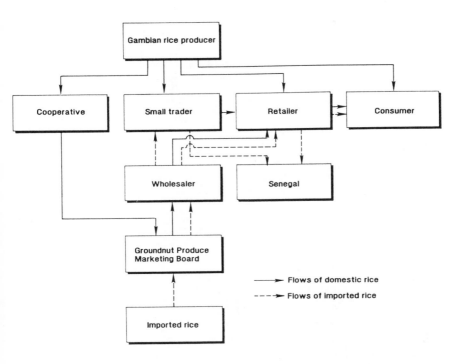

Figure 7:3   The marketing of both imported and domestically produced rice after 1973

In Senegal a similar situation occurs, with ONCAD (National Office of Cooperation and Assistance for Development) being the government agency responsible for marketing all agricultural outputs, including imported and domestically produced rice. Producer prices are fixed by the government in collaboration with the Comite des Grands Produits. Prices are announced to the public annually, but the buying season is not opened until the cooperatives repay ONCAD 80 per cent of the seed debts received on credit by the cooperatives as a group. This causes delays in farmers getting cash for their output. All these rigid institutional constraints have resulted in the emergence of an illegal parallel marketing circuit for rice in Senegal, which by all accounts is more active than the official one. Despite the fact that farmers are not permitted to sell milled rice, this is very common, being more lucrative for both middlemen and farmers.[7]

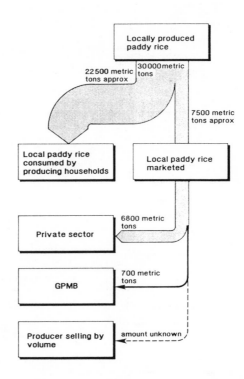

Figure 7:4 Destination of locally produced paddy rice in 1976/77

The policy of controlling both wholesale and retail prices of paddy and clean rice in The Gambia until 1986 eliminated the excessive profits which had been made by traders dealing in imported rice in the 1950s, and has meant a guaranteed price for locally produced rice, but it has not stimulated domestic production as much as the government had hoped for. The pricing policy was partly to blame. The price structure of local rice purchased by the GPMB at controlled prices from 1973–1979 can be seen in Table 7:5. This shows that in 1978/79, the consumer price for clean rice was 13 per cent less than the price paid for the

Table 7:5

The price structure of local rice in The Gambia

Year	Producer price for paddy rice	Producer price for paddy at milled rice equivalent*	Buying Allowance	Cost of Milling	Cost of Marketing	Overheads	Total Cost	Price paid by Consumer in Banjul	Implied Level of Subsidy
	D/met.ton	D/met.ton	D/met.ton	D/met.ton	D/met.ton	D/met.ton	D/met.ton	D/met.ton	D/met.ton
1972/3	154	265	49	198	11	1.81	525	352	173
1973/4	242	418	49	102	20	4.36	593	484	109
1974/5	309	533	49	200	16	5.06	803	572	231
1975/6	353	608	54	231	24	7.34	924	638	286
1976/7	397	684	49	218	27	5.98	984	638	346
1977/8	441	760	68	187	38	10.26	1,063	695	368
1978/9	463	798	68	NA	NA	NA	NA	695	NA

Source: GPMB Annual Reports and Financial Accounts

* One metric ton of milled rice is equivalent to 1.724 metric tons of paddy rice, when converted at the Kuntaur mill, (58 per cent conversion rate).

equivalent amount of paddy [8] before taking into account additional costs for milling, handling and transportation. This implies a government subsidy of over D 368 per metric ton of milled locally produced rice in 1977/78, a subsidy of almost 50 per cent. In the marketplace in 1979/80, a kilogram of rice cost D 0.70, the government subsidy was D 0.32. This subsidy is financed from the GPMB's rice stabilisation fund, which is ultimately financed from groundnut trading profits. With these prices, the rice producer could attain greater benefit by selling her paddy rice to the GPMB at the fixed price, then purchasing clean rice from the market at the controlled price. In 1978/9 a farmer with a metric ton of paddy rice could sell it to the GPMB for D 463, with this sum she could purchase approximately 667 kilograms of clean rice (at the controlled price of D 695 per metric ton). If she decided to consume her own rice, she could only do so after having it milled. Figure 7:5 shows the amount of clean rice that could be obtained from the various milling procedures available. From the diagram it can be seen that if the producer takes her rice to a small mill, she would receive 550 kilograms of clean rice. SONED (1977) estimate that these small mills average an out turn of about 65 per cent (with an average capacity of 350 kilograms of paddy per hour), with a charge made to the customer of ten per cent of the paddy rice. If instead the producer processed her own rice, it is possible for her to have an end product of 700 kilograms of clean rice, as SONED estimate an out turn by hand milling of 70 per cent. However, this would take her twenty days [9] and produce poor quality rice, with about 60 per cent broken grains. Using these figures, most women would find it beneficial to sell their own produce and buy imported rice in the marketplace. This is particularly the case if the producer is able to participate in the 'parallel' market, and receive a price above that fixed by the government. Thus it can be seen that such a policy stimulated the sale of domestically produced rice (see Table 7:4), even if, as Haswell, Dey and Weil believe, it did not stimulate production.

The Gambian Government was faced with a dilemma. If they stopped the subsidy on imported rice and/or raised the producer price, then Gambian farmers may concentrate on rice production to the detriment of groundnut production. Because the economy relies so heavily on groundnut exports, the government cannot afford to take the risk of affecting groundnut production - the encouragement of rice cultivation in The Gambia by the government is therefore only a half-hearted attempt at self-sufficiency. However in 1986 the Gambian government, in serious financial difficulties, did deregulate the pricing and marketing structure for both domestically produced and imported rice. The effects of this on the economy have yet to be assessed.

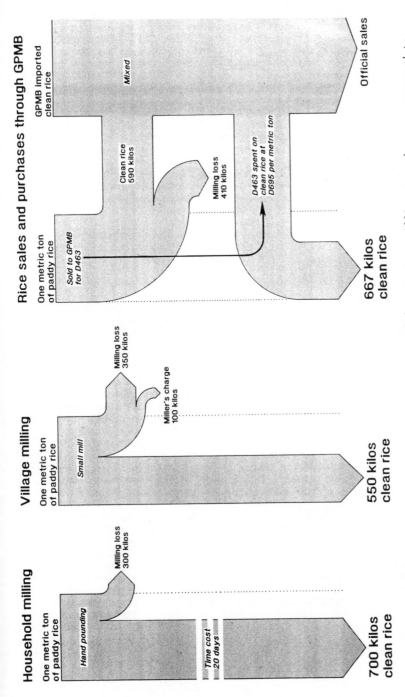

Household milling

One metric ton of paddy rice

Hand pounding

Milling loss 300 kilos

Time cost 20 days

700 kilos clean rice

Village milling

One metric ton of paddy rice

Small mill

Milling loss 350 kilos

Miller's charge 100 kilos

550 kilos clean rice

Rice sales and purchases through GPMB

One metric ton of paddy rice

GPMB imported clean rice

Mixed

Sold to GPMB for D463

Clean rice 590 kilos

Milling loss 410 kilos

D463 spent on clean rice at D695 per metric ton

Official sales

667 kilos clean rice

Figure 7:5   The quantity of clean rice that can be obtained from various milling procedures as compared to selling paddy rice directly to the GPMB

Upland cereals

The principal upland cereals grown in The Gambia are millet and sorghum, with maize and findo being produced on a smaller scale. These upland crops are grown on the plateau and colluvial soils, and as such compete for land with the groundnut. The most important determinant of the area allocated to each crop is not the availability of suitable land, but the supply of labour which is exacerbated by the short five month growing season imposed by the seasonal patterns of the moisture climate.

The farmers' staggering preference for growing groundnuts to the neglect of other upland crops has already been discussed. It is necessary here only to give some indication of the areas involved. In 1976/7, of the total area under cultivation in The Gambia, only 14 per cent was planted with millets, seven per cent with sorghums, two and a half per cent with findo, and two and a quarter per cent with maize. This contrasts significantly with the 61 per cent of the total area devoted to groundnut cultivation (see Table 3:7).

Although all four types of upland cereals are found in all parts of the country, there are variations, dependent on ecological conditions and dietary preferences. The most obvious example is that of millet and sorghum. Millet tends to be dominant in the western half of the country and sorghum in the east. The two are to some extent complementary, in that millet can be grown on poor sandy soils if they are well drained, and will thrive with a lower total rainfall than sorghum. Millet can also tolerate a greater degree of salinity than sorghum. An example of dietary preferences affecting acreage is that of maize. Maize is grown in all parts of the country mainly as a backyard crop, except in Upper River Division, where the Serahuli people consume it as a major food item; here it is planted on a field scale.

Local varieties of millet can be broadly divided according to their period to maturity into early forms which take up to 95 days to mature, known locally as suno (Pennisetum, gambieuse) and late forms which may take up to 150 days, that are known as sanyo (Pennisetum typhoideum). Suno is planted in July and harvested in September, and is cultivated usually as a pure crop, mainly in MacCarthy Island Division, North Bank Division, and Lower River Division. The main advantage in growing suno is its early harvesting date, so that it is able to supplement dwindling household food stocks. Sanyo, the late millet, is planted in late July and is harvested in early November. Since its growing season is much the same as the groundnut the two are often intercropped. It is grown extensively throughout the country, but is more important in Western Division than elsewhere. Millet is usually grown as a pure stand on land near the village which has been manured by tethered cattle in the previous dry season, or mixed cropping, usually with groundnuts, in areas farther from the compound. The Department of Agriculture recommends the planting of early maturing millets in dry soil before the onset of the rains, and of late millet in wet soil. In practice, both are usually planted following the onset of the rains.

Sorghum (sorghum gambicum Snowden) is grown on similar land to millet, but cultivation to a depth of eight inches is recommended by the Department of Agriculture, before the crop is sown in June to July. Cultivars currently used are of the guinea family and have a maturation period of 90-150 days, most lying between 120 and 130 days. Two types of sorghum are cultivated, a red variety known locally as basso and a white variety known as kinto. All are photoperiodic and flower with the shorter days of September, coinciding usually with the termination of the rains. They therefore mature when there is still adequate soil moisture for grain development. The highest acreages are to be found in MacCarthy Island Division and Upper River Division.

Maize (Zea mays Linn) is widely grown as a compound crop throughout The Gambia, but it is only in Wuli that it is planted as a field crop. It occupies the smallest acreage of all the cereals, yet has certain advantages over other grains. It matures early and is harvested in September thus avoiding the peak labour constraints of the November/December groundnut harvest. Further, the local variety jeka, becomes available only 70-80 days after sowing, when other locally grown foodstuffs are generally scarce.

Findo (Digitaria exilis stapf.) is widely grown, but individual plots are small and little information is available on the total area harvested and on yields. The crop is commonly sown broadcast before or soon after the onset of the rains, on land which has had little if any preparation. This apparent lack of care reflects the role of findo as an insurance against the failure of the other upland cereals, and there is seldom any weeding or attention given to the crop until the September harvest.

Upland crops are cultivated in the same way as for centuries, by hand and hoe. Their improvement has been neglected by successive governments that have instead encouraged the cultivation of groundnuts. But in the 1978 rainy season the Department of Agriculture did introduce an upland cereal programme designed to increase food production. This programme included the provision of improved varieties of seed, fertilisers, insecticides and extension advice. Fertiliser was provided free, but farmers were to repay the seed loan in kind. In 1979, 1,416 ha of each of the following, suno, sanyo, sorghum, and maize (total of 5,666 ha) were included in the programme. Also included was 283 ha of upland rice, which unlike the rest of the upland cereals is cultivated by women. The programme encountered a large number of problems and was judged to be only partially successful. The failure of the project was the result of a number of factors including a shortage of improved seed; fertiliser not reaching the farmers in time; considerable damage by pests that were not controlled; and the drought, which led to complete crop failure in many areas.

Of total upland cereal production, only about ten per cent reaches commercial channels, the rest being consumed by the producing household. Few, if any, cultivate these cereals commercially. Most of the domestic crop that does reach the market comes from producers who have achieved a fortuitous surplus above their domestic requirements, or by farmers whose cash needs compel them to sell.

The marketing of upland cereals

In contrast to the marketing of rice, there is no legal or actual intervention by any government agency in the marketing of upland cereals. The movement of these cereals from producer to consumer is effected through a small scale traditional marketing system, illustrated in Figure 7:6. As most rural families in most years grow enough upland cereals to satisfy their annual needs, the main demand for these cereals is in the urban areas, where cous (a general term for millets and sorghums) is eaten on special feast days, when important guests are visiting, or is just used as a change from imported rice. It is not eaten daily due to the length of time that it takes to prepare. For example in the preparation of findi nyelengo the grain has to be washed up to about six times to remove impurities such as grass seeds. With sanyo and suno nyelengo the grain is washed, pounded and the flour removed before it is steamed. Cherreh, one of the more popular cous dishes, is made from the flour obtained from pounded cous. It is then sifted to make it evenly fine and a little water is added so that when it is stirred small balls or clumps of flour are formed. These are then steamed, broken down and resteamed. Finally they are sifted and steamed again, producing a 'dry' food which can easily be carried in a cloth. It is therefore understandable why easily cooked imported rice is the preferred staple.

The bulk of marketable surpluses of upland cereals are sold to small traders, although some producers sell directly to consumers in the rural markets. It is, in the main, the small trader who represents the primary link in the marketing chain as is shown in Figure 7:6. He generally buys in small lots from producers and disposes of his purchases in three ways. He may either sell to families within the village who are short of food supplies, secondly, he may sell to petty traders who perform the functions of assembling, or thirdly, he may sell to merchants located in larger markets. The petty traders may act for themselves, or for larger merchants. It is reported by the FAO adviser in Banjul that there are some 2,500 petty traders permanently involved in the food trade, especially the trade in upland cereals, in The Gambia. Neither the average volume handled by these traders nor the margins they received could be estimated. Even for those retailers located in Banjul such estimates are very difficult.

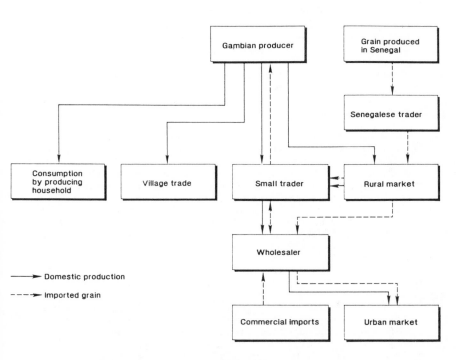

Figure 7:6   The marketing of millet and sorghum, 1980

In the major consumer markets, prices for millet and sorghums are officially recorded, but the prices paid at the various stages of the marketing chain are difficult to ascertain. Two comments can be made, based on the officially recorded retail prices. Firstly, (and surprisingly) there appears to be neither seasonal nor geographic variation among consumer prices. Secondly, a smooth continuous increase in price seems to be taking place. The lack of geographical variation in prices can be explained by the relatively small size of the country, its efficient transportation network and the fact that millet and sorghum are cultivated in all rural areas. For example in May 1980, the price of sanyo was D 0.58 per kilogram in Banjul and was the same in Kaur, whilst in Farafenni it was D 0.54 per kilogram. Similarly with sorghum, the price in Farafenni was only D 0.02 per kilogram less than in

Banjul. Although not controlled cous prices are fairly uniform
throughout the country. The lack of seasonal variation in prices
(see Table 7:6) can be attributed to the availability of imported
rice, in sufficient quantities, throughout the year and at a
constant price. During the months of June through to October when
cous is in short supply, consumer demand shifts instead to rice
and the price of cous thus remains constant. Niane (1980),
investigating the marketing of millet and sorghum in Senegal, has
found the existence of a price ratio between upland cereals and
imported rice, equal to about 0.68, above which the demand for
cous may drop and theoretically become close to zero, because of
its substitution with rice in consumption. The more this ratio
decreases, the more the demand for millet and sorghum increases.
So by controlling the price of rice to the consumer, the Gambian
government also in effect stabilises the price of the upland
cereals, both geographically and seasonally.

There has, however, been a steady increase in the retail price
of cereals in The Gambia since 1973 (see Table 7:7) that can be
attributed to increased OPEC prices and an overall inflationary
trend in the world economy. More locally, steady increases in
purchasing power, which are the result of higher groundnut prices,
have contributed to inflation of approximately 15 per cent per
annum from January 1974 to January 1979 in The Gambia. Also, with
losses due to pests and poor rains, as well as shifts of labour
and land away from upland cereals to the production of a more
profitable crop, groundnuts, the supply of cous has been either
constant or falling. Thus with slightly increasing rice prices
accompanied by population growth, all these factors have resulted
in the slight price increase of upland cereals since 1973.

The largest markets for cous in The Gambia are the urban areas
of Banjul and Kombo St. Mary. As we have seen, despite
transportation and handling costs, the price for these cereals in
these markets compares very favourably with prices in the rural
markets. This can be partly explained by the way in which the
urban markets are supplied with these cereals. Consumers in
Banjul are supplied by five wholesale traders and an unknown
number of retailers. Only one of these wholesalers appears to
have adequate storage facilities. He is based in the Albert
market in Banjul and claims to handle some 200 metric tons of
millet and sorghum per annum. The remaining wholesale traders
each handle about 50 metric tons in the average year. Their
storage facilities are inadequate with all of them storing sacks
of cereals, covered with tarpaulin covers in the kwiang. Each
hires a night watchman to guard his stock. Only the largest
wholsesaler had access to institutional credit via the Commercial
and Development Bank, the others had very limited access to credit
facilities, mainly because they are not able to keep adequate
records of their business transactions.

Table 7:6

The consumer price of millet and sorghum in Banjul Market, from May 1979 to May 1980
(Price in Dalasi per kilogram)

| | 1979 | | | | | | | | | 1980 | | | |
	M	J	J	A	S	O	N	D	J	F	M	A	M
Late Millet	0.56	0.56	0.54	0.54	0.52	0.54	0.54	0.54	0.54	0.54	NA	0.52	0.58
Sorghum	0.56	0.56	0.56	0.56	0.52	0.54	0.54	0.54	0.54	0.54	NA	0.58	0.60

Source: Central Statistics, Retail Price Index

These wholesalers are supplied from two sources; petty traders operating in the rural markets; and from the luma markets. The petty traders assemble the produce at convenient points in the rural markets. When there is enough grain for a full consignment it is transported by lorry to Banjul. The petty trader acquires his shipment by buying small quantities of cereals from individual farmers, who either have a surplus or need ready cash. Supplies from these traders are therefore irregular and unreliable. The other important source of supply are the luma markets, particularly the one held at Farafenni every Sunday. Although this market is 185 km east of Banjul, sufficient supplies of cous can be bought in a single day, mainly through Senegalese traders, and can be transported to the capital in the same day. The difference in the price paid by consumers in Banjul, and that paid for the cereals in Farafenni, appears to be attractive enough to encourage wholesale traders in the urban markets to make regular weekly trips to Farafenni to secure supplies. The economic breakdown of this business transaction is shown on Table 7:8. The trip to Farafenni to buy supplies is clearly profitable. A wholesaler handling an average of 50 metric tons per annum of millet and sorghum purchased in Farafenni, may have a net return of D71 per metric ton or D296 per month, if he sells to a retailer in Banjul. However, by selling direct to the consumer, his profit would be D141 per metric ton, or D587.5 per month. Most of the millet and sorghum for sale in the urban markets in 1979/80 was of Senegalese origin and had been purchased in the lumas. This is due to advantageous price differentials existing in The Gambia, in comparison to Senegal.

Table 7:7
The retail price of cereals in Banjul Market 1974-1980
(Price in Dalasi per kilogram)

Year	Rice	Millet	Sorghum
1974	0.47	0.29	0.28
1975	0.60	0.33	0.31
1976	0.63	0.56	0.54
1977	0.68	0.62	0.60
1978	0.70	0.57	0.57
1979	0.70	0.56	0.56
1980	0.70	0.58	0.60

Source: Department of Central Statistics

In 1976 substantial quantities of millet and sorghum began to be legally imported into The Gambia, when price differentials between Senegal/Mali and The Gambia were sufficiently large. The procedure was for a trader to obtain an import permit from the Gambian government, and have the imported product inspected by the

Gambia Crop Protection Unit, to ensure against the importation of pests and diseases. In 1976 three permits totalling 5,000 metric tons were granted, and imports of 2,000 metric tons of millet and sorghum from Mali and 3,000 metric tons of millet from Senegal were authorised. These were imported by lorry to Banjul, where they were purchased by retailers and sold in both rural and urban markets. Currently, an increased price for cereals in Senegal, a depreciation of the dalasi vis-a-vis the CFA franc and a shortage of upland cereals in the exporting countries concerned, has resulted in the termination of these large scale commercial imports of millet and sorghum. In fact, no major commercial imports have occurred since September 1976. However, price differentials between Senegal and The Gambia are such that it is still profitable for individuals to participate in the clandestine trade in upland cereals between the two countries. This occurs mainly between villages near the border, but more especially in the luma markets, where lorry loads of Senegalese cereals are openly sold to the Gambian wholesaler, with no legal intervention.

Table 7:8

The price structure for millet and sorghum purchased at Farafenni luma and sold in Banjul Market in 1980

	Purchase Price	Other Costs	
	D/100 kg	D/100 kg	%
Price paid at Farafenni luma	25.0	–	58
Cost of handling and transportation to Banjul	–	5.89	13
Wholesale traders' margin	–	7.11	14
Price paid by retailers at Banjul Market	38.0	–	–
Retailers' gross margin	–	7.00	15
Price paid by consumer at Banjul Market	45.0	–	–
TOTAL	–	20.00	100

Source: Based on the author's discussions with wholesalers and retailers in both Farafenni luma and Banjul Market, 1980

In Senegal, the government marketing board, ONCAD, has had a legal monopoly on the primary collection and marketing of millet and sorghum since 1975. ONCAD collects the production from cooperatives, stores a security stock and sells the rest to deficit producers and consumer cooperatives. But in addition to the official ONCAD marketing network, a parallel millet and sorghum marketing system exists. Producers, instead of selling their surpluses to the local cooperative agency, sell to local traders, who in turn either sell to wholesalers or directly to consumers. In theory ONCAD purchases from producers at 35 CFA per kg, while in the parallel market the producer can sell directly to a trader at 40 CFA per kg, with both producer and trader receiving a better price. The better price offered on the parallel market has therefore encouraged its expansion, and it is this market that crosses the border and takes advantage of the higher grain prices in The Gambia. In 1979/80 the controlled price for millet and sorghum paid to producers in Senegal by ONCAD was 35 CFA per kg, that is the equivalent to D0.29 in The Gambia. During the same period, the price paid by traders for cous at Farafenni luma was D0.58 (equivalent to 70 CFA). So the trader buying upland cereals on the parallel market in Senegal for 40 CFA per kg (equivalent to D0.33) could sell it in Farafenni luma for D0.58. A gain of D0.25 per kg (30 CFA), despite handling and transportation costs, is well worth the risk of being caught by the Senegalese authorities and being fined. The low controlled price of upland crops in Senegal has therefore encouraged the development of a parallel market within Senegal which is important in supplying the Gambian market. This, along with a constant supply of subsidised imported rice, has helped depress the price of upland cereals in The Gambia, and has not produced the expansion in the production of these cereals that the government envisaged.

Conclusion

In view of the preponderance of subsistence orientated production and the growing demand for rice, two rather distinct marketing channels for cereals have evolved in The Gambia. The private trade handles the marketing of the upland cereals, whilst the government controls the marketing of rice. Although the marketing system which has developed for the sale of upland cereals is lacking in many of the facilities associated with modern marketing, such as adequate storage facilities and access to credit, the essential functions are still being performed satisfactorily. Trading in rice prior to deregulation was more organised and systematised under the GPMB, and in the view of the government's policy of protecting consumers against high prices and local producers against low prices, its performance was acceptable.

Although these marketing channels appear to adjust supply with demand adequately in the short run, they do not stimulate production in the long run. Rice is the primary substitute for cous in the rural everyday meal. If the price of rice increases, then the farmer will prefer to keep his millet and sorghum for his family's own consumption and will consume less rice. A rise in the price of rice will therefore result in a decline in the amount of upland cereals marketed and may even result in an increase in the acreage being planted in the following season. Millet and sorghum production in any given year is thus positively responsive to the previous year's producer price for these cereals and the consumer price of rice, and is negatively responsive to the previous year's producer price for groundnuts. [10] If, as the government is hoping for, there is to be greater production of cereals in The Gambia, then the marketing system and the price policy for them viz-a-viz the groundnut and imported rice, must be revised. The government's programme of subsidised rice imports has had a definite adverse effect on upland cereal producers. It has transferred welfare from producers to consumers and has meant that resources are pulled out of domestic cereal production in order to pay the subsidy and to keep the country's balance of payments in order. [11]

Notes

[1] Nyankantango This refers to a further steaming of already cooked cereals, together with pounded raw groundnuts and locust beans.

[2] The Department of Agriculture has four main stations, Yundum, Jenoi, Sapu and Basse. Additionally the Jenoi station has a sub-station at Kerewan and the Sapu station has one at Kuntaur. It is from these centres that the agricultural programming on the level of the farmers is coordinated. The area under the jurisdiction of each main station is known as its "circle".

[3] At the height of the wet season the salt/freshwater mixing zone may be located near Kerewan; as the flood declines this zone moves up river affecting areas 220 km upstream (Kaur/Kuntaur). See Chapter One.

[4] In 1974 the charge was D37 per ha. (Dunsmore 1976, p.184)

[5] In January 1986 the government deregulated the rice market in The Gambia.

[6] In the 1972/3 season, output at the Kuntaur rice mill was very low, only 57.4 per cent, in 1973/4 it improved to 59.4 per cent. (WARDA 1976)

[7] For fuller discussion see Rigoulot (1980).

[8] It takes 1.724 metric tons of paddy rice to produce one metric ton of clean rice at the Kuntaur rice mill, at a 58 per cent conversion rate.

[9] SONED estimate it takes two days to mill 100 kg of paddy rice by hand.

[10] As was found to be the case in both Senegal and Mali. See Niane (1980) and Sako and Cotterill (1981).

[11] Airey (1981) describes a similar situation in Sierra Leone where the Rice Corporation has followed a classic low price consumer subsidising policy and as a result rice producers have been reluctant to grow and market a surplus.

8   The marketing of fish and livestock

Introduction

In the last chapter the government controlled network for the distribution of rice was discussed, along with its attendant effect on the traditional marketing sector for upland cereals. In this chapter the marketing of fish and livestock will be investigated, paying special attention to government intervention. This took the form of the setting up of the Livestock Marketing Board (LMB) and Fish Marketing Corporation (FMC) to take formal control of these sectors fo the economy. However, neither were successful and both ultimately stopped trading.

Meat and fish are the chief sources of protein in the average Gambian's diet. In a study undertaken by SEDES [1] in 1970, the per capita consumption of meat in The Gambia was estimated at 10.4 kg, and fish at 10 kg. This gives a total consumption of 20.4 kg, which compares very unfavourable with other West African countries, particularly Senegal (66 kg) and Mauritania (52 kg) (see Table 8:1). However, these figures mask internal differences in consumption. It is estimated that consumption of meat in the Banjul area is about 21.3 kg per capita per annum (which compares favourably with the SEDES estimates for Senegal), but consumption in the rural areas was estimated at only 8.1 kg.

Fish is eaten more frequently than meat in The Gambia, [2] so the SEDES estimate of per capita consumption of only 10 kg in 1970 seems low, and actual levels would appear from observation to be more in the region of 23.7 kg per capita per annum as estimated by the Fisheries Department in 1978. This would place the Gambian combined per capita consumption of meat and fish more in line with other West African countries. Of course, these figures are estimates subject to wide margins of error. There are no overall nutritional or household consumption surveys, and as such all figures must be used tentatively. Average figures not only hide differences in consumption patterns within the country itself, but also mask differences within the family. [3] As will be seen, there are adequate supplies of both meat and fish within the country to satisfy domestic demand, the problem appears to be one of marketing (and to a certain degree consumer purchasing power[4]) accompanied by poor communications and storage facilities. The existing market network for fish and livestock, and government attempts to improve the system will be discussed below.

Table 8:1
Per capita consumption of meat and other animal products
in West Africa in 1970 (kg)

	Mali	Mauritania	Senegal	Gambia	Sierra Leone	Liberia
Beef and offal	9.7	10.5	13.4	6.8	2.2	2.2
Goat meat and offal	9.5	15.7	5.2	1.9	0.5	0.8
Pork and offal	0.2	0	1.5	0.6	0.6	1.9
Camel meat and offal	0.6	9.5	0.1	0	0	0
Poultry	1.8	0	1.3	1.0	1.0	1.0
Other meat Products	0	0.2	0	0.1	0.5	1.8
TOTAL MEAT	21.8	35.9	21.5	10.4	4.8	8.7
FISH (fresh equiv)	10.0	16.1	46.5	10.0	14.1	13.2
TOTAL MEAT AND FISH	31.8	52.0	66.0	20.4	18.9	21.9

Source: Adapted from SEDES, 1970

Livestock

The main classes of domestic stock to be found in The Gambia are cattle, sheep, goats and poultry, with pigs, donkeys and horses being found in small numbers. In 1978, the cattle population of the country stood at 293,211, with 62 per cent being found in the eastern part of the country, namely Upper River and MacCarthy Island Divisions (see Table 8:2). This is a reflection of the available pasturage and the pattern of ethnic settlement - the Fula and Serahuli cattle keeping peoples being predominantly located in the eastern half of the country.

The indigenous cattle are the N'dama breed. Their milk and meat productivity is low, but they are the most suitable breed for Gambian conditions. This is due to their trypanotolerance, hardiness and ability to produce beef on poor pastures. Because of these features the N'dama is in much demand in other parts of West Africa, as a practical alternative to other methods of trypanosomiasis control. So, in line with its policy of increasing the volume and value of take-off from the cattle herd to 26,000 per annum in 1979/80 and a possible 35,000 per annum. in 1984/5 (of which up to 10,000 will be for export) the Gambian government signed an agreement with Nigeria in 1980 for the export of 5,000 N'dama annually over a five year period for breeding purposes. Similar negotiations are under way for the export of Gambian N'dama breeding stock to Ghana, Liberia and Sierra Leone.

Table 8:2
Cattle census figures, 1977/78

Division	Number of Herds	Number of cattle			
		Male	Female	Total	Distribution
Upper River Division	1269	30,238	52,314	82,552	28
MacCarthy Island Division	1596	27,677	72,007	99,684	34
Lower River Division	381	6,666	15,578	22,244	8
North Bank Division	706	13,722	31,796	45,518	15.5
Western Division	662	14,731	28,482	43,213	14.5
The Gambia	4614	93,034	200,177	293,211	100

Source: Adapted from UNDP Preparation Working Paper No.3, Annex 1

The government's policy of increasing off-take is linked to a policy of reducing the national herd, in order to conserve pasture resources which towards the end of the long dry season are reduced and become inadequate. An ODA report published in 1971 recommends that The Gambia should aim at a breeding herd of not more than 70,000 cows and 7,000 bulls in addition to 20,000 oxen, as the dry season fodder is sufficient, it was estimated, to support only 150,000 adult cattle. Using these figures as the ideal, in 1977/78 the Gambian national herd was overstocked by 95 per cent. For this reason the report states:

> The first objective for The Gambia is to reduce the size of and to restructure, the national herd. (ODA 1971, p.38)

The Government believes that this problem can only be overcome when cattle owners are persuaded to regard their cattle in purely economic terms and not as a form of status value within the village hierarchy; and when the current unregulated pastoralism is phased out in favour of herding the animals within rangeland that is controlled by the village or groups of villages. At present, cattle are kept under traditional systems of husbandry, involving extensive grazing on poor pastures or bush, with little regard being paid to the carrying capacity of the pasture.

Nearly every compound in the rural areas owns at least one beef animal, with the wealthier families owning large herds. As the Mandinka (who make up over 42 per cent of the population) [5] are sedentary arable people, they hire Fula cattlemen to tend their animals. Cattle are not regarded as a primary source of income by the Mandinka, but are seen as an economic asset only to be sold when the household cannot obtain cash by other means. However, these herds do provide the family with meat and dairy products. During the dry season, the cattle are allowed to graze on the harvested fields near the village. They benefit from farm by-products such as groundnut haulms and rice and cous bran, which supplement the poor pasturage at this time, whilst the fields are in turn manured. In the rainy season the cattle are herded away from the village to avoid damage to the cultivated crops.

No reliable figures are available for the population of sheep and goats in The Gambia, and estimates vary from 180,000 to 300,000 for each species. These small ruminants are generally given no special attention by their owners and are left to fend for themselves throughout the year, except during the cropping season, when they are herded or tethered away from the village to avoid destruction to crops.

Sheep and goats play an important economic role, and are sold whenever cash is needed. While these animals could contribute significantly to the improvement of the diet of the population if consumed regularly, they are reared primarily for eating at ceremonial occasions such as naming ceremonies, weddings and the muslim feast of tobaski. [6] It is estimated that small ruminants provide about 31 per cent of the meat supply in The Gambia. For the numbers of animals slaughtered and inspected by the health officer before sale in markets, see Table 8:3. This does not, however, include an unknown number of beasts which are slaughtered for household or village consumption that do not enter the marketing system.

Table 8:3
Summary of animals slaughtered and inspected after slaughter, 1977

Location	Cattle	Sheep	Goats	Pigs	Total
Banjul	4,271	1,521	3,653	1,524	10,969
Bakau	602	118	126	1	847
Serrekunda	1,982	682	1,421	114	4,119
Yundum	238	13	25	2	278
Brikama	583	168	1,012	16	1,779
Gunjur	113	5	13	-	131
Bwiam	129	17	9	-	155
Mansakonko	782	24	950	-	1,756
Georgetown	517	64	359	-	940
Bansang	621	400	984	-	2,005
Basse	1,128	579	1,189	3	2,899
Fatoto	241	40	70	-	351
Kuntaur	336	544	649	44	1,573
Kaur	682	240	393	2	1,317
Farafenni	552	262	631	-	1,445
Kerewan	32	1	5	-	38
Barra	147	76	153	-	376
Dankunku	136	45	32	-	213
Diabugu	69	13	55	-	137
TOTAL	13,161	4,812	11,729	1,706	32,408

Source: Livestock Marketing Board, 1978

Horses and donkeys are not eaten in The Gambia and are used mainly as beasts of burden and for other agricultural functions such as pulling ploughs and harrows, in addition to their important role in rural transportation. No reliable data is available on the numbers of these animals in the country, but there are believed to be only a few thousand.

Poultry is commonly kept throughout the rural areas, mainly by women. The indigenous bird is of low productivity, but provides a useful source of animal protein in the form of eggs and meat. Their numbers are not known.

The only attempt at a large scale livestock development scheme in The Gambia involved poultry. In 1948 the Colonial Developement Corporation proposed the establishment of an egg producing unit. It was agreed that 4,000 ha of forest and bush should be cleared to create a poultry farm capable of "producing in two or three years time" 20 million eggs per annum (for the domestic and European markets), to be followed by subsequent expansion if justified by the results. However, a feasibility study was never undertaken, many mistakes were made and in 1951 the project was wound up with a loss of some £628,000. Despite this set back the importance of the poultry industry has been recognised and the present government has four aims for the industry:

i)   improving the nutritional standard of the nation by providing an adequate supply of eggs and poultry meat.

ii)   meeting the requirements of the tourist industry, thereby increasing net foreign exchange earnings.

iii) diversifying the source of cash income of the rural population.

iv)   providing employment opportunities.

In response, a few projects have been set up by private individuals, notably an egg unit at Yundum and a poultry producing plant at Farafenni. These enterprises are still in their early stages; for any conclusion to be drawn from them would be premature.

Livestock marketing

Traditionally, livestock marketing in The Gambia was very similar to that described by Hill (1966) as it operated in Kumasi Market, Ghana, and by Cohen (1965) in the cattle market of Ibadan in Nigeria. It was the cattle dealers, mainly of Mauritanian origin, who would act as middlemen between the farmers in the rural areas and the butchers in the urban areas, to whom they offered very favourable credit terms. The dealers operated through agents who travelled from village to village seeking suitable animals to purchase. The transactions leading to the purchase were conducted privately and were based on sight estimation of the value of the animal. This type of transaction seemed to be preferred by the farmers, who are in general suspicious of weighing scales that they cannot read. After purchase the animals were assembled and trekked to the urban centres, where they were sold on a credit basis.

This system obviously resulted in several problems, mainly high prices, indebtedness and erratic suuplies. Recognising these problems, in March 1953 a modest cattle marketing scheme was started by the Colonial Office, under the control of the senior vetinary officer. Difficulties in transportation of the animals hampered any rapid expansion of the scheme. In 1953, 161 animals were shipped to Bathurst, with 301 animals arriving during the first ten months on 1954. The relative success of the scheme resulted in the first Cattle Marketing Act being passed in 1955. This act formed the basis for tentative government attempts at intervention in livestock marketing and resulted in the cattle dealers losing their monopoly of the cattle trade. In 1972, the Cattle Marketing Act was redrawn to restructure the Cattle Marketing Board and to expand its scope, based on the ODA mission's recommendations. However, in 1975 the Act was again amended to become the Gambia Livestock Marketing Act, but it did not come into force until 1st July 1978. The 1975 Act, in addition to the responsibility of ensuring an adequate supply of cattle for the local markets, charged the Livestock Marketing Board (LMB) with the development of an export trade and the control of livestock importation.

The legal intent of the LMB, which was instituted in 1978, was to strengthen, control and administer more closely the livestock trade and to assist in any way the development of the industry in The Gambia. The LMB was set up as an autonomous quasi government commercial institution, with four divisions:

i)   the Gamhides Division, formally known as the Gambian Hides Export Company Limited, which was to be responsible for the purchase and export of hides and skins.

ii)   the Field Division, which was to be responsible for the procurement of livestock from farmers.

iii)   the Abattoir Division, which would slaughter cattle to supply the markets in Banjul and the Kombos.

iv)   the Sales Division, which would be responsible for the sale of animals purchased by the Field Division, either live, or in the form of dressed carcasses from the abattoir.

The buying operations of the LMB were carried out by a field manager assisted by two buying agents employed by the LMB. In addition there were a larger number of licenced buying agents operating on behalf of the board. The licensed agents used the traditional method of negotiating the price of an animal, on the basis of sight estimation. The animal purchased in this manner was then sold to the LMB agents at the buying points, on a live weight basis. Buying points were set up at various strategic villages, whence the animals were evacuated by truck or cattle boat. The transportation of the beasts was done by a fleet of four Berliet trucks, each with a capacity to carry 15 to 18 animals, and a cattle boat which could carry up to 120 head per trip. [7] Evacuation of cattle by the boat was undertaken from the upper reaches of the river, as far as Basse. The animals were off loaded at Bintang (85 km east of Banjul), where the cattle were held and grazed until they were required. From Bintang they were transported to Banjul and environs by truck. It was hoped that the boat would do six round trips per month, but the maximum achieved was only five. From Bintang, the animals were sent to the abbatoir at Abuko, which was opened in June 1979. The abbatoir is designed to take a throughput of thirty cattle (and a similar number of small ruminants) per eight hour shift. It has been built to European Economic Community standards with a view to export possibilities and has both chilling and freezing facilities. But it has never been fully operational and in April 1980, due to the economic difficulties of the LMB, and a boycott of meat slaughtered there by the predominantly muslim population, because Islamic rites did not take place, the abbatoir was closed down.

The LMB has never been fully operational, and by late 1979 the board was experiencing serious financial difficulties. In March 1980 the LMB's buyers were reduced to two, assigned only D10,000 per week with which to buy cattle and by April the board had only one buyer in its employ, assigned only D900 per week with which to purchase animals. By May 1980, the LMB had ceased trading, without ever operating at full capacity.

The major problem for the LMB has been the rigidity of the Gambian official pricing system. The LMB purchased animals on the basis of live weight using weighing scales. Purchasing prices and selling prices were set by government and are shown in table 8:4. These fixed prices allow the LMB D60 per head of cattle to cover operating costs. As the actual operating costs of the LMB was D193 per animal in 1978, the LMB was experiencing a heavy loss in its operations, which amounted to D377,548 in 1978. This meant that in order to break even, the LMB would have to sell to the butchers at D4.05 per kg carcass weight. This was not economical for the butcher at the prevailing price control levels, which are shown in table 8:5. At the government controlled prices, the butchers claimed to be operating at a loss. This has not been supported by investigation. No butcher is known to have gone out of business and many have built themselves new houses and own new cars. [8]

Table 8:4
Purchasing and selling prices of animals by the
Livestock Marketing Board in 1980

LMB Purchasing Prices

273 kg and over	D1.32 per kg
200 - 272 kg	D1.20 per kg
below 200 kg	D1.10 per kg
females (depending on condition)	D0.75 - D1.00 per kg

LMB Sale Prices

Live animals 273 kg and over	D1.54 per kg
200 - 272 kg	D1.50 per kg
below 200 kg	D1.20 per kg
females	D1.00 per kg
carcass	D3.08 per kg

Source: Author's fieldwork, 1980

Table 8:5
Government controlled retail price of beef in 1980

fillet	D4.94 per kg
steak	D3.85 per kg
meat and bone	D2.75 per kg
liver and heart	D3.85 per kg

Source: Author's fieldwork, 1980

As the LMB's revenue was limited to D60 per head of cattle handled, in order to meet its overheads, the board had to purchase at least 10,000 cattle per annum. This it was unable to do, partly due to the fact that an unknown number of Gambian cattle cross the border into Senegal. This is the direct result of the low meat prices in The Gambia viz-a-viz Senegal. In 1980 the price of beef was 40-45 per cent higher in Senegal. For this reason Senegalese dealers could afford to pay more for Gambian cattle than the LMB, and as a result many Gambian cattle were illegally sold across the border. For example, in 1980 a 300 kg steer brought about D560 in Senegal while the same beast would raise only D360 from LMB buying agents. The LMB was thus locked in a price structure set up by the government. Beef prices, which are government controlled, had not altered since 1975. In order for the LMB to be commercially viable, the government had the choice of raising the price controls, or subsidising LMB operations. The government chose neither, and hence since May 1980 the LMB has ceased trading, and the marketing of beef has now reverted to the traditional system.

The marketing of meat and dairy products can be divided into three: the sale of beef, the sale of sour milk and the sale of other meat. The following is a description of the system as it was found in 1979-80, during a survey of sixteen markets by the author. [9]

Domestic marketing of beef There are three main cattle markets in the country, Banjul market and the lumas at Farafenni and Kaur. Of these, Farafenni luma attracts livestock from Senegal which have illegally crossed the border, [10] and is the busiest livestock fair. There is no formal organisation. The owner brings his livestock to the market and waits for a potential purchaser to come forward. The animal is not weighed and a price is arrived at by haggling after assessment by prodding the beast. Most purchasers are either farmers buying animals to replace slaughtered or old stock, or butchers from neighbouring markets. It is interesting to note that both Farafenni and Kaur lumas supply the daily markets in these villages with meat. The beasts sold in the lumas are said to be cheaper than equivalent animals sold in the surrounding villages. This is particularly the case in the dry season when some farmers will sell their beasts at very reasonable prices, to obtain money to buy rice for their household's sustenance during the hungry season. This was particularly the case in the drought years of the early and late 1970s.

The livestock market in Banjul, which is situated right next to the abbatoir, is run by the city council. The animals are penned, and then auctioned. Most of these beasts go to supply the meat needs of the urban and peri-urban areas nearby, hence its location. In other areas, butchers may be supplied by agents. In all the markets where surveys were undertaken, the butchers interviewed had purchased their beef cattle no more than 5 km from the village in which they did business (except Banjul, where meat came from a 14 km range). This indicates that most butchers had reverted quite smoothly to the pre LMB system. Apart from the urban markets all butchers slaughtered their own animals, but had

to have them inspected by the district health officer before
selling any meat in the market.

Marketing of sour milk   Sour milk is regarded as a luxury food
item in all parts of the country, and those who can afford it
clamour to buy it.   It is prepared by leaving milk to go sour in a
covered container.   No starter is added as the containers harbour
a mixed culture, including the yogurt bacillus.   Milk is collected
over a period of seven days and added to the container.   When the
milk is considered sour enough it is taken to the local market.
In the Basse area, women will walk up to 10 kilometres through the
bush, crossing the river by canoe, in order to sell the milk
collected from their husbands' herd.   These women tend to be of
Fula extraction, as members of this ethnic group are the largest
cattle owners in the country.

Of all the markets visited, sour milk was found to be sold only
in Serrekunda, Central Sabigi, Barra, Farafenni and Basse.
Central Sabigi, Farafenni and Basse were supplied locally.
However, in Barra market, a wholesaler was interviewed, whose
supplies of sour milk came from Kaolack, and it is suspected that
some of this milk crossed the river to be retailed in Banjul and
Serrekunda markets.

Marketing of other meat   Small ruminants were mostly marketed in
an informal way at the village level, except for the sheep trade
before the muslim feast of tobaski.   At this time, many people in
the urban areas purchase sheep in the rural areas, frequently from
relatives in their home village, to re-sell at inflated prices in
the urban areas, when a sheep can cost as much as D200.   The
prices of small ruminants, pigs and poultry have traditionally
been higher weight for weight than for beef, but in recent years,
the price of sheep in particular has gone up dramatically, mainly
because of the effect of the Sahelian drought which has killed
many of these animals.   Sheep and goat meat is sold in most
markets, usually on the days when a cow has not been slaughtered.
But it is more common for a village or compound to kill one of its
own herd and distribute the meat amongst the occupants on a
reciprocal basis.

As most of the population are muslim, pig meat is consumed in
very small quantities.   Pork is sold in both Banjul and Serrekunda
markets on three days a week, but was not found in any other
market.   This is probably due to the Christian and expatriate
communities, who tend to live in Banjul and Kombo St. Mary.   The
Jola group, who are either animist or Christian, also eat pork and
keep pigs.   These people live chiefly in the Fonis and hunt a lot
of bush pigs, which are regarded as agricultural pests.   This meat
is highly prized by the pork eating population but is never seen
in the markets.

179

Poultry is found in every market, and often hawkers will go from compound to compound trying to sell live birds. The local birds, although very tasty, tend to be small, due to the fact that they are left to scavenge for themselves. Most compounds contain hens, which are an important source of protein, and a ready meat supply for unexpected guests. Eggs are not an important component of the local diet and taboos restrict their consumption by certain groups. [11]

Fish

Although The Gambia has a limited coastline, it is said to be one of the richest fishing zones in West Africa, due to the vast reservoir of the Atlantic Ocean continental shelf and the river itself. Yet despite this potential, the fish resources of the area are under exploited and fishing in The Gambia is to a large extent an artisanal, small scale activity. A survey undertaken by the Fisheries Department in 1978 revealed that 582 boats (mainly canoes) were involved in fishing that year, with the majority of them based on the Atlantic coastline and the river estuary. It is estimated that five thousand fishermen are involved, with the majority engaged in fishing full time. But a large number of Senegalese fishermen also fish in Gambian waters, mostly seasonally for lobsters and groupers.

The fishing industry in The Gambia can be divided into two very different sections, the marine sector and the inland fishing sector. Of the inland sector very little is known, and very little government attention is paid to it, due to the relatively lucrative nature and potential profitability of the marine sector. This bias is reflected in the data available.

Marine sector

Although The Gambia has a small coastline, it has 2,500 square kilometres of territorial waters and a large river estuary. A survey undertaken in 1976 estimated that there was an annual stock of commercially exploitable demersal species in these waters of approximately 4,000 metric tons. No surveys have yet been carried out for pelagic species, though the Fisheries Department estimate that from current landings there is a harvest of 12,000 to 15,000 metric tons each year, with a potential sustainable yield of 30,000 to 50,000 metric tons per year. The coastline and estuary are also a source of lobsters, shrimps, oysters and cockles.

As Table 8:6 shows, bonga fish (Ethmalosa fimbriata), a pelagic species, forms the bulk of fish landings in The Gambia, an estimated 20,000 metric tons being harvested in 1974/75. The majority of the landings are on the Atlantic seaboard, at coastal villages such as Gunjur, Tanjai and Brufut, where up to 50 per cent of the catch is smoked for export, mainly to Ghana, the rest being marketed by middlemen for domestic consumption. An average landing per day is estimated by the Fisheries Department to be one ton, though at the peak of the season (November/December) this figure may reach as much as two and a half tons per day. Apart from bonga, the rest of the fishery, covering most of the demersal species, can be classified as mixed. There is an export market for catfish (<u>Crysichthys</u> spp.), groupers (<u>Rypticus</u> spp., <u>Epinephalus</u> spp.), ladyfish (<u>Pseudotholithus senegalensis</u>) and barracuda (<u>Syhyraena syhyraena</u>). Figures from vessels licenced to fish in Gambian waters show monthly production figures for 1978 to be well over 100 metric tons per vessel.

Lobster fishing is a traditional activity along the Gambian coastline, mainly involving Senegalese fishermen. The catch has traditionally been taken to Senegal, where it is exported as Senegalese produce. Recently, controls have been more effective and buyers are required to pay duties and declare their catch before going to Senegal. It is estimated that between 70 to 100 metric tons of lobster are exploited annually in this manner.

Shellfish are seasonally harvested by women on a rather limited scale. Oysters and cockles are gathered in the dry season from the stems of mangrove plants in the tidal swamps of the estuary. Further upriver, shell fish are collected at the start of the rice harvest from the bolongs near the rice fields. Crabs and snails are also collected, especially in April. Because of the sporadic nature of their exploitation and the isolated and scattered distribution of locations, it is difficult to estimate the annual harvest. However, some 150 metric tons of dried cockles are exported to other West African countries each year.

Inland fishing sector

Estimates for harvests of fish from the River Gambia are hard to arrive at, as no reliable statistics are available. In 1951, Hickling reported to the Secretary of State:

> As far as I know there is no information at all as to the present numbers of fishermen, part time and whole time, nor of the number of fishing craft of different types, nor of the varieties and quantities of fish which are landed at each place by each method of fishing. (Hickling 1951, p.6)

Thirty years later the situation is much the same in this sector. In 1950, a Swedish expedition did carry out a survey of the river. They identified 81 species of fish, but unfortunately no scientific experiments were undertaken, and no estimates of potential or actual yield were made. But it is clear that the inland waterways of The Gambia are totally underexploited. The Fisheries Department estimate that in 1977 only 3,000 metric tons of fish were harvested from the inland sector, a very marginal figure indeed. The rate of exploitation could increase drastically with the introduction of improved gear and implements, and with the exploitation of presently unexploited species.

The recent proposal to construct a barrage-bridge across the river has important considerations for the inland fishing sector. The suggested barrage will be built across the river at Yellitenda, the ferry crossing point of Trans-Gambian highway which links northern Senegal with Casamance. Apart from improving communications, one of the main reasons given for the construction of a barrage is to stop upriver intrusion of salt water, which is presently damaging rice fields as far upstream as Kuntaur(256 km). However, this saline intrusion has some advantages for the inland fishing industry, for due to the high salinity gradient of the river, several marine species of fish are found in the river. Fish such as bullshark, saw-fish and shrimps are harvested regularly from the river and contribute greatly to the local economy, and, more importantly, to local diet. Constructing a barrage will undoubtedly change the characteristics inherent in the natural systems of the river. The effect on the inland fisheries may be dramatic.

The export of fish

The exact rates of fish catches are unavailable, but an overall estimate of total production of both marine and inland sectors is made in the 1975/80 Development Plan, showing the estimated production in 1974/75 and the target production the plan envisaged by 1979/80 (see Table 8:6). It is shown in the table that of the estimated production of 30,715 metric tons in 1974/5, that 20,579 metric tons would be exported, bringing an estimated D4,621,660 of foreign exchange into the country.

Most of the fish exported is handled by the country's two industrial fisheries, the "Sea Gull Fisheries" and "Gambia Fisheries Limited". "Sea Gull Fisheries" was established in Banjul in 1973 by "Mankoadze Fisheries" of Ghana. The catch is supplied by the company's own trawlers. These have a cold storage facility but no processing is undertaken on board. On shore there is a cold storage capacity of around 750 metric tons (at -18°C) and three freezers that can hold up to 40 metric tons each. In addition, an ice plant produces 30 metric tons of ice a day. The catches are almost completely exported to Ghana by ship. Although The Gambia does not benefit directly from this operation, it does benefit through licences, salaries and taxes, which were estimated at $250,000 in 1975. "Gambia Fisheries Limited", the second of the country's industrial fisheries was established in Banjul in 1971. The Gambian government has a minority share of 20 per cent in this company, the balance being owned by Japanese firms. The plant purchases, freezes and exports mainly crustaceans for the Senegalese and French markets. It has a cold storage capacity of 750 metric tons (at -25°C) and an ice plant with a daily capacity of 20 metric tons. In 1973 and 1974 annual quantities frozen by the company amounted to around 2,000 metric tons.

182

Table 8:6

Estimated production and export of marine products from Gambian waters

| | Estimated production | | Estimated value | | Estimated % exported | |
| | metric tons | | D'000 | | % | |
	1974/75	1979/80	1974/75	1979/80	1974/75	1979/80
Bonga and herrings	20,000	30,000	1,120	1,680	50	60
Black grouper, choff, snapper	2,000	4,800	896	1,792	80	50
Shark, rays, catfish	6,000	7,800	672	784	80	90
Other fish	2,000	3,000	896	1,344	10	20
Lobster	65	85	728	952	90	80
Oyster	100	150	562	840	50	60
Cockles	150	200	8	23	80	80
Shrimps	400	450	2,016	2,016	90	80
TOTAL	30,715	46,485	6,898	9,431	67	61

Source: Weitenberg, 1977

The total recorded exports of fish from The Gambia in 1973 were as follows: fresh, chilled or frozen fish, 832 metric tons; preserved fish, 956 metric tons; lobsters, 23 metric tons; other crustaceans, 208 metric tons; the total being 2,019 metric tons, worth an estimated $580,720. More than 50 per cent was destined for other African countries (33 per cent exported value). Italy was the major importing country, receiving 610 metric tons, worth $180,000. Exporting fish is a profitable business and although the two industrial companies dominate the export market in frozen and chilled fish, nearly 50 per cent of the exports are of preserved fish, whose production is in the hands of native entrepreneurs. Smoked bonga and catfish, dried bonga, catfish and seasnails are the main items. Methods of preservation are very primitive and quality is low.

The two main methods of fish preservation used in The Gambia are drying and smoking. Fish are smoked, after they have been cleaned and parboiled. This is done over a charcoal or wood fire covered by a sack. The process is long and some fish are spoiled. Fish which is successfully smoked will not deteriorate for some time, and many cartons of smoked fish, originating in the coastal areas, are to be found in every wharf town along the river. Fish is dried naturally. After cleaning, including gutting and the removal of scales, the fish is laid out to dry in the sun. Losses and spoilage are high, as flies and seagulls are to be found in large numbers at these sites. Once dried, the fish can be kept for many months.

Preserving fish is the job of women, who tend to be relatives of the fishermen. When the canoes come home the women come down to the beach, purchase the catch and begin processing the fish immediately. If the catch is landed in the morning, then some of the fresh fish will be held back by the fishermen who will take it to the nearest market or sell it to a middleman. But as deterioration is very rapid most of the morning catch and all of an evening catch will be processed as soon as possible. To save time, most of the fish is processed on the beach, where fires will have already been lit and areas prepared for the drying or smoking process.

All the fishing villages, including Gunjur, Tanjai and Kartong along the Atlantic coast process their surplus fish, but the main centres for the smoking of fish are Banjul and Brufut, with Brufut being the largest producer of dried fish. In Banjul, fish are processed on the beach, here many women spend their days cleaning, boiling and smoking fish. These are fish which had been landed on Banjul beach, or were fish that the fishmongers could not sell that day and let the women have at cost price. Most of the fish processed here either re-enters the market, or is crated up for shipment upriver. The business appears to be profitable. None of the women give any indication of their income, although many other traders in the market talked of their wealth with envy.

Brufut, the most successful fishing village in the country is a unique case. It is an isolated village on the Atlantic coast, populated solely by immigrant Fanti Ghanaian fishermen. These men fish in large canoes, with a crew of six to ten men. All the canoes have outboard motors. The catches are large, consisting mainly of bonga and catfish, with a few barracuda and ladyfish. Most of the catch is smoked or dried on the beach, but some is sold fresh to middlemen who come to the village by taxi or bicycle, and who resell in local markets. Some of the preserved fish also enters the domestic marketing system in this way, but when asking what happened to the rest of the preserved fish, the author was told by the fishermen that they are crated up in large tea chests, and taken by canoe to Ghana. This seems implausible and it is suspected that the canoe makes the journey to Banjul, where the fish is sold either to enterprising sailors on board the Ghanaian Black Star Line vessels that have business in Banjul, thus probably avoiding payment of export duties, or alternatively, may be sold to the "Sea Gull Fisheries" for export to Ghana.

The domestic marketing of fish

The Gambian government has recognised the potential of the fishing sector, and stated the following objectives in its 1975/80 Development Plan:

i)   to use local fish as a means of improving the nutritional standards of the population

ii)   to effect a rational long term utilisation of coastal and inland fisheries resources

iii) to the extent that it will be consistent with the above, increase employment and net foreign exchange earnings in the sector

iv)   to achieve a 10 per cent annual rate of growth in production.

In order to achieve these objectives, a multi disciplinary mission was invited to the country, to study the situation of the fisheries. (Weitenberg, 1977) It was upon the recommendations made by the mission that in 1977 the Fish Marketing Corporation (FMC) was created. The Fish Marketing Corporation Act (1977) gave the FMC wide powers, including the power to licence and register fishing vessels, the responsibility of developing fisheries and the task of improving internal fish distribution and export sales. But the FMC, like the LMB, has never been fully operational, and in 1980 the statutory powers of the corporation were temporarily withdrawn, due to irregularities in its accounts. So in 1980, the fishing industry in The Gambia was in the same position as it had been in 1977, with marketing in the hands of local entrepreneurs.

The marketing of fish is a major problem, as the 1975/80 Development Plan acknowledges:

> At the moment there are no proper landing, wholesale, or cold storage facilities readily available to Gambian fishermen and this has discouraged the distribution of fish within the country. (Gambian Government, 1976)

The lack of ice, cold storage facilities and poor road transport, make the distribution of fresh fish virtually impossible. The seriousness of the problem is demonstrated by the fact that per capita consumption of fresh fish in the Banjul area and along the Atlantic coastline is over 45 kg, whereas consumption in the interior is only 15 kg or less, [12] a very sharp contrast.

Fish is a highly perishable commodity and must be either preserved or eaten within hours of being caught. [13] The marketing of preserved fish does not pose as many problems as the marketing of fresh fish, and for this reason a distinction must be made between the two.

The marketing of fresh fish   The marketing of fresh fish is an extremely difficult task in The Gambia, with poor communications and little if any refrigeration. Fish is sold in the market, on concrete tables in the open with no fly screens or ice, consequently there is a lot of spoilage. The country can be divided into two parts as concerns the marketing of fresh fish, firstly, those areas within relatively easy reach of the Atlantic and estuarine fishing villages, namely the Banjul and Kombo regions, and secondly, the rest of the country which is primarily supplied from the river and its tributaries. The two regions can be differentiated by the quality of their communications network which is crucial in the marketing of fresh fish where no cold storage facilities exist.

In the western part of the country and particularly in the Kombos, the roads are reasonably well maintained, consisting of either all weather surfaces or laterite, with most villages being well served. In this part of the country there are also plenty of taxis available, the charges of which are fixed by the government and are very reasonable. [14]   A publicly owned bus service is also operated where the roads are suitable. In this area fish is supplied directly from the Atlantic coast and river estuary. The major centres of distribution are the fishing villages on Tanjai, Old Jeswang, Bakau, Brufut, Gunjur, Kaimbujae, Barra and Banjul itself. Due to the abundance of fish in the area and the size and shape of the region, fish has only to travel a few kilometres from beach to market, the longest journey being 20 km from Tanjai to Serrekunda market. Fresh fish is therefore readily available and plentiful in the markets of this region. As one moves eastwards the situation rapidly deteriorates. In 1981 an all weather road from Banjul to Basse was opened along the south bank, but only a very badly maintained laterite road was available along the north bank. Many villages are accessible only by mud tracks, which become totally impassable in the rainy season and, although since 1981 an infrequent bus service runs from Banjul to Basse along the south bank, most travellers have to rely upon either a taxi or government vehicle stopping with a spare place.

Due to the inefficient nature of the communications system as one moves eastwards, fish tends to be caught and landed near the village in which it will be sold. The fish found in Basse, Georgetown, Kaur, Kerewan and Barra markets were caught in the river off these villages and were sold within hours of being landed. There are exceptions however. Kerewan is supplied in part from Jorunku Creek, 31 km away. Kuntaur is supplied from Panchang, 38 km away, where the fish is caught in Nianija Bolon. But it must be remembered that both these centres have reasonably good road networks and in addition they are both administrative headquarters, with a large demand for fish from resident civil servants and their families.

Farafenni is somewhat of an oddity, not being supplied with fresh fish from Gambian waters. Here, supplies come by taxi from Kaolack. (The same taxi takes supplies to Kaur once or twice each week). This occurrence is obviously facilitated by the presence of the all weather Trans-Gambian Highway, which links Kaolack with Farafenni. This enables fish supplies from Senegal to reach the market in Farafenni faster than supplies from Gambian coastal waters. It was difficult to ascertain the origin of this fish, but it is thought that it came from the Senegalese coast in a refrigerated railway container before being distributed either from a cold store or directly from the train in Kaolack.

Marketing of preserved fish Smoked and dried fish will, if cured and stored properly, keep several months. These types of fish, and especially smoked bonga, were found in every market that was visited. Smoked fish, especially, is in great demand everywhere, as it is a key ingredient in many sauces, particularly in areas where fresh fish are not plentiful.

There are two major supply centres of preserved fish in The Gambia. Firstly, there are the Gambian Atlantic seaboard fishing villages, particularly Brufut, Gunjur, Kartong and Banjul itself. Secondly, supplies enter the network via the luma markets of Farafenni and Kaur, whose supplies originate in Senegal. Most Gambian markets are supplied from the Kombo fishing villages, supplies being sent mainly by truck, but with Georgetown and Basse receiving the majority of their supplies from the river boat, the Lady Chilel. The fish arrives packed in tea chests, which have been bought and transported by middlemen. They are then sold to groups of retailers, who split the contents between themselves. The fish is not sold by weight, but in small lots of maybe two or three fish. The price varies with the amount charged by the middlemen. Most middlemen, as happened in Basse, will travel to

the coast and purchase five to ten chests of fish at a time.
There are, however, no storage facilities in the rural markets and
the boxes are piled up in the sun all day, until they are sold,
which may take some months. Often by the time the last few chests
are sold, the percentage of unsaleable fish in each has risen, and
the retailer charges accordingly, to cover these spoilages.

The markets at Kerewan, Farafenni, Kaur and Kuntaur do not
receive any supplies of preserved fish from the Kombos. These
markets are all situated on the north bank and have very poor
communications with the coast. Kerewan market is supplied from
its own beach, the other markets are supplied from Senegal. Most
of the Senegalese supplies of preserved fish which enter The
Gambia, come from Kaolack, Koungel, and M'Bar and enter the
marketing network by way of the luma markets at Farafenni and
Kaur. At these lumas large quantities of poor quality broken
smoked bonga fish are sold. Here it is sold by weight, not volume
as in other Gambian markets. This fish is mostly purchased by
local market women, who sell it in the daily market the next day,
in small piles or "lots".

The influx of Senegalese fish into this central north bank area
of The Gambia is the result of poor communications with the rest
of the country, and the relatively easy access with Senegal via
the highway. It is also beneficial for Senegalese traders to
cross the border, particularly to trade in the luma markets,
where, as was discussed in Chapter Five, there are very little if
any border controls. The Senegalese traders deal in local
currency and use their takings to buy imported consumer goods,
such as cloth, radios and enamelware, as well as imported food
such as rice, which are cheaper in The Gambia. This exchange of
goods is therefore beneficial to both parties. The Senegalese
trader acquires goods that are more expensive or are in short
supply back home, whilst the occupants of this remote region are
supplied with a valuable source of protein.

Imported meat, dairy and fish products

Except for milk and dairy products, local supplies of meat and
fish are adequate to meet demand, and only small quantities are
imported into The Gambia. Table 8:7 shows that in 1977/78, only
51 metric tons of meat was imported into the country. This
consisted mainly of frozen and canned meats, as the importation of
slaughter stock has been banned since 1968. [15] The amount of
fish and fish products imported is greater, and in 1973 (the most
recent figures available), a total of 148 metric tons was
imported. This comprised 86 metric tons of fresh, chilled or
frozen fish, 50 metric tons of canned sardines (96 per cent from
Spain), and 12 metric tons of other processed fish. Most of these
products are imported by the hotels and supermarkets, and consumed
primarily by the tourist and expatriate communities. [16] In

contrast, dairy products consisting mainly of condensed and dried milk, are among the country's major imported agricultural products. In 1973, 465 metric tons of dairy produce was imported (see Table 8:8), these coming mainly from the European Economic Community, especially The Netherlands, which supplied 60 per cent of the total imported dairy products in that year.

Table 8:7
Meat legally imported into The Gambia, 1977/78

Category	Quantity (metric tons)	Value (dalasis)
Fresh, chilled and frozen meat	21	152,092
Dried, smoked and salted meat	10	64,816
Canned and other prepared meat	20	108,073
TOTAL	51	325,041

Source: Central Statistics Department

Table 8:8
Dairy products legally imported into The Gambia, 1973

Category	Quantity (metric tons)
Evaporated milk	353
Dried milk	88
Butter	17
Cheese and curd	7
TOTAL	465

Source: Weitenberg, 1977

  These imported meat and fish products are not distributed through the traditional marketing network, but instead can only be purchased in retail store outlets. Fresh, frozen or chilled products can only be obtained in the large supermarkets in the urban areas, such as CFAO, Maurel et Prom and the NTC. It is only these stores that have the refrigeration facilities (and generators to keep them running when there is a power cut) to stock large quantities of these highly perishable foodstuffs.

Canned or dried products such as tinned sardines and dried milk powder can be bought in any small family store throughout the country, as well as in the large urban supermarkets. Store keepers in the rural areas usually buy their supplies of these goods from their nearest NTC store, or may occasionally travel into the urban areas to renew their stocks.

These imported meat and fish products are not important constituents of the rural Gambian's diet. They are regarded as luxuries and not essentials, and when money is short they are the first food items to be dropped from the menu.

Conclusion

From this discussion it is clear that there is a need for an improved marketing system for meat and fish in The Gambia. This is especially the case as the national herd and territorial waters are more than adequate to provide the needs of the population.

The network has many problems, not least the lack of quick, efficient communications and adequate cold storage facilities. Without these capital investments, it is not surprising that neither the LMB nor FMC ever operated at full capacity and that both experienced financial difficulties, leading to liquidation after only a few years trading. In fact, when the marketing boards were operating it was only the urban areas and the Kombos, an area already well supplied with meat and fish, that were directly affected. Areas where fish and meat supplies are very spasmodic and unsatisfactory, such as the north bank and upper river, did not benefit from their activities at all.

The LMB had its own unforeseen problems, with the strict government price controls on meat, as well as with muslim customers (95 per cent) who refused to buy meat slaughtered at the new abbatoir at Abuko, because Islamic religious rites were not observed there. This is a problem which should have been recognised and discussed with the Imam before the slaughterhouse was built.

The failure of both marketing boards indicate that the system of meat and fish marketing was not fully understood and investigated before their formation. If a study had been performed taking into account social as well as economic variables, many problems would have been avoided.

Notes

[1]   Quoted by Livestock Marketing Board, 1978.
[2]   McCrae and Paul, 1979, p.9.

[3]   The best food is given to the men, the women and children
      eating inferior food out of a separate bowl.

[4]   Of course there may be a demand or need for supplies of meat
      and fish, but the money to buy it may not be available,
      particularly during the hungry season.

[5]   The other groups include Fula (18 per cent), Wolof (16 per
      cent), Jola (ten per cent) and Serahuli (nine per cent).
      (Census, 1973)

[6]   L'aide el Kebir, the feast day held 70 days after the end of
      Ramadan.

[7]   The boat was received in 1978 as part of a grant from the
      British Government.

[8]   "The butchering trade in West Africa is a very lucrative
      one, whatever the butchers may say to the contrary, as
      almost everything including the hide is sold. No butcher,
      however, will admit this, and will always maintain that he
      sells every beast at a loss. One can only admire, the
      philanthropic spirit and devotion to the public welfare of
      these men who for so many years have supplied meat not only
      without any profit, but at an actual loss. Their spiritual
      rewards must however be great, as very few of them ever
      leave the butchering trade". (Letter to Senior
      Commissionier from Senior Veterinary Officer, The Gambia,
      15.1.53). This view is still held by many.

[9]   Banjul, Serrekunda, Bakau, Central Sabigi, Sukuta, Gunjur,
      Brikama, Barra, Kerewan, Farafenni, Kaur, Kuntaur,
      Georgetown, Basse and the lumas at Farafenni and Kaur.

[10] There seems to be no monetary reason why Senegalese
      livestock should be sold in Gambian markets, as prices are
      higher in Senegal. This phenomenon, however, was observed
      and it can only be assumed that the Senegalese livestock
      owner wishes to obtain Gambian currency in order to buy
      consumer goods which are cheaper in The Gambia.

[11] Mandinka custom states that pregnant women and young
      children should not eat eggs.

[12] Trupke, 1976. The 1975/80 Development Plan puts the figures
      higher - Banjul area averaging 91 kg per capita per year,
      and the provinces only 23 kg.

[13] Few have electricity, let alone a fridge.

[14] The taxi fare from Banjul to Serrekunda, a journey of 14 km
      in 1980 was fixed at DO.50. The journey from Serrekunda to
      Bakau (7 km) was fixed at DO.25. All taxi fares are fixed
      even for long distance journeys. Passengers make sure they
      are adhered to!

[15] In effect slaughter stock is still illegally imported,
      especially in rural areas near the border, and could be seen
      for sale in the luma markets.

[16] 1975/80 Development Plan estimates that "85% of the
      foodstuffs consumed by the tourists is now imported, more
      because of the absence of proper marketing channels and
      storage facilities than because of production problems."

9 The marketing of fruit, vegetables and cooking oils

Introduction

In this chapter, the marketing of fruit, vegetables and cooking oils will be discussed. The importance of these foods in the Gambian diet varies from season to season and from location to location. Cooking oils are used every day by most families, in every sauce, along with whatever vegetables are in season, particularly onions and tomatoes. [1] Fruit, however, is not an important constituent of the Gambian diet, and is used in principal meals only in times of extreme shortage of staples, but more regularly as a snack in between meals.

Each of these categories of food will be described in turn, followed by a discussion of the marketing system that has evolved for them. Unlike the marketing of cereals, fish and meat, this is one area of food marketing in The Gambia where government intervention has been minimal.

Fruit

Although there are numerous edible fruit species in The Gambia, there is little in the way of orchard or commercial scale planting. This is in part due to the unfavourable climatic conditions and colonial government policy. In all parts of the country rainfall is sub-optimal for tree fruits, with maximum yields only being obtained using irrigation. Such fruits as bananas (Musa cvv.) and paw paws (Carica papaya Linn.) will not normally produce any fruit and may even die if they are not irrigated in the dry season. As the Western Division receives the heaviest rainfall, it is in this region that most fruit production is to be found, mainly as a backyard crop. The only fruits which have been grown on a commercial basis are limes (Citrus aurantifolia Swingle) and cashews (Anacardium occidentale Linn.) But both projects were economically impractical and have now been discontinued.

The possibility of establishing a citrus fruit industry in The Gambia was explored shortly after World War II, as a joint venture between the colonial government and Messrs. Rose & Co. Rose agreed to establish a lime factory if the government would guarantee 121 ha of limes in bearing. In 1947 the government planted 40.5 ha of lime seedlings at Abuko on an experimental basis. The project never succeeded as the limes needed extensive irrigation facilities which were not available and produced poor grade oil. At the same time, the bottom dropped out of the lime oil market, making it totally uneconomic for Rose to set up a factory in The Gambia. The project was therefore abandoned.

The cashew is one of the few tree crops which is well adapted to local climatic conditions. During the Second World War, with the shortage of oils in mind, the colonial government investigated the possibility of setting up a cashew nut industry. But it was discovered that cashew nuts are very sensitive and must be handled quickly and efficiently to be of any use. Decortication is the major difficulty and is a highly skilled hand operation. When the kernel is exposed to the air for any length of time, it loses its whiteness and crispness and becomes soapy. To avoid this the kernels are therefore packed for export in four gallon containers of carbon dioxide gas. The value of the nuts falls rapidly if they are damaged. In The Gambia, producers were totally inexperienced in cashew preparation. The skilled work of decortication was done successfully in India, and cashews produced in East Africa at this time were shipped to India for decortication. Such a proposition for Gambian cashews would have made the whole operation uneconomic. These difficulties therefore led the colonial government to abandon the scheme in 1953:

> In view of the difficulties of preparing the nut for market, and the fact that these nuts supply a rather limited luxury demand, it is not considered that the production of cashewnuts for export would be a paying proposition. (BA 2/3267, 1953)

At the present time, only one large scale fruit tree project is operating. This is a privately owned orchard of mango (Mangifera indica Linn.), avocado pear (Persea americana Mill.), orange (Citrus sinensis Osbeck.), and grapefruit (Citrus paradisi) at Mandinari. Most of the produce of this venture is exported, although no production figures are available. The ecological conditions in The Gambia are very suitable for the mango tree which is found throughout the country. Most trees give good yields of clean fruit and there is a ready local market, but they are mainly unimproved cultivars and the fruit is frequently fibrous and tastes of turpentine. However, the Department of Agriculture has imported some improved varieties which are being cultivated on the tree farm in Mandinari and which produce fruit of high enough quality to export. Good specimens of orange and grapefruit can also be found on this farm, as well as avocados. However, the possibility of air freighting the fruit to Europe has come up against one large problem: the Gambian season coincides with that of Israel and South Africa, and the Gambian crop is not able to compete economically.

Most fruit trees are grown as backyard crops, particularly mangos which are semi-wild, originating from chance seedlings. Good yields of bananas and paw paws are possible in favoured sites with efficient management, but there is the problem of obtaining good planting material. Some fruits are gathered wild from the bush, such as tamarind (<u>Tamarindus indica</u> Linn.), juss (<u>Icacina senegalensis</u> A.), soursop (<u>Anona sp. Anona muricata</u> Linn.) and bush mango (<u>Cordyla africana</u> Lour.). These fruits are often added to sauces in time of shortage. For example, bush mangos may be harvested before they are ripe and cooked with raw groundnuts. They may also be dried. The fruits are cut in half and then dried in the sun for about five days and stored, the kernel being discarded. When needed they are pounded in a mortar with a little water, steamed twice, baobab leaves are added and they are steamed again. Wolof people sometimes use the dried fruit as a substitute for meat. Juss berries are used in the same way. The tamarind tree grows mostly in MacCarthy Island Division and Upper River Division. Its fruit is very acidic and is used as a drink or to flavour sauces, the kernels of the seeds may also be eaten in times of scarcity. The seeds of several fruits such as cashew, locust bean (<u>Parkia biglobosa</u> Benth.) baobab (<u>Adansonia digitato</u> Linn.) and gingerbread plum (<u>Parinari macrophylla</u>) are also eaten, often by pounding and using in sauces in addition to or instead of groundnuts.

The baobab tree is one of the most useful trees of The Gambia. The fruits are large and are available for most of the year, although they are most abundant from December to April. The white or pinkish 'bread' (or lumps of 'flesh' which is hard and dry) is squeezed in water for use as a drink. It may also be mixed with milk or groundnut paste and sugar. Baobab fruit juice is rich in cream of tartar, pectin, glucose and mucilage. During Ramadan, particularly, rice balls may be made and served in baobab juice. The seeds that are found embedded in the bread are rich in potassium and phosphate. They are eaten especially in August and September. In some districts, especially the Kiangs, these seeds are roasted, ground and used instead of groundnuts or may be used to supplement them in time of scarcity. Similarly, gingerbread plum nuts and cashew kernels may also be used instead of groundnuts in sauces.

Another useful fruit is the locust bean which is a long black pod that contains yellow floury flesh and black seeds, available from April to August. The flesh can be eaten raw or cooked after first soaking in water and squeezing out the fibrous material and seeds. The seeds are used as a valuable flavouring in several dishes, but they must first be 'treated'. This treatment takes the form of fermentation, before pressing into balls. These balls are usually pounded with chilli pepper before adding them to groundnut sauces, sour leaf sauces and palm oil stews. Because most of these 'bush' fruits are collected by children for their mothers, few are found for sale in markets. However, locust bean balls and baobab flour are available in all markets all year round.

Production figures for fruit in The Gambian are very unreliable, but a survey was carried out by the Central Statistics Department in 1979/80 and the results are shown in Table 9:1. The price of fruit varies seasonally with demand and supply, so the prices given in the table are averages of the prices found in the urban markets; further inland, where fruit is not so widely available, prices are higher.

Marketing of fruit

As fruit growing is not undertaken on a commercial basis, any fruit that comes into the market is the surplus from a compound's trees. The main fruits to be found in the market are oranges, mangoes, bananas and limes. Mangoes are usually available in most markets from April until August, but are most abundant and cheap in May and June, with oranges in good supply from November to February. During these periods the urban and coastal markets are inundated with them. Individual producers transport surplus mangoes and oranges to neighbouring markets, such as Brikama and Serrekunda, usually by taxi. The fruit is generally sold by the sack or basket, to a consortium of two or more small traders. These traders divide the sack and then hawk the fruit either in the market or around the streets. The street activity is usually undertaken by young children who carry the fruit in bowls on their heads. Fruit, especially oranges, is sold individually to thirsty customers, who eat the fruit immediately, and is also often sold from tables at busy points by the roadside. These are usually at ferry crossings, such as the Barra-Banjul ferry terminals or near taxi parks. These vendors pay no rent and are often moved on by the police for causing an obstruction.

Unlike most vegetables, oranges, mangoes, limes and some other fruits are often transported from the coastal areas of surplus to the deficit inland regions. The fruit is transported in sacks, mainly by lorry but also occasionally on the <u>Lady Chilel</u> river boat. However, supplies are irregular and consignments are sold quickly. This trade is undertaken by rural businessmen, who travel down to the coast irregularly to buy supplies. These

Table 9:1

Production of fruit in The Gambia, 1979/80

Crop	Local unit	Normal weight of unit	Production in units	Production in kilos	Value per unit	Value per kg	Total value
		kg		kg	D	D	D
Mango	50 kg bag	45	197,331	8,879,895	5.16	0.11	1,020,201
Orange	50 kg bag	38	111,565	4,239,470	10.75	0.28	1,200,438
Lime	small basket	5	5,808	29,040	5.06	1.12	32,524
Banana	bunches	?	33,865	?	?	?	245,525

Source: Adapted from a personal communication, Mr. M. Gibril, 1981

196

traders transport them back to the market and then sell off individual sacks to other smaller traders within the market, who in turn retail the fruit.

One exception to this coastal-inland flow of fruit is the lorry traffic from Guinea Conakry, Guinea Bissau, and Sierra Leone, which supplies the market at Basse with coconuts, pineapples and oranges. This trade was discussed in Chapter Five. It must be noted here that there are signs that some of the markets near Basse are being supplied with fruit from this lorry trade. At least one trader, interviewed in Farafenni Luma, makes the journey every week from Basse, usually with a sack of fruit purchased from the lorries. He reported that he also regularly visited Bansang market to sell fruit.

In general the supply of fruit to the rural markets is small. In all the rural markets where surveys were undertaken, only six per cent of all the vendors interviewed were selling fruit. In the urban markets of Banjul and Serrekunda, the number rose to eight per cent. This contrasts significantly with the percentage of vendors selling vegetables. In the rural markets, the average number of sellers offering horticultural produce for sale was on average 22 per cent and in the urban markets the percentage was as high as 39 per cent. In fact, in five markets, over a quarter of the traders interviewed were selling vegetables; Banjul (33 per cent), Serrekunda (38 per cent), Bakau (42 per cent), Brikama (27 per cent) and Basse (32 per cent). In no market did the percentage of vendors selling fruit exceed 12 per cent. These statistics indicate the relative unimportance of fruit in the Gambian diet, in comparison to vegetables, and indicates the limited nature of the market for fruit, unless demand in the rural areas can be stimulated.

Vegetables

A wide variety of vegetables are eaten in The Gambia, including leaf, root and fruit vegetables. Leaf vegetables are gathered mainly from the bush; their availability is restricted to the rainy season, and they are therefore most commonly eaten from June to October. Of the other vegetables eaten, tropical vegetables, including tomatoes (Solanum incanum Linn.), hot peppers (Capsicum frutescens Linn.) and Okra (Hibiscus esculentus Linn.) are produced mainly in the wet season, with the production of exotic vegetables being restricted to the dry season. This is partly due to physiological reasons, such as temperature and humidity conditions, and partly because of the lower incidence of pests and diseases.

Of the leaf vegetables eaten, red sorrel or sour leaves (Hibiscus sabdariffa Linn.) are the most favoured. These leaves are used fresh in groundnut sauces and leaf stews, they have a sour taste and go viscous when cooked. Bush green (Amaranthus

<u>candatus</u> Linn.) are also commonly used, and taste like spinach beet (<u>Beta vulgaris</u>) but are used only in palm oil sauces. These plants are sometimes cultivated, particularly near large centres of population, in watered vegetable gardens, which means they are available in the markets throughout the year. More commonly in the more remote rural areas, however, they are harvested from the bush during the rainy season only.

Root vegetables such as cassava (<u>Manihot utilissima</u> Pohl.), and yams are eaten in small quantities, more especially near the coast, and are useful in that they are available during the rainy season before the cereal crops are harvested. They are not a major constituent of the Gambian diet, as they are in other parts of West Africa. The most widespread root vegetable available is cassava. Both the root and leaves are consumed. The root is peeled and boiled with salt, or pounded and made into cassava porridge. It may also be dried, peeled, split and stored. When needed it is pounded into flour and steamed or boiled. The sweet potato (<u>Ipomoea batatas</u> Polr.) is eaten mainly at the coast. Again both roots and leaves are used, the root being boiled and eaten with Jolof rice or groundnut sauce. Yams are rarely eaten except in times of scarcity when both the aerial and underground tubers of the potato yam (<u>Dioscorea bulbifera</u> Lingr.) are gathered from the bush. The coco yam (<u>Colocasia esculentum</u> Schott.) is grown only by the Fula people in Upper River Division, where it is eaten both fried and boiled.

Fruit vegetables are usually planted by women in vegetable gardens near the house. These include bitter tomatoes (<u>Solanium incanum</u> Linn.), onions, tomatoes, aubergines (<u>Solanum melongena</u> Linn.) and okra, and are more frequently eaten during the dry season. The bitter tomato is a common vegetable, and the fruits resemble immature tomatoes. They are green, white or red in colour and have a very bitter flavour that complements the blandness of groundnut sauce. Okra is used to give food a glutinous texture. They are harvested before they become stringy and are sliced and boiled in sauces such as okra soup and palm oil stew. The local tomatoes are cherry sized, and are cultivated in irrigated vegetable gardens, but do not grow well in the rainy season. They first ripen in November and December and are available only at this time in some remote areas, though elsewhere they may be available until March. They are used in nearly every soup. When fresh tomatoes are not available, tomato paste is used.

Fruit vegetables are the most commonly cultivated vegetables in The Gambia, and production usually takes place in low lying areas, where water is available either from shallow wells or from streams. The bulk of production is from communal groups, many of which were originally established in the early 1970s for the primary purpose of producing onions. For the reasons discussed below (particularly the problem of marketing) many women no longer cultivate onions, but have opted to grow other vegetables. Currently there are a number of small vegetable farms around major settlements in the provinces, but most are concentrated in the Kombo region, where the climate and soil is more suitable. The major centres of production are Bakau, Brikama and Sukuta, where farmers (mostly women) have taken up vegetable gardening activities with assistance from the Department of Agriculture and other agencies. It is difficult to assess how well these farms are doing as no factual information is available. Following the implementation of the onion growing scheme in 1972, it was claimed by the government that some success had been achieved in various parts of the country. Production in 1977/78 was estimated at 300 metric tons. In the same year, however, official imports of onions, mainly from The Netherlands, had reached a record high of 310 metric tons (Table 9:3). This suggests that the onion growing scheme may not be progressing as well as expected. This scheme and its implications for planning policy are discussed later.

Production figures of the various vegetables are unknown, particularly as many households supply their own needs before marketing surpluses, and others collect vegetables from the bush. But in 1979/80 the Central Statistics Department carried out a survey, with results shown in Table 9:2. From this it can be seen that the production of tomatoes, aubergines, green leaves and peppers are significant, both in quantity and value. It is interesting to note that the value of the onions produced in this season was the lowest of all the vegetables surveyed, despite a seven year old scheme to try to raise yields.

The consumption of vegetables in The Gambia is also an unknown factor, but an estimation can be put forward. In assessing vegetable consumption two types of consumer can be distinguished, namely the tourist and the urban consumer; most rural families are self-sufficient. In December 1978, one tourist hotel with 165 beds consumed 1,089 kg of vegetables. The breakdown of this total is shown in Table 9:4 and indicates the importance of onions and tomatoes (accounting for 52 per cent of vegetables consumed) in the tourist diet. If we assume that the occupancy rate in the hotel is 64 per cent (an average based on the period 1973/4 to 1977/8) it is possible to arrive at a rough figure for the consumption of each vegetable per guest night. If this is multiplied by the number of guest nights spent in The Gambia, a rough idea can be obtained of the amount of vegetables consumed by tourists. During the period 1973/4 to 1977/8 an average of well over 18,000 tourists came to The Gambia and it was recently predicted that the number of tourists by 1985/6 would reach 45,000, although recent statistics show that there has been a decline since 1978. The tourist figures for the period 1978/9 to 1981/2 are shown in Table 9:5.

Table 9:2
The production of vegetables in The Gambia, 1979/80

	Local units	Normal weight of unit	Production in units	Production in kilos	Cost per kg	Cost per unit	Total value
		kg		kg	D	D	D
Tomato	Big basket	20	69,325	1,386,500	0.63	12.75	883,900
Bitter tomato	Big basket	20	13,876	277,520	0.65	13.00	180,388
Onions	Bag	29	7,050	204,450	0.73	21.31	150,236
Okra	Small basket	6	12,656	75,936	1.98	11.88	150,353
Pepper	Big basket	6	7,458	44,748	8.33	50.00	372,900
Aubergines	Big basket	13	33,764	438,932	0.76	10.00	337,640
Green leaves	Basket	10	22,691	226,910	0.92	9.24	209,665

Source: Personal communication, Mr. Gibril (Central Statistics Department), 1981

Table 9:3
Imports of vegetables into The Gambia, 1972/73 to 1977/78*

	Onions and garlic		Tomatoes		Other fresh vegetables	
	Quantity metric tons	Value D	Quantity metric tons	Value D	Quantity metric tons	Value D
1972/73	136.3	42,071	0.05	49	1.1	2,600
1973/74	110.2	42,917	15.08	30,115	3.3	8,359
1974/75	98.3	33,404	4.5	1,784	0.5	3,440
1975/76	66.9	33,736	1.9	3,772	7.1	5,143
1976/77	5.4	5,693	-	-	5.1	16,342
1977/78	310.0	325,010	0.2	690	1.2	3,967

Source: Central Statistics Department, Banjul, 1979

* not including illegal imports across the land frontier with Senegal

Table 9:4
Vegetable consumption in Hotel 'X' in December, 1978

Type of vegetable	Consumption (kg) December 1978	Consumption (kg) Per guest night
Onions	300	0.09
Tomatoes	266	0.08
Pumpkin	30	0.01
Lettuce	213	0.06
Cucumber	104	0.03
Melon	176	0.05
TOTAL	1089	0.32

Source: Gebre-Mariam, 1979

Table 9:5
The number of tourists visiting The Gambia, (Year Ends in April)

1974/75	21,586
1975/76	25,287
1976/77	22,888
1977/78	19,657
1978/79	29,572
1979/80	25,391
1980/81	21,347
1981/82	21,300

Source: Standard and Chartered Review and Annual Reports of
         Central Bank of The Gambia

Tourist consumption of vegetables is therefore quite substantial,
particularly tomatoes and onions. Fortunately tourist demand
coincides with the dry season (November until April) when there
are plentiful supplies of vegetables.

The estimation of vegetable consumption by urban consumers,
other than tourists, is also difficult. The only data available
is from the Household Expenditure Survey of Banjul which was
conducted in 1968/9. According to this survey, households in
Banjul made an average expenditure of D 87.30 in 1968/9 on five
types of vegetables, with onions accounting for 52 per cent of the
total expenditure made. The figures are shown in Table 9:6.
Incomes have, however, lagged far behind prices. During the 1960s
the economy grew at an average annual rate of four and a half per
cent, well above population growth of two point six per cent. Per
capita incomes reached an all time high of US$260 in 1967/8 (at
1976/7 prices) as good growth in the output of groundnuts was
accompanied by increases in processing and growth in some import
substitution industries. However, between 1969 and 1977 severe
droughts affected groundnut production and dampened overall
economic performance – annual growth was a mere one and a half per
cent on average and per capita GDP dropped to US$200 in 1977. The
average standard of living seems to have declined to about the
same level in 1977 as in 1961. It may be assumed then that under
such conditions vegetable consumption will have at best remained
stable, but will probably have declined (due to the rise in urban
populations). In 1974, the consumer price index was initiated,
and by September 1980 had risen 118 per cent from its 1974 base.
The category 'fruit and vegetables' (shown on Figure 9:1) also

experienced an increase, with the price of onions more than doubling.

Table 9:6
Reported expenditure on and estimated quantity of vegetables bought by the 'average' household in Banjul, 1968/9

Type of vegetable	Reported expenditure	Estimated quantity that could have been bought
	Dalasi	Kilograms
Onions	45.19	125.6
Tomatoes	25.63	23.2
Pumpkins	8.84	13.2
Lettuce	7.15	7.6
Cucumber	0.49	0.6
TOTAL	87.30	170.2

Source: Gebre-Mariam, 1979

Combining tourist demand with urban consumption of vegetables, it is possible to get some idea of the demand for vegetables in The Gambia, although actual figures are impossible to produce. Demand is significant, with onions, tomatoes, pumpkins and lettuce being consumed in the most quantities.

Because the supply of vegetables is highly seasonal, demand cannot always be supplied domestically and vegetables have to be imported. The quantity and the value of imported fresh vegetables are shown on Table 9:3. This table shows that 311.4 metric tons of fresh vegetables were imported into The Gambia in 1977/78, of which 310 metric tons were onions and garlic. Imports supplied 19.3 per cent of the total consumption of onions in the Banjul-Kombo St. Mary region in that year. This is quite an import bill. For the period 1972/3 to 1977/8, the average value of imported fresh vegetables was D 93,182 at current prices. This bill could be avoided (and the foreign exchange spent on capital equipment for agricultural projects, such as irrigation pumps) if more research was done on the production of vegetables under Gambian conditions, with the investigation of possible irrigation projects to even out the supply of vegetables throughout the year. A further improvement in the situation would be the provision of better and more storage facilities, along with an improved marketing system, so that areas of surplus vegetable production can easily and quickly supply deficit areas. The example of the

'Collective Onion Growing Scheme' of the 1970s, which will be discussed below, demonstrates this.

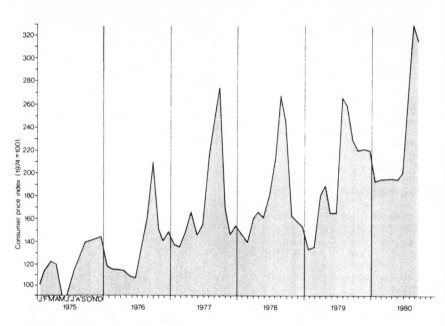

Figure 9:1   Consumer price index of 'fruit and vegetable' category
Source: Central Statistics

The 'Collective Onion Growing Schemes'

As we have seen, onions are an important constituent of The Gambian diet. Being the major vegetable ingredient in all sauces, it is not surprising that over 50 per cent of money spent on vegetables buys onions. The traditionally grown local variety is known as <u>Mandingo jabo</u>, and is small and similar to garlic. Introduced varieties are also grown, but yields are low. In order to meet demand, onions from The Netherlands have had to be imported. In an effort to try to phase out these imports, onion demonstration schemes were started in 1971/2 at Gunjur and Njougou, and in 1972/3 a further eighteen schemes were established all over the country with a total membership of 903 farmers. By 1977/8 the number of farmers participating in the schemes had reached over 4,000.

The system of production used on these schemes is based on a collective effort by a group of farmers (mainly women from one village) which establishes and cultivates a vegetable garden. This group, led by an elected president, applies to be recognised as a 'Collective Onion Growing Scheme' and become eligible for government assistance. This includes the provision of inputs, advice from the extension service and marketing support.

The scheme was not initially well planned, and the first season was disastrous, as no ready market was available for this first crop. The local trade had not been informed about the scheme and importation had not been restricted. As a result, farmers could not sell their produce. In order not to discourage the participants in the scheme, the government had to step in as an emergency buyer. The producer price offered by the government was D 7.50 per 25 kg bag. Altogether 4,008 bags were bought, unfortunately field grading was not carefully done and the major part of the produce was of short keeping quality. This resulted in heavy losses. Of the total amount purchased, 1,827 bags were sold locally, 1,001 were exported to the UK and 1,180 bags rotted in storage. The UK export returns did not even cover the freight charges as the produce arrived in a deplorable condition. [2] The net loss suffered by The Gambian government was D 16,252.

The situation was as bad in the 1973/4 season. Once again the government guaranteed to buy the crop through the Cooperative Union at a fixed price of D 7.50. A total of 6,196 bags were purchased. Unfortunately subsequent marketing resulted in heavy losses. Only 750 bags could be sold for D 5.75 cash and 335 bags for D 6.00 on credit. The remaining 5,111 bags were left to rot. After these two disastrous marketing seasons the government requested the help of an FAO Regional Marketing Adviser, and improvements in the marketing of the 1974/5 crop are due to his advice.

Once again in the 1974/5 season the producer price was fixed at D 7.50. But it was decided to build open sided thatched roof onion stores in all divisions, near the main roads. A card-cum-number system was successfully introduced to facilitate the buying operation. Cards were distributed to scheme members one to two days before the actual buying took place. Buying of the crop and disbursing of the cash was then carried out in numerical order to facilitate record keeping and to avoid confusion. In general the system worked very satisfactorily but substantial time had to be spent on field grading, due to the poor quality of the crop. Crops which were below standard were returned to the respective farmer for her own consumption. Altogether 1,824 bags were bought. The divisional onion stores were designed to store onions for a period of up to two months, under dry weather conditions, thereby allowing additional drying and also to ease the transport situation, as evacuation of the crop could be spread over the whole period. However, by the time the rains arrived in July

1975, onions were still in the divisional stores. The rising humidity and direct exposure to rain accelerated the rotting of the onions, and over five tons of onions were lost.

Lessons were learned, and in the 1975/6 season all seeds and fertiliser were distributed in October. Only 'Golden Creole' seed was given out to assure uniform variety production in all official schemes. The producer price was also fixed well in advance, at D 9.00. But the quality of the crop was very low and only 2,500 bags were bought. This was due to a lack of field supervision, which resulted in late transplanting in many schemes, irregular irrigation, field drying was not properly carried out, and the leaves were not left to dry off, but were cut off at an early stage, therefore damaging the bulbs and causing early rotting.

In 1976/7, the schemes were still quite a heavy liability to the government and it was decided to reduce the government's direct involvement, by promoting the direct sale of onions from the schemes to local traders on a country-wide basis. This proved much more successful. Practically all onion scheme members in Western Division sold their produce to traders, [3] with 51 per cent going into Banjul market, 24 per cent into Serrekunda market, and the remainder to the markets in Brikama and Bakau. In North Bank Division, 89 per cent of onion production was sold to traders, with once again the majority of the produce going into Banjul market (55 per cent). Twenty-four per cent was sold to traders from Farafenni market and 16 per cent crossed the border. The balance was sold in the production area. In Lower River Division, 86 per cent was sold to traders, with 43 per cent to Basse market, 32 per cent to Banjul, 10 per cent to Farafenni and smaller quantities being sold in Kaur and Brikama. In Upper River Division and MacCarthy Island Division, over 27 per cent (by far the highest percentage in the country) was sold by the producer directly to the consumer. The majority of the produce (54 per cent) went to Basse market, 18 per cent to Bansang, with the balance mainly sold in the Kantora and Kaur areas.

Summarising, it can be said that out of the 12,739 bags of onions produced for marketing in the 1976/7 season, the bulk was sold in Banjul market, closely followed by Basse. Substantial quantities also found their way into Farafenni and Serrekunda markets. Table 9:7 shows the actual destination of the 1976/7 crop.

Looking back at the marketing problems in the initial stage, it is not surprising that heavy losses resulted. The main reasons for these difficulties were inadequate marketing arrangements, the selection of an unsuitable variety of seed, and the purchase of onions from the farmer without any prior quality control. After 1975, new marketing arrangements were introduced which centred on an integrated system of field purchasing and grading arrangements, combined with the improvement of marketing facilities and

streamlining of the whole operation. Some of these problems are
still not adequately solved and onions are still being imported
from The Netherlands, particularly in the four months before the
local onion harvest. This is due principally to the poor storing
quality of the local onions and inadequate storage facilities.

Table 9:7
Markets in which 1976/7 onion crop was sold

Market	% of total
Banjul	34.2
Basse	27.1
Farafenni	8.4
Serrekunda	5.5
Senegal	3.7
Area of production	21.1
TOTAL	100.0

Source: Adapted from Trupke, 1977

This example shows just how difficult the marketing of
vegetables in The Gambia can be, with no centralised marketing
agency, inadequate storage facilities and little information on
prices and areas of demand and supply. The scheme has had some
benefits, despite its problems. The domestic production of onions
has increased supplies throughout the country, which in turn has
reduced the retail price in the marketplace vis-a-vis imported
onions. This has brought onions, that have a high nutritional
value, within the reach of the lower income groups in both rural
and urban areas. Secondly, the scheme has demonstrated to farmers
the benefits of vegetable production and has familiarised them
with dry season production techniques, enabling them to cultivate
other dry season vegetables. Thirdly, the export trial has
generated the awareness that The Gambia is potentially a good
producer for horticultural export crops.

Perhaps with the marketing problems of the onion scheme
(particularly export prospects) in mind, the Gambian government
requested that a team be sent from the Tropical Products Institute
in London, to undertake a design study for a 'Horticultural
Produce Centre' and to assess its profitability. The mission was
also asked to consider the possible incorporation of lime
processing within the complex. The mission arrived in The Gambia
in 1975. The mission came to the conclusion that the potential

207

domestic market for fresh horticultural produce, including the tourist trade, by the year 1985 would be too small to justify the building of a large complex, and it was suggested that the possibility of building a smaller complex be investigated. The report came to the conclusion that the following cold stores would be required for fresh vegetables:

1) Two onion stores. a) 60 metric tons capacity for long term storage to meet tourist demand.

b) 200 metric tons, to meet local/ supermarket demand.

2) Two stores each of 15 metric tons capacity, to handle other vegetables. (Two because of the different storage temperatures required by various vegetables).

They also suggested that provision should be made for a 50 metric ton capacity cold store for the storing of chillies, pending their export. This could alternatively be used for onions in the late 1980s. The mission concluded that it would not be advisable to include tomato canning in the complex for three reasons:

a) that an adequate supply of tomatoes suitable for processing might not be available at a price which would make the product competitive with the imported product.
b) yields of tomatoes are low.
c) inputs, such as cans, which have to be imported, are expensive. [4]

It was decided that the canning of mango products would be uneconomic if not undertaken as part of a general operation, to include tomato canning. The processing of limes into oil and single strength juice was also deemed to be unprofitable by the mission, due to the very high cost of transporting empty drums to The Gambia, and full drums to UK. The mission came to the basic conclusion that the prospects for exporting horticultural products from The Gambia were small, and that supplying the domestic market, including the tourist sector, should be the government's main priority.

Since 1975 the government has done very little to encourage horticultural production, and the suggested construction of storage facilities is still only a dream. Imports remain high. Even a chain of supply from producers to hotels has not been established and most hotel still import their vegetable requirements, to ensure reliable supplies. The producer, then, still has no option other than personally to take her surplus produce, to the local market for sale.

Vegetable marketing

There are no government organised or controlled means of marketing vegetables in The Gambia, apart from onions grown on the

Collective Onion Growing Scheme, as discussed above, In most cases, it is the grower herself who brings the produce to the market. As far as could be ascertained, there are no farmgate sales or middlemen involved in the trade (except for cassava, see below).

In the provinces, most producers sell in their local market, generally a journey of no more than five miles from home. Most women headload their produce to market, with some occasionally hiring a donkey cart. In Basse market, for example, a large proportion of the horticultural produce for sale was grown in Damfa Kunda, Alohungari and Chamoi, all within a radius of 6 km. However, as one moves westwards, hinterlands become larger. Brikama received vegetable supplies from Sanyang, Basori, Sifoe and Pirang, within a 14 km radius of the market. Bakau is supplied from a radius of 20 km which includes the villages of Sukuta, Lamin and Yundum. Of course, the urban hinterlands are larger, with vegetables entering Banjul market from places up to 40 kilometres away. This means that producers in the Kombo region do not necessarily trade in their local market; many travel by taxi or bus to the urban markets of Banjul and Serrekunda. This trade was discussed in Chapter Five.

There is hardly any interregional trade in vegetables, apart from onions. The marketing of vegetables is unorganised and seemingly chaotic and in virtually all cases it is the producer herself that brings the vegetables to market. There is, however, one exception, the case of cassava. Tubers play only a small role in the local diet and only limited amounts of cassava are grown, and only as a backyard crop, in the area to the west of Brikama. It is usually planted as a pure stand in small fields, and is useful as a hungry season crop because it is available during the rainy season before the cereal crops are harvested. In general it is not harvested by the producer, but is sold unharvested in the field. The trader that buys the crop will then employ labourers to harvest the crop when he needs it. The sacks of cassava are then taken either to Banjul or Serrekunda markets by lorry, where they are sold by the sack to retail traders. This type of transaction was common practice in the villages of Sanyang, Brufut and N'Yoffelleh in 1979/80 and also occurred at Sifoe, Jambur, Sukuta and Brikama. This method of marketing is attractive to the producer as it eases his labour demands, and means that his other crops do not suffer from neglect at this busy time. In 1973 the Department of Agriculture began a campaign to increase the acreage under cassava, but the total area under the crop remains at less than 800 ha. This, it is suggested by Dunsmore (1976), is due to the limited market for the crop within The Gambia — cassava was only found to be on sale in six markets: Banjul, Serrekunda, Bakau, Brikama, Georgetown and Basse.

Cassava and onions are amongst the least perishable vegetables and as such can be stored for limited periods of time and are not easily damaged during transportation, but other vegetables do not have these advantages. In many instances, vegetable produce is already spoiled upon arrival at the market. In the majority of cases this is due to careless handling by the farmer, with the lack of proper display space and facilities within the market aggravating the situation. Due to the lack of adequate storage facilities, perishable produce deteriorates quickly under Gambian climatic conditions, and therefore the sale of the remaining produce on the following day is often impossible. It is estimated that during these peak periods of supply, waste can be as high as 40-50 per cent for the highly perishable commodities such as lettuce, tomatoes and aubergines, and within the range of 30 per cent for less perishable goods such as sweet potatoes, cassava and onions. During the off-season, perishable vegetables for local consumption (mainly Irish potatoes and onions) are imported into the country; for these commodities, losses are considerably lower and are estimated to be in the range of ten per cent during the marketing process.

As well as experiencing large losses, the vegetable seller also faces the problem of large fluctuations in price. There are no price controls for vegetables in The Gambia, and prices respond to demand and supply. The consumer price index for the category 'fruit and vegetables' is plotted on Figure 9:1. From this it can be seen that fruit and vegetables are cheapest in the dry season and are at their most expensive from July to September, the peak agricultural season. This is because vegetable gardening is not a major activity for the farming household. Most attention is given to the production of groundnuts and rice, and in general women turn to the task of gardening only after they are through with their major activity of rice harvesting. As a result, there are delays in planting vegetables and shortages occur.

Monthly price data is available for bitter tomatoes and aubergines. The figures show that the price charged for bitter tomatoes in Banjul market varies in 1978 from a low of D 0.47 in November to a high of D 1.26 in August (per 500 gram), in 1979 the lowest price was recorded in January (D 0.51) and the highest in July (D 1.64), and by August 1980 had reached an all time high of D 2.29. In other markets the seasonal difference in price was just as marked. In Farafenni the variation in price in 1978 was D 0.97 and in 1978 was D 0.93. In Basse market the fluctuations in price for bitter tomatoes were D 0.54 in 1978 and D 1.55 in 1979. The annual price variation for aubergines are smaller. In 1978 the price for aubergines in Banjul market varied from D 0.33 (per 500 gm) in December to D 0.55 in July and August, and in 1979 from D 0.35 in January to D 0.61 in May, reaching a record high of D 0.96 in August 1980. In Farafenni market, price fluctuations were recorded as D 0.42 in 1978 and D 0.62 in 1979. In Basse market the variations in price in the two years were D 0.38 and D 0.43 respectively. It can thus be seen that in the dry season vegetables are very cheap and are virtually given away, and the

210

'lots' of vegetables offered for a fixed price are large, whilst in the off-season, the 'lots' are very small.

It may be because of seasonal price variations that most vegetable sellers supplement their income by selling more than one item, usually vending condiments, spices and dried fish in addition to their home produced vegetables. Of all the vendors interviewed in the urban markets, 55 per cent were displaying for sale two or more food items, with 14 per cent offering six or more items. In the rural markets the percentage is higher, with 64 per cent offering two or more items for sale, and 24 per cent selling six or more. In six of the markets where surveys were undertaken, over a quarter of the sellers interviewed were selling a combination of vegetables, condiments and dried fish. The highest number was found in Kaur market, where nearly half (44 per cent) of the traders were selling these items; Central Sabigi (38 per cent), Sukuta (36 per cent), and Kuntaur (32 per cent) markets the percentage was over 30 per cent with the markets at Gunjur (27 per cent) and Kerewan (26 per cent) following close behind. This perhaps indicates the insecurity of the vegetable seller, particularly in the rural markets where, to try to cushion themselves against fluctuating prices, these traders have had to broaden their economic base.

Cooking oils

The other major constituent of the Gambian diet, which has not so far been discussed, are the cooking oils - both groundnut and palm oil - which are the basis of all cuisine. The groundnut is not only the chief cash crop of the country, but is also an important item of food. It provides not only oil, but a paste (peanut butter), which is used in many sauces. All the groundnut oil that is consumed is industrially refined either by the GPMB oil mill at Denton Bridge, or across the border in Senegal. For health reasons this is the best oil to use, as the toxin levels in the groundnuts are carefully measured in the refinery, and any oils with excessive toxin levels are destroyed. Groundnut paste, on the other hand, is all produced in the compound - there are as yet no plans to produce it industrially. The paste is produced by pounding (in a pestle and mortar) freshly roasted groundnuts, until a smooth paste has been formed. The groundnut butter is then transferred to a basin and covered until it is needed. In all markets and at all times of the year, groundnut paste was available, being sold by women in lots about the size of tennis balls.

The Gambia is on the northern limit of the oil palm belt, and it grows wild in the coastal regions, and it is here that palm oil is produced and is abundant. Palm oil from the coastal region is eaten in all parts of the country. The oil palm (Elaeis guineensis Jacq.) is a typical palm, with long fronds. The tree

211

is cultivated by the Manjago and Jola ethnic groups for its wine, which is tapped from the terminal bud vase; and for its oil, which is extracted from both the fruit and its kernel. Palm oil is made in the compound, usually using the oil palm fruit – the kernels are generally sold for commercial extraction. The orange fruit is boiled for about an hour. The fruits are then removed and pounded in a mortar until the flesh is separated from the nuts. The flesh is then reboiled and used for palm fruit sauce, and the orange oil that rises to the top is skimmed off and stored for home consumption or sale. To extract the kernel oil, the kernels are pounded to release the seeds, which are then themselves pounded. Water is added and the mixture is left to stand overnight. This is repounded the next day and kneaded in water. If left, the oil rises to the surface and can be skimmed off. Palm oil which is orange on colour, is particularly rich in carotene and the principle fats are olein and palmitin, which are particualrly resistant to rancidity. It can therefore be kept for long periods without spoiling. Palm oil is well liked in The Gambia and is used in many dishes. Most palm oil production takes place between February and August, when the fruits are ready, but due to its keeping qualities, palm oil is found in all markets at all times of the year.

Marketing of cooking oils

The marketing of the GPMB refined groundnut oil, is undertaken by the NTC. The GPMB sells bottled groundnut oil to the NTC who are the sole distributors, utilising their nationwide network of retail stores to supply the public. Consumers and traders alike can buy the oil from the NTC. This groundnut oil is rarely seen for sale in the market, but is found in small retail stores. However, in 1979/80, Senegalese refined groundnut oil, bottled under the label Niani, was found to be in every market and most retail stores. This was due to high toxin levels in the Gambian oil, which meant that domestic supplies were inadequate. Most of this Senegalese oil was brought by lorry from across the border by wealthy Lebanese businessmen, who distributed supplies through Lebanese retail outlets. In the rural areas, some traders did cross the border to buy a few cartons of oil, but their access to ready capital is limited – a problem that faces most market traders.

In order for a trader to deal in palm oil, he must have enough capital to buy and transport a 45 gallon (204.5 litre) drum of oil from the coastal producing areas to his place of business. This is costly and may mean that the capital is tied up for many months. For this reason the number of traders dealing in palm oil is low, the average in the urban markets is five per cent, dropping to four per cent in the rural markets. In some markets, for example Central Sabigi and Kerewan, no palm oil at all was found. Most palm oil sellers were men, who had been given the initial capital by relatives, usually brothers or uncles. The few women trading in palm oil said that their husbands had given them their first drum of oil and they had continued from there.

Palm oil is sold by volume, usually a cigarette tin full with the customer bringing her own bottle or container to put it in. Many sellers just bring a bucket of oil each day to market, leaving the drum in the safety of the compound. In other markets, where security is good, the trader may leave the drum permanently in the market, although this was found to be the case only in one market - Basse. It is only in the coastal markets west of Brikama, that the producer will market her own oil.

The production and marketing of groundnut paste requires less capital, and is a function performed only by women. Most of the women producing groundnut paste purchase the groundnuts necessary for the next day's trade in the market in the late afternoon. The groundnuts are roasted and pounded in the compound the same evening, ready for sale the following morning. In no case did the men of the compound give or sell part of their groundnut crop to the women.

In Gambian society, men and women's money is separate, any money made by an individual on the sale of their Kamanyago crop belongs to that individual; similarly with trading. However, when asked, many women market vendors did say that part of their day's takings would be used to buy vegetables or palm oil, to supplement and add variety to the household's diet. [5] So, for many women, marketing is regarded as a form of bartering one good for another, with money as an intermediary to enable this transaction to take place, and not as a means of making monetary profit. [6] In this sense, then, the fruit, vegetables and groundnut paste marketing sector has changed very little over the last few centuries.

Conclusion

The poor performance of the Collective Onion Growing Scheme has demonstrated the importance of the marketing network and the need to improve it, if fruit and vegetable production is to be increased, and deficit areas are to be adequately supplied. In the coastal areas, where transportation is generally good the marketing of these foodcrops is satisfactory but not ideal. In the more remote parts of the country, however, this sector of the economy has changed very little since the first European travellers visited the river in the fifteenth century. Cadamosto's account of a market held in a field outside present day Kaur in 1455-6, could be used today to describe many modern rural markets. Even the goods offered for sale are the same.

Men and women came to it from the neighbourhood country within a distance of four or five miles, for those who dwelt farther off attended other markets. In this market I perceive quite clearly that these people are exceedingly poor, judging from the wares they brought for sale - that is, cotton, but not in large quantities, cotton thread and cloth, vegetables, oil and millet, wooden bowls, palm leaf mats, and all other articles they use in their daily life. (Cadamosto 1937, pp.48-9)

Despite proposals by the Tropical Products Institute and the resident FAO marketing adviser in The Gambia for the expansion and improvement of the urban markets and the following government statement contained in the 1975/80 Five Year Development Plan, nothing had been done.

The Government will (also) affect commercial development more directly by assisting in the provision of necessary storage wholesale and retail facilities . . . it is foreseen that a wholesale centre will be constructed outside Banjul in 1978/9 and the public market facilities in Farafenni and Basse will be expanded and improved in 1977/8. A national wholesale centre for imported and domestic goods is a pre-requisite to an increase in the efficiency of, and the local participation in, the trade of the nation. (Gambian Government 1976)

The government appears to be aware of the problems but has done nothing to alleviate them, and none of the above proposals have been put into action. The marketing of fruit, vegetables and cooking oils is therefore the most unorganised, least financed and under researched sector of the marketing network.

Notes

[1] For the sake of convenience, in this chapter, tomatoes are classified as a vegetable.

[2] A drum of groundnut oil leaked and contaminated many of the onions, which had to be jettisoned.

[3] The balance was either consumed by the producing household, or was sold in the local market by the producer herself.

[4] This had already been tried in 1947, when the colonial government built a small tomato puree factory. It was closed down after a year as it cost £2,000 to run the factory and produce 10 tons of puree which could only be sold for £1,000. (BA 2/3285, 1947)

[5] Yoon (1983) found the same in Casamance, Senegal. "Women do not generally spend money on luxury goods or cattle, but on food, clothing, housing and education" (p.150).

[6] Marx (1977) "Money functions as a means of circulation only because in it the values of commodities have independent reality. Hence its movement as the medium of circulation is, in fact, merely the movement of commodities while changing their forms" (p.117).

10   Conclusion

Gambian marketplaces have not been studied before, perhaps because the principal article of trade, groundnuts, is marketed through other channels.   The author was therefore working in unexplored territory, which necessitated: an exhaustive search through the archives held both in Banjul and London; thorough reading of early European travel accounts; and a twelve-month investigation of marketplace activity in The Gambia.   During the field work, which began in September 1979 and finished in October 1980, surveys were undertaken in sixteen markets in all parts of the country.   It is the information collected from these varied sources that forms the basis of this study and from which the following general conclusions about the traditional marketing network for foodstuffs in The Gambia will be drawn.

During the colonial period, it was strongly believed that marketplaces were a new phenomenon brought to the region by the European colonisers.   Even eminent scholars such as Ames, an anthropological specialist on the country, subscribed to this view.   The author's research has shown that this is not the case. Both long distance trade and local exchange were important in the region long before the first Europeans arrived on the coast. Cadamosto, Pereira, Donhela and Jobson, all visitors to the River Gambia in the fifteenth and sixteenth centuries, describe flourishing markets in the area.   From the evidence presented, it can be said that two market networks existed in the region in the early contact period: firstly, the local subsistence-oriented marketing network, which supplied local people with their everyday needs; and secondly, similar markets that had been temporarily given added economic importance by the stimulus of long distance trade. These marketplaces were periodic and regionally restricted to up-river locations associated with the interior, trans-Sudanic salt trade.

With the growth of the slave trade in the eighteenth century, and the disruption to the region in the second half of the nineteenth century caused by the outbreak of the Sonike-Marabout wars, these markets disappeared, not to be re-established until colonial pacification of the river at the beginning of the twentieth century. As no written record of a Gambian marketplace appears to have survived from these two centuries, the problem is whether there were functioning marketplaces during this period which went unrecorded, or did they temporarily disappear, trade and exchange being effected through other mechanisms? Evidence is scant, but it is hypothesised in this study that marketplaces did in fact disappear, but that exchange continued through other mechanisms. What these 'other mechanisms' were is unclear.

In the twentieth century, marketplaces re-emerge, but now as daily (rather than periodic) institutions. They are, however, restricted to the eastern part of the country, where markets had previously been recorded. It was not until 1950 that the marketplace idea was universally accepted and markets were to be found in all parts of the country. Two components of growth have been identified, firstly, that related to increased purchasing power associated with cash-crop production, and the consequent neglect of food crop cultivation. Marketplace development associated with this component, occurred in the eastern part of the country, being connected to the capital, Bathurst, by the transportation role of the river. The spatial pattern was of a key-hole, the intervening areas having no marketplaces. It is a unique situation, and none of the existing theoretical models provides an adequate explanation of the pattern. The second component of growth, that of marketplace diffusion from the urban centre, Bathurst, is associated with improved road communications and the growing demands of the ever increasing Bathurst-Kombo St. Mary population. By 1950 the two components had joined up and by this date marketplaces covered the whole country. Of the twenty-eight markets operating in the protectorate, half were now located west of Kaur. After this date the 'system' underwent a period of adjustment, when marketplaces were relocated in reaction to such factors as the increased use of road transportation, as advocated by the independent government. The Gambian situation is therefore quite different from that described by others studying marketplace evolution, particularly Good and Bromley. None of the models provide an adequate explanation for the Gambian data. Population characteristics and transportation improvements, although influencing the system, do not appear to be the principal factors affecting the evolution of marketplaces in The Gambia. It is argued that purchasing power potentials, associated mainly with groundnut cultivation, are much more important.

The author's field research identified three types of market; rural, peri-urban and urban. In 1979, there were forty-three official markets operating within The Gambia. There were also fourteen unofficial markets. With the exception of the two Upper River Division districts of Wuli and Sandu, the whole country is served by marketplaces. However, the network cannot be regarded as a 'system', since functional connectivity only occurs in the western parts of the country, around the urban centres. Rural markets are only very loosely interconnected, each one serving a very limited cellular area of about 15 kilometre radius.

Since 1979 a new type of entirely unofficial rural market has sprung up. These are luma markets, periodic phenomena, which have extended into middle-Gambia from adjacent Senegal. They are partly supplied locally, but also receive supplies from across the border. Because of this cross-border trade, the lumas are beginning to perform a valuable wholesale function. Traders from all over The Gambia travel to them to replenish their stocks. An important element in this trade are the various cereals, particularly cous. Most of the cous for sale in the urban markets of Banjul and Serrekunda, during the author's period of fieldwork, was purchased in the lumas of Farafenni and Kaur.

As one moves westwards, towards the urban centres, market connectivity in general becomes more developed, being most advanced in the peri-urban markets. These markets differ from the strictly rural markets, in that there is a direct link between them and the urban markets - both for commodity supplies and as a wholesale outlet. The urban markets therefore contribute to the redistribution of produce from areas of plenty to those of demand within the peri-urban region. There are only two urban markets in The Gambia, sited in the largest settlements, Banjul and Serrekunda. It is here that the wholesale trade is beginning to develop. The only wholesale trade proper to be undertaken in these markets is that of imported onions and Irish potatoes. Other wholesale trade is still in its infancy. There is therefore in The Gambia a loosely connected system of markets of various categories. It is a system that is most developed in the western part of the country, with a wholesaling and bulking network beginning to develop there. However, in the centre of the country another nucleus of a connected wholesale/retail system is evolving in the form of the luma markets.

Although other channels operate, most food purchases occur in the marketplace. The supermarkets and retail stores tend only to provide imported consumer articles of a luxury nature. On the other hand, the country's chief marketing activity, the collection, grading and shipment of export groundnuts totally by-passes the traditional marketplaces, being managed entirely by the government-controlled marketing board (GPMB). All commercial activity in The Gambia is critically dependent on the expanded sale of groundnuts produced by small-scale farmers, whose degree of auto-subsistence has correspondingly diminished. With the introduction of groundnuts as a cash crop in the nineteenth century, food production began to suffer. The men began to neglect their role as providers of upland cereals, in favour of cultivating a seemingly more profitable cash crop, leaving women as the major suppliers of food for the household. This situation has continued, with groundnuts being exported in larger quantities, whilst rice is imported in increasing amounts. The Gambian case does not therefore fit the "vent-for-surplus" theory for cash crop adoption, as many commentators, such as Hogendorn, argue. Since 1974 the actual tonnage of domestically produced cereals has declined. Haswell in her study of Genieri over the period 1949 to 1973 found an increasing neglect of food crops in favour of groundnuts. A similar situation was found by Weil in his study village, Bumari.

This lack of self-sufficiency in food means that food has to be purchased in the marketplace, and helps explain why, after their brief disappearance in the eighteenth and nineteenth centuries, markets reappear as daily phenomenon and not as the periodic occurrences they had been in pre-colonial times. Not only has the groundnut affected the periodicity of the marketing system, it has also produced a marked seasonal bias in market activity. This is due to the large amounts of money that come into circulation after the groundnut crop has been sold. The government determines when the groundnut crop can be sold, by fixing the opening and closing dates of the buying season. This period, known as the 'trade season', usually stretches from December through to early March. Officially, groundnuts cannot be sold in bulk at any other time of the year. As groundnuts are the main source of cash income for the majority of the population, this period obviously necessitates relatively large payments of money. The seasonal nature of the money supply is pronounced, with a peak occurring during the trade season.

The seasonality of the money supply is reflected in merchandise sales which reach a peak in the trade season, and were one of the early incentives for the Gambian farmer to grow groundnuts as a cash crop. Figures from the United Africa Company in 1954 show that half the merchandise sales were transacted during the trade season. It is a trend that is present today. This strong seasonal element is reflected in the marketing network, with some markets opening only during the trade season whilst others, such as that at Basse, experience an expansion of the market at this time.

The strong association of marketplaces with groundnut sales is shown by the number of marketplaces sited near buying stations.

It is known that in the majority of cases, the establishment of a centre for the purchase of groundnuts, initially by the commercial trading companies, preceded the establishment of the foodstuff market. The buying stations were not, in this case, taking advantage of 'traditional' market gatherings, it was the other way round. In 1953, out of the twenty-eight markets operating, twenty were located near groundnut buying stations or in the same villages as the buying stations. Of these, seven were only open during the trade season. In 1979/80, out of the forty-three official markets operating, twenty-four were located near buying stations, with seven of these open daily during the trade season.

With independence, there has been a swing towards road transportation and, as would be expected, the location of markets shifted accordingly, from the wharftowns to the road side. This trend has been very noticeable on the north bank of the river, particularly the area between Barra and Farafenni. One good example of how the development of road transportation has affected markets, is that of Farafenni, which has thrived since the opening of the Trans-Gambian Highway in 1957.

With the development of a marketing system for the disposal of the groundnut crop that by-passes the traditional marketplace, the latter has been neglected. The marketplace system is not well integrated, and it was for this reason that the marketing of imported rice was put under the control of the GPMB in the early 1970s. The marketing and controlled price structure for rice appeared to function smoothly, although it was biased towards urban and elite consumers, however, since 1986 rice marketing has been deregulated. Much more research needs to be done on this particular topic and the contradiction between stated government policy of attaining rice self-sufficiency and the reality, which is increasing rice imports. It would appear to the author that it is against the interests of the government to raise rice prices and encourage domestic cereal production, as this would take capital and labour away from the groundnut sector.

In controlling the price of rice to the consumer, the Gambian government in effect stabilised the price of upland cereals, both geographically and seasonally. The constant price of imported rice, meant that during the months of June to October, when the upland cereals are in short supply, consumer demand shifts instead to rice, and the price of cous remains constant. The government therefore has no need to interfere in this sector of the marketing network.

Perhaps because the GPMB has been such a success in organising the efficient marketing of groundnuts, the government has tried to improve other sectors of the commercial economy, by setting up other marketing boards along similar lines. Most notable are the abortive attempts by the government to create controlled marketing facilities for meat and fish. The Livestock Marketing Board (LMB)

was set up in 1978 to guarantee supplies of meat to the urban
areas, and to encourage meat and livestock exports. It has,
however, never worked at its full potential, and after only two
years' trading it was closed down. The main reasons for the
failure of the LMB was the government's low price controls, and
its refusal to subsidise LMB operations, which meant that the
Board was working at a loss. Its ultimate collapse was therefore
inevitable. The LMB was a half-hearted attempt to interfere with
meat marketing by the government, which was really designed to
benefit only the urban consumers of meat. After the closure of
the LMB, the system quite smoothly slipped back into the pre-
marketing board traditional system. Whether government's aims
could have been better served by improving facilities in the
traditional sector, is a moot point. It could not have been less
successful nor more costly.

The Fish Marketing Corporation (FMC) was set up with the same
intention as the LMB, which was to supply the urban consumer and
exploit the lucrative export market. Inland areas, where there
are acute shortages of fish and demand is high, were not included
in planned FMC operations, and there were no plans to build cold
storage facilities and supply these deficit areas. The FMC which
was set up in 1977, has never been fully operational, and like the
LMB, its statutory powers were withdrawn in 1980, due to
irregularities in its accounts. As happened with the meat sector,
the fish industry reverted quite smoothly to its pre-1977 pattern
of marketing, and there is little evidence now to show that the
FMC ever existed.

In contrast, government interference in the sale of fruit and
vegetables has been minimal. However, the government did
intervene in the marketing of onions, when it was realised that
poor marketing arranagements were jeopardising the success of the
Collective Onion Growing Schemes. Even then, the arrangements
made were incompetent and eventually the process was handed over
to the private sector.

In fact, government intervention in the marketing of foodstuffs
in the form of administrative structures has been half-hearted,
incompetent and usually ending in failure. There are many reasons
for this lack of success: firstly, an absence of understanding of
the marketing network; secondly, insufficient infrastructural
development; thirdly, no, or an inadequate, financial commitment
by the government.

The lack of understanding of the network is demonstrated by the
Collective Onion Growing Scheme, and to a lesser extent by the
LMB's failure to take into account Muslim religious rites with
regard to the slaughter of animals. However, these lessons were
eventually learned. But an even more important drawback to the
extension of government intervention in the marketing of
foodstuffs is the absence of basic infrastructures. Without

adequate cold storage facilities, good roads and refrigerated lorries, it is not surprising that the LMB and FMC could not operate fully. Even the provision of simple lock-up stores at reasonable rents in the environs of the marketplace would help tremendously in preventing damage and spoilage to foodstuffs. Perhaps with the provision of more capital inputs, such as improved communications and storage facilities, the Gambian traders themselves would take the initiative, and government intervention in order to control prices and supplies would not be found necessary. The third drawback to improvements in the marketing system is the half-hearted financial commitment by the government. With limited economic resources, the government channels large sums of money into the collection, storage and marketing of groundnuts, whilst virtually ignoring the subsistence sector. This lack of commitment is demonstrated by the examples of the LMB and FMC. After having set up these marketing boards, the government was unwilling to subsidise them or even to adjust price controls in their favour. They ultimately had to cease their operations. Without full support, not only in terms of administration, but also of capital, any government intervention in the subsistence marketing network in The Gambia is doomed to failure. A look at the level of government commitment to and the success of the GPMB in comparison to the LMB and FMC demonstrates this.

In conclusion, it can be said that two major factors have emerged as important in the development of the traditional marketing network for foodstuffs in present-day Gambia. Firstly, spatial patterns of marketplace development have been and are distorted by the abherrant spatial structures of this tiny state, especially its small size and more particularly the long, narrow nature of the country, which is also bisected by the River Gambia. Secondly, commercial patterns, especially the dominance of the cash crop, groundnuts, and the government's interest in export revenue, have had a profound effect on traditional marketplaces, both on their location and timing. Seasonality of the money supply, levels of purchasing power, the level and location of demand for bought-in foodstuffs, all reflect the 'groundnut economy'.

This book has concerned itself with the marketing of foodstuffs in The Gambia; for this reason markets have been regarded essentially as sites of economic transactions and the exchange of commodities. It must be remembered, however, that markets do fulfil other functions, particularly a social usefulness, and Gambian markets are no exception. The author herself has spent many a happy hour sitting and chatting with market sellers and other market users. Without this social contact and the kind, cooperative response of the Gambian people, especially in the marketplace, this study would not have been possible.

Bibliography

Official Records

Public Record Office, London

CO   87   Official and unofficial correspondence
CO   88   Gambia Ordinances
CO   89   Sessional paper
CO   90   Miscellanea including the Blue Books of Statistics (also
           to be found in the Royal Commonwealth Society Library,
           London, and the Banjul Archives, The Gambia).
CO 460   Government gazettes

Banjul Archives, Banjul, The Gambia

BA   2   Colonial secretaries correspondence
BA   3   Confidential files
BA   4   Secret correspondence
BA   5   Customs department, correspondence
BA   9   Senior Commissioner, correspondence
BA   13   Blue Books of Statistics
BA   16   Registrar of cooperative societies, annual reports
BA   32   Ordinances, rules, regulations and proclamations
BA   52/10 Report on river and road transportation
BA   53   Customs, department annual reports
BA   54   Miscellanea
BA   75   Commissioner North Bank Province, correspondence
BA   76   Dr. D.P. Gamble's files
BA   84   The secretariat, confidential correspondence
BA 100   Thesis and articles

Dissertations and unpublished works

Airey, A., (1981), The role of feeder-roads in promoting rural change in Eastern Province, Sierra Leone, Unpublished Ph.D. thesis, University of Birmingham.

Barrett, H.R., (1984), The traditional marketing network of The Gambia, West Africa, with special reference to foodstuffs, Unpublished Ph.D. thesis, University of Birmingham

Benini, A.A., (1980), The community development agency and its village project: "Community Services Basse" and the "Koina Rice Project" in the U.R.D. of The Gambia, West Africa, Unpublished typescript, University of Bielefield.

Blandford, D., (1976), A study of the framework and implementation of public policy, with special reference to export monopoly marketing boards in West Africa, Unpublished Ph.D. thesis, University of Manchester.

Clough, P. and Williams, G., (1983), Marketing with and without marketing boards, Unpublished conference paper, ASA, Boston.

Cooperative Department, (1977), Cooperatives in The Gambia, Unpublished typescript.

Dey, J., (1977), A Socio-economic study of the effects of an irrigated rice development project on women's role in agricultural production in The Gambia, Unpublished Seminar report, University of Birmingham.

Dey, J., (1980), Women and rice in The Gambia: The impact of irrigated rice development projects on the farming system, Unpublished Ph.D. thesis, University of Reading.

Gamble, D.P., (1958), Kerewan: an analysis of the economic conditions and underlying factors in a Gambian Mandinka community, Unpublished Ph.D. thesis, University of London.

Gebre-Mariam, Z., (1979), Preliminary investigation of market prospects for selected vegetables, Unpublished monograph.

Gebre-Mariam, Z., (1979a), Tentative proposal for the improvement of the onion growing scheme, Unpublished monograph.

Gebre-Mariam, Z., (1980), Preliminary study on the marketing of cereals in The Gambia, Unpublished monography.

Hogendorn, J.S., (1966), The origins of the groundnut trade in Northern Nigeria, Unpublished Ph.D. thesis, University of London.

Isaac, B.L., (1969), Traders in Pendembu, Sierra Leone: a case study in entrepreneurship, Unpublished Ph.D. thesis, University of Oregon.

Jarrett, H.R., (1950), The Gambia, a study in tropical environment, Unpublished Ph.D. thesis, University of London.

Jeng, A.A.O., (1978), An economic history of The Gambian groundnut industry, 1830-1924: the evolution of an export economy, Unpublished Ph.D. thesis, University of Birmingham.

Livestock Marketing Board, (1978), R.D.P. Phase II - livestock component, livestock marketing, Unpublished typescript.

Mahoney, F.K.O., (1963), Government and opinion in The Gambia: 1816-1901, Unpublished Ph.D. thesis, University of London.

Paul, A.A. and Muller, E.M., (1979), Seasonal variations in dietary intake in pregnant and lactating women in a rural Gambian village, Paper for Nestle Foundation Workshop, Lausanne, Switzerland.

U.N.D.P., (1978), <u>Crop and farm development</u>, preparation working paper number 1.

U.N.D.P., (1978), <u>Irrigation development</u>, preparation working paper number 2.

U.N.D.P., (1978), <u>Livestock development</u>, preparation working paper number 3.

U.N.D.P., (1978), <u>Fisheries development</u>, preparation working paper number 5.

U.N.D.P., (1978), <u>Input, supply, credit, marketing outlets and cooperatives</u>, preparation working paper number 8.

U.N.D.P., (1978), <u>Marketing and prices</u>, preparation working paper number 12.

U.N.D.P., (1978), <u>Programme area</u>, preparation working paper number 13.

U.N.D.P., (1978), <u>Progress review of rural development project, 1976-79</u>, preparation working paper number 14.

U.N.D.P., (1979), <u>Report on the agro-economic impact of the package programme, 1978/9 crop season</u>

Senghor, J.C., (1979), <u>Politics and the functional strategy to international integration: Gambian Senegambian integration, 1958-1974</u>, Unpublished Ph.D. thesis, University of Yale.

Sidibe, B.K. and Galloway, W.F., (1975), <u>Senegambian traditional families and women in traditional Senegambian society - past, present and future</u>, Occasional paper of the Gambia Cultural Archives, number 1.

Trupke, H., (1976), <u>Increasing food availability through waste reduction and improvement of the marketing system in The Gambia</u>, Unpublished typescript.

Trupke, H., (1977), <u>Onion marketing system 1976/77; preliminary findings and recommendations</u>, Unpublished typescript.

Verdellen, J.A.J.M., (1973), <u>The ecological basis of agriculture and production patterns in the U.R.D. of The Gambia</u>, Unpublished monograph.

Printed Sources

Official Publications and Reports

Ames, C.G., (1965), <u>Laws of The Gambia, Vol. V. revised edition</u>, Bathurst, Government Printer.

Bannister, T.H., (1971), <u>Considerations for horticultural development in The Gambia</u>, Department of Agriculture, The Gambia.

Bunning, A.J.F., (1952), <u>Report of a commission on road and river transport in The Gambia</u>, Sessional Paper 6/52, Bathurst, Government Printer.

Central Bank of The Gambia, <u>Quarterly Bulletins</u>

Central Statistics Division of The Gambia, (1974), <u>Household budget survey, Banjul area 1968/69</u>, Banjul, Government Printer.

Central Statistics Division of The Gambia, (1974), <u>National sample survey of agriculture, 1973/4</u>, Banjul, Government Printer.

Central Statistics Division of The Gambia, (1974), <u>Quarterly survey of employment and earnings</u>.

Central Statistics Division of The Gambia, (1965), Report on the census of population of The Gambia, taken on 17/18 April 1963, by H.A. Oliver, Sessional Paper 13 of 1965, Bathurst, Government Printer.

Central Statistics Division of The Gambia, (1974), The Gambia Produce Marketing Board, 1963/64 to 1972/73, Banjul, Government Printer.

Central Statistics Division of The Gambia, (1975), Urban Labour Force Survey, 1974/75, Banjul, Government Printer

Central Statistics Division of The Gambia, (1976), Population census 1973, Vol. II, General Report, Banjul, Government Printer.

Central Statistics Division of The Gambia, (1986), Population and housing census 1983: Provisional Report, Banjul, Government Printer.

Colonial Office, (1953), Report on farmers' fund, 1951-52, Sessional Paper 7/53, Bathurst, Government Printer.

Colonial Office, (1956), Trans-Gambian road and ferry: agreements with the governor-general of French West Africa, Sessional Paper 3/56, Bathurst, Government Printer

Crowther, P.C. et al, (1976), Report of the agro-industrial storage complex design/evaluation mission to The Gambia, London, Tropical Products Institute.

Dunsmore, J.R., (1976), The agricultural development of The Gambia: an agricultural environmental and socio-economic analysis, Land Resource Study, 22, London, Overseas Development Ministry.

Food and Agriculture Organization, UN, (1980), Appraisal of crop production deficits and food aid measures proposed, Report of FAO/WFP, Rome, UN, FAO.

Gambia Government, (1975), Report on the commission of enquiry on the cooperative movement in The Gambia, Sessional Paper 4 of 1975, Banjul, Government Printer.

Gambia Government, (1976), Five year plan for economic and social development, July 1975 - June 1980, Banjul, Government Printer, 195/2150/76.

Gambia Government, (1978), Employment and earnings: trends since independence with prospects for 1980-85 and beyond, Banjul, Government Printer.

Gambia Oilseeds Marketing Board, Gambia Oilseeds Marketing Board, Reports 1957/58 to 1966/67, Bathurst, Government Printer.

Gamble, D.P., (1955), Economic conditions in two Gambian Mandinka villages - Kerewan and Keniba, London, Colonial Office.

Haswell, M.R., (1953), Economics of agriculture in a Savannah Village, London, HSO.

Haswell, M.R., (1963), The changing pattern of economic activity in a Gambian Village, London, HSO.

Hickling, C.F., (1951), Report by C.F. Hickling, fisheries advisor to the Secretary of State for the colonies of his visit to The Gambia in November 1950, Sessional Paper 9/51, Bathurst, Government Printer.

Hill, I.D., (1969), An assessment of the possibilities of oil palm cultivation in W.D., The Gambia, Land Resource Study 6, London, Overseas Development Ministry.

Hireh, R.D., (1979), Cereals policy in Sahel countries. Case study
    – millet marketing: ONCAD, Rome, UN, FAO.
International Labour Office, (1980), Employment, incomes and
    production in the informal sector in The Gambia, Addis Ababa,
    ILO.
MacLuskie, H., (1958), Report on the Gambia Rice Farm, 1952-58,
    London, Colonial Office.
Mettrick, H., (1978), Oxenisation in The Gambia: an evaluation,
    London, Overseas Development Ministry.
Nasta, V., (1964), Report to the Government of Gambia on rice
    marketing, FAO Report number 1910, Rome, UN, FAO.
O.D.A., (1971) Report of The Gambian livestock marketing Vol. I
    and Vol. II, London, HSO.
Palmer, J.H., (1946), Notes on strange farmers, Sessional Paper
    15/1946, Bathurst, Government Printer.
SONED, (1977), Etude sur la commercialisation et le stockage des
    cereales au Senegal, Tomes 1, 2 et 3, Dakar.
Trupke, H., (1978), Expansion and rehabilitation of the Albert
    Market, Banjul, Banjul, Government Printer.
U.N.D.P., (1977), The external sector of The Gambia: analysis and
    proposals, Mission Report, Geneva, U.N.D.P.
U.N.D.P., (1976), Consolidated report on development assistance:
    The Gambia 1976-77, Banjul, U.N.D.P.
Van der Plas, C.O., (1957), Report of a survey of rice areas in
    the Central Division of The Gambia Protectorate, August 1955,
    Bathurst, Government Printer.
Weitenberg, A.J., (1977), Food and agricultural products
    processing in The Gambia Mission Report, UN Economic Commission
    for Africa, Industry Division, IND-171/MR-122, Addis Ababa, UN,
    ECA.
West Africa Rice Development Association, (1976), The MacCarthy
    Island irrigation project in The Gambia economy, Banjul,
    Government Printer.
Winter, J.D. and Gilman, G.A., (1975), Report of the grain
    storage/marketing evaluation mission to The Gambia, London,
    Tropical Products Institute.
World Bank, (1980), Basic needs in The Gambia, Report number 2656-
    GM, World Bank.
Zachariah, K.C., (1979), Migration in The Gambia, Washington,
    World Bank.

Other Published Material

Adanson, M., (1759), A voyage to Senegal, the Isle of Goree and
    the River Gambia, London, Nourse
Ames, D., (1962), 'The Rural Wolof of The Gambia' in Bohannan and
    Dalton (eds).
Amin, S., (1972), 'Underdevelopment and dependence in Black Africa
    – origins and contemporary forms', Journal of Modern African
    Studies, 10, pp.503-24.
Amin, S., (1973), Neo-Colonialism in West Africa, London, Penguin.
Barrett, H.R., (1986), 'The evolution of the marketing network in
    The Gambia in the twentieth century, Tijdschrift voor
    Economische en Sociale Geographie, 77, pp.205-12

Barth, H., (1859), Travels and discoveries in North and Central Africa, New York, Harper and Brothers

Bauer, P.T., (1954), West African Trade, Cambridge, Cambridge University Press.

Beavon, K.S.O. and Mabin, A.S., (1975), The Losch system of market areas: derivation and extention, Geographical Analysis, 7, pp.131-51.

Benini, A.A., (1980), Community developement in a multi-ethnic society: the URD of The Gambia, West Africa, Saarbrucken, verlag breitenbach.

Berry, B.J.L., (1967), Geography of market centres and retail distribution, Englewood Cliffs, New Jersey, Prentice-Hall Inc.

Bohannan, P. and Dalton, G. (eds), (1962), Markets in Africa, Evanston, North Western University Press.

Bovill, E.W., (1958), The Golden trade of the Moors, London, Oxford University Press.

Bridges, R.C. (ed) (1974), Senegambia, Proceedings of a colloquium at Aberdeen University.

Bromley, R.J., (1978), 'Traditional and modern change in the growth of systems of market centres in highland Ecuador', in R.H.T. Smith (ed).

Brooks, G.E., (1975), 'Peanuts and colonialism: consequences of the commercialisation of peanuts in West Africa, 1830-1870', Journal of African History, 16, pp.29-54

Brooks, G.E., (1980), Luso-African commerce and settlement in The Gambia and Guinea-Bissau Region, sixteenth to nineteenth centuries, African Studies Centre Working Papers, No. 24, Boston University.

Burton, R., (1863), Wanderings in West Africa, Vol I, London, Tinsley Brothers.

Cadamosto, (1937), The voyages of Cadamosto, translated and edited by G.R. Crone, London, Hakluyt Society.

Caldwell, J.S., (1975), Population growth and socio-economic change in West Africa, London, Columbia University Press.

Christaller, W., (1966), Central places in Southern Germany, translated by C.W. Baskin, Englewood Cliffs, New Jersey, Prentice-Hall Inc.

Clarke, J.I. and Kosinski, L.A. (eds), (1982), Redistribution of population in Africa, London, Heinemann.

CILSS (Club du Sahel), (1977), Marketing, price policy and storage of food grains in the Sahel: a survey. Vol. II Country Studies, Michigan, University of Michigan Press.

Cohen, A., (1965), 'The social organisation of credit in a West African cattle market', Africa, 35, pp.8-20.

Colvin, L.G. et al, (1982), The uprooted of the Western Sahel: migrants quest for cash on the Senegambia, New York, Praeger Publishers.

Crampton, P.D., (1972) 'The population geography of Gambia', Geography, 57, pp.153-158.

Crowder, M., (1968), West Africa under Colonial Rule, London, Hutchinson.

Cruise O'Brien, D.B., (1971), The Mourides of Senegal, Oxford, Clarendon Press.

Crummey, D. and Stewart, C.C. (eds), (1981), Modes of production in Africa: the pre-colonial era, London, Sage Publications.

Curtin, P.D., (1969), The Atlantic slave trade: a census, London, University of Wisconsin Press.

Curtin, P.D., (1972), 'Prices and market mechanisms of the Senegambia, 1680-1790', Ghana Social Science Journal, 2, pp.19-41.

Curtin, P.D., (1975), Economic change in pre-colonial Africa: Senegambia in the era of the slave trade, London, University of Wisconsin Press.

Dacey, M.F., (1960), 'The spacing of river towns', Annals of the Association of American Geographers, 50, pp.59-61

Dey, J., (1981), 'Gambian women: unequal partners in rice development projects?' Journal of Development Studies, 17, pp.109-122

Donelha, A., (1977), An account of Sierra Leone and the rivers of Guinea of Cape Verde, translated by P.E.H. Hair, Lisboa, Junta de investigacoes cientificasdo ultramar.

Dorjahn, V.R., (1962), African traders in Central Sierra Leone, in Bohannan and Dalton (eds).

Duignan, P. and Gann, L.H. (eds), (1969), Colonialism in Africa, 1870-1960, Vol. I. History and politics of colonialism 1870-1914, Cambridge, Cambridge University Press.

Duignan, P. and Gann, L.H. (eds), (1975), Colonialism in Africa, 1870-1960, Vol. IV, The economics of colonialism, Cambridge University Press.

Eighmy, T.H., (1972), 'Rural periodic markets and the extension of an urban system: a western Nigerian example', Economic Geography, 48, pp.229-315

Fage, J.D., (1969), A history of West Africa, Cambridge, Cambridge University Press.

Fagerlund, V.G. and Smith, R.H.T., (1970), 'A preliminary map of market periodicities in Ghana', Journal of Developing Areas, 4, pp.333-48.

Floyd, B.N., (1966), 'Gambia: a case study of the role of historical accident in political geography', Bulletin of the Journal of the Sierra Leone Geographical Association, 10, pp.22-38.

Frank, A.G., (1969), Latin America: underdevelopment or revolution, New York, Monthly Review Press.

Freund, W.M. and Shenton, R.W., (1977), '"Vent-for-surplus" theory and the economic history of West Africa', Savanna, 6, pp.191-195.

Gailey, H.A., (1964), A history of The Gambia, London, Routledge and Kegan Paul.

Gamble, D.P., (1967), The Wolof of Senegambia, London, IAI.

Gibril, M.A., (1979), Population size evaluation in African countries: Gambia, Group de demographie Africaine, Monograph number 16, Paris.

Good, C.M., (1970), Rural markets and trade in East Africa, University of Chicago, Department of Geography research paper number 128.

Good, C.M., (1973), 'Markets in Africa: a review of research themes and the question of market origins', Cahiers d'Etudes Africaines, 13, pp.769-780

Gray, J.M., (1966), A history of The Gambia, London, Frank Cass and Co.

Hagerstrand, T., (1952), 'The population of innovation waves' Lund Studies in Geography, Series B, 4, pp.3-19.

Hailey (Lord), (1951), Native administration in the British West African Territories, London.

Hart, K., (1982), The political economy of West African agriculture, Cambridge, Cambridge University Press.

Haswell, M.R., (1975), The nature of poverty, London, Macmillan Press.

Hill, P., (1966), 'Landlords and brokers: a West African trading system', Cahiers d'Etudes Africaines, 6, pp.349-66

Hill, P., (1966a), 'Notes on the traditional market authority and market periodicity in West Africa', Journal of African History, 7, pp.295-311.

Hill, P., (1969), 'Hidden trade in Hausaland', Man-newseries, 4, pp.392-409.

Hill, P., (1971), 'Two types of West African housetrade', in Meillassoux (ed).

Hodder, B.W., (1961), 'Rural periodic day markets in part of Yorubaland', Transactions of the Institute of British Geographers, 29, pp.149-159.

Hodder, B.W., (1965), 'Some comments on the origins of traditional markets in Africa South of the Sahara', Transactions of the Institute of British Geographers, 36, pp.97-105

Hodder, B.W., (1971), 'Periodic and daily markets in West Africa', in Meillassoux (ed).

Hodder, B.W., (1980), Economic development in the Tropics, London, Methuen.

Hodder, B.W. and Ukwu, U.I., (1969), Markets in West Africa, Ibadan, Ibadan University Press.

Hodge, C.T. (ed), (1971), Papers on the Manding, The Hague, Mouton & Co.

Hogendorn, J.S., (1975), 'Economic initiative and African cash farming: pre-colonial origins and early colonial developments', in Duignan and Gann (eds).

Hogendorn, J.S., (1976), 'The "vent-for-surplus" model and African cash agriculture to 1914', Savanna, 5, pp.15-28

Hopkins, A.G., (1973), An economic history of West Africa, London, Longman.

Howard, A.M., (1981), 'Trade without marketplaces: the spatial organisation of exchange in North-Western Sierra Leone to 1930', African Urban Studies, 11, pp.1-22

Ingram (Governor), (1847), 'Abridged account of an expedition of about 200 miles up the Gambia by Governor Ingram', Journal of the Royal Geographical Society, 17, pp.150-55

Jarrett, H.R., (1948), 'Population settlement in The Gambia', Geographical Review, 38, pp.633-36

Jarrett, H.R., (1949), 'Strange farmers of The Gambia', Geographical Review, 39, pp.649157

Jobson, R., (1932), The Golden Trade, London, Penguin.

Johnson, F.R., (1964), The Peanut Story, Murfreesboro, N.C., Johnson Publishing Co.

Klein, M.A., (1977), 'Servitude among the Wolof and Sereer of Senegambia' in Miers and Kopytoff (eds).

Kolp, P.W., (1976), Sene-Gambian transport survey, Virginia, Research Analysis Corporation.

229

Little, K., (1949), 'The organisation of communal farms in The Gambia', Journal of African Administration, 1, pp.76-82

McCrae, J.E. and Paul, A.A., (1979), Foods of rural Gambia, Medical Research Centre, Dunn Nutrition Unit, Cambridge.

McIntosh, S.K., (1981), 'A reconsideration of Wangara/Palolus, Island of Gold, Journal of African History, 22, pp.145-58

McKim, W., (1972), 'The periodic market system in N.E. Ghana', Economic Geography, 48, pp.333-344

McLoughlin, P.F.M. (ed), (1970), African food production systems, Baltimore, J. Hopkins Press.

McPhee, A., (1926), The economic revolution in British West Africa, London, Frank Cass and Co.

Marx, K., (1977), Capital Vol. I, London, Lawrence and Wishart.

Masefield, G.B. (1972), A history of the colonial agricultural service, Oxford, Clarendon Press.

Meillassoux, C. (ed), (1971), The development of indigenous trade and markets in West Africa, London, Oxford University Press.

Miers, S. and Kopytoff, I. (eds), (1977), Slavery in Africa, London, University of Wisconsin Press.

Mollien, G., (1820), Travels in the interior of Africa, London, Colburn.

Moore, F., (1738), Travels into the inland parts of Africa, London, Edward Cave.

Morgan, W.B. and Pugh, J.C., (1969), West Africa, London, Methuen & Co.

Myint, H., (1958), 'The "classical theory" of international trade and the underdeveloped countries', Economic Journal, 68, pp.317-337

Newbury, C.W., (1969), 'Trade and authority in West Africa from 1850-1890' in Duignan and Gann (eds).

Niane, A.D., (1980), Supply and demand of millet and sorghum in Senegal, Michigan State University, African Rural Economy Programme, Working Paper number 32.

Park, M., (1878), Travels in the interior of Africa, Edinburgh, Adam and Charles Black.

Pedler, F., (1974), The lion and the unicorn in Africa: a history of the origins of the United Africa Company, 1787-1931, London, Heinemann.

Pereira, D.P., (1937), Esmeraldo de situ orbis, translated by G.H.T. Kimble, London, Hakluyt Society.

Pitts, F.R. (ed), (1962), Urban systems and economic development, Oregon, Eugene.

Quinn, C.A., (1971), 'Mandingo states in nineteenth century Gambia' in Hodge (ed).

Quinn, C.A., (1972), Mandingo kingdoms of the Senegambia: traditionalism, Islam and European expansion, Evanston, North-Western University Press.

Reeve, H.F., (1912), The Gambia: its history, ancient, medieval and modern, together with its geographical, geological and ethnological conditions, London

Richardson, D.A.R., (1966), 'Private enterprise on the River Gambia', Progress (Unilever), 51, pp.229-38

Riddell, J.B., (1972), 'A note on the origin conditions of periodic marketing systems', International Geography, 1, pp.584-86

Riddell, J.B., (1974), 'Periodic markets in Sierra Leone', <u>Annals of the Association of American Geographers</u>, 64, pp.541-48

Rigoulot, J.P., (1980), <u>An analysis of constraints on expanding rice output in the Casamance region of Senegal</u>, African Rural Economy Programme, Working Paper number 31, Michigan State University.

Sako, B. and Cotterill, R.W., (1981), <u>An economic analysis of supply responsiveness in traditional agriculture: millet, sorghum and rice farmers in Mali</u>, African Rural Economy Programme, Working Paper number 36, Michigan State University.

Skinner, G.W., (1964), 'Marketing and social structure in rural China', <u>Journal of Asian Studies</u>, 24, pp.3-43, pp.195-228, pp.363-399

Smith, M.G., (1962), 'Exchange and marketing among the Hausa', in Bohannan and Dalton (eds).

Smith, R.H.T., (1970), 'A note on periodic markets in West Africa, <u>African Urban Notes</u>, 5, pp.29-37

Smith, R.H.T., (1971), 'West African market places: temporal periodicity and locational spacing,' in Meillassoux (ed).

Smith, R.H.T. (ed), (1978), <u>Marketplace trade</u>, Vancouver, University of British Columbia.

Stine, J.H., (1962), 'Temporal aspects of tertiary production elements in Korea', in Pitts (ed).

Sundstrom, L., (1965), <u>The trade of Guinea</u>, Lund, Hakan Oulssons Boktrycken.

Swindell, K., (1979), 'Serawoolies Tillibunkas and strange farmers: the development of migrant groundnut farming along the Gambia River, 1848-1895', <u>Journal of African History</u>, 21, pp.93-104

Swindell, K., (1982), 'From migrant farmer to permanent settler: the strange farmers of The Gambia', in Clarke and Kosinski (eds)

United Africa Company, (1953), 'Trading in The Gambia', <u>United Africa Company Limited, Statistical and Economic Review</u>, 11.

Van der Laan, H.L., (1975), <u>The Lebanese traders in Sierra Leone</u>, Paris, Mouton.

Venema, L.B., (1978), <u>The Wolof of Saloum: social structure and rural development in Senegal</u>, Wageningen, Centre for agricultural publishing and documentation.

Weil, P.M., (1970), 'The introduction of the ox plow in central Gambia', in McLoughlin (ed).

Weil, P.M., (1971), 'Political structure and processes among the Gambia Mandinka: the village parapolitical system', in Hodge (ed).

Weil, P.M., (1973), 'Wet rice, women and adaptation in The Gambia', <u>Rural Africana</u>, 19, pp.20-29

Whitford, J., (1967), <u>Trading life in West and Central Africa</u>, London, Frank Cass

Wright, D.R., (1977), 'Darbo jula: the role of a Mandinka jula clan in the long-distance trade of the Gambia River and its hinterland', <u>African Economic History</u>, 3, pp.33-45

Yoon, S.Y., (1983), 'Women's garden groups in Casamance, Senegal', <u>Assignment Children</u>, 63/64, pp.133-153